the
hell
world

n o o n e

First published 2015
By Rowanvale Books Ltd
2nd Floor
220 High Street
Swansea
SA1 1NW
www.rowanvalebooks.com

A CIP catalogue record for this book is available from the British Library.
ISBN: 978-1-910607-78-7

part one

chapter one

It was, without doubt, a beautiful planet.

From their vantage point in space – beyond the grey, pock-marked, rocky and lifeless little satellite moon, the ever-scudding, whirling and twirling clouds obscured much of the predominately blue world below, interspersed, as it was, with large, hotchpotch patches of green, brown, yellow and white land-masses – it looked magnificent. Those meteorological blobs of dark-grey or grey-white water vapours were, on closer inspection, circulating the world within the confines of a narrow layer of planetary atmosphere; a thin film of gases a mere one-hundred or so kilometres deep – such a slender and fragile envelope of life-giving sustenance.

Indeed, it *was* a beautiful planet, teeming with millions of beautiful species of precious life.

Beneath those scurrying, billowing mists of water vapour, however, on all of those green, brown, yellow and white surfaces of that beautiful globe, lived a notable anomaly. That exception was a species of animal with a dreadful, if not unique, gift – unique on their world, at least. Everything about this species was wrong; they appeared to have no definable good qualities whatsoever. They could, it seemed, kill any life-form, animal or vegetable, by their mere touch; be it a member of their own species or any other form of life on the planet that, at a distance, looked so serene, so peaceful and so beautiful. The deaths these animals meted out could be an instantaneous, gone in the blink-of-an-eye, kind of killing, or a long, drawn-out, lingering death – they could do either, depending on what *they* required at the time; what would be most advantageous to *them*, how *they* themselves felt. For much of the preceding four and a half billion years, life on the planet had evolved in a natural manner – species came, mutated, thrived or died out. There *were* mass extinctions caused by asteroidal impacts and climate changes, yet these events were to be expected as the world matured. However, as if in a geological flash, those nightmarish animals developed and began to dominate, spread themselves across the planet and started their campaign of terror against all other species of life; in less than a comparative nanosecond they came, saw and were, at that point in time, well on the way to destroying their world. In real time, every instant that elapsed beneath those clouds, *every* single second of *every* single minute of *every* single day, some gross atrocity was being perpetrated by these animals; against themselves, against other species of life and, indeed, against the planet itself somewhere on that tortured world – non-stop.

Touch and die, touch and die.

Though not literally, of course.

Their skin was very rarely in actual contact with their victims. They preferred, instead, to use their tools and technologies to accomplish their aims, be it their percussive-explosive weapons, their bricks and mortar, their manufacturing processes or a myriad of other devices, materials and practices. Whatever, their hands were behind it, their touch upon it. They thought themselves so ingenious.

The female of this reckless, murderous and uncaring species was capable of producing issue every year, for around twenty-five or so years – though, thankfully, few seldom did. And, although the norm was for the female to produce one offspring per pregnancy, multiple births of two, three or four were not unheard of. In many cases the female would produce just the single infant in her life time, though many would have given birth to ten, eleven, twelve or more during their periods of fecundity. An infant was not born with this perceived ability to kill by mere touch. It was not innate, the gift would be theirs post-natal – well, just afterwards – until their ultimate demise some sixty or seventy years later, some more, some less. The toxin required to produce a death-touch animal would be introduced to the infant by its parents, its grand-parents and any other adult animal of its own species it came into contact with throughout its infancy, during its formative years and beyond, as if, a drip at a time, poisons were being poured into its tiny ears. Before too long, the young animal would mature and produce offspring of its own, whereupon the corrupting process would repeat itself.

Again and again and again – all across the planet – all of the time.

Over the course of its lifetime, just one of these animals would be responsible for the deaths of billions of animals, millions of hectares of deforested and deserted land; billions of litres of water, both oceanic and fresh, polluted by carbon deposits, pathogens and their faeces; an atmosphere befouled by mega-tonnes of ruinous pollutants, if not always directly, at least by their commission. Almost from birth, the infants of this species would be infected – drip, drip – with those evil poisons of their antecedents, whispering hate and superstitious nonsense into their ears, encouraging them to continue the mistakes of their predecessors. Almost from birth, every action undertaken by the infants would, in overt, unambiguous ways, adversely affect the world around them, destroying multiple lives, destroying the planet. So the planet wasn't just dying – there were no natural causes underlying its ill-health – it was being murdered by these animals and these animals alone. In the blink of an eye, after billions of years of maturing into a beautiful, life-giving and life-sustaining world, this indigenous species had turned stupid and, in that relative, geological nanosecond, applied a lightning-fast, fatal blow. An alternative version, perhaps, would be of a slow, drawn-out execution, over a couple of centuries, where, increasing by degree, the emission of noxious substances into the oceans and atmosphere eventually smothered and strangled, befouled and blighted the planet into submission, into annihilation.

Some animals of that species would claim no responsibility for the steady decline in the quality of life they were experiencing, by, perhaps, one chance in multiple trillions; they would deny they had anything to do with the thickening atmosphere or the corrupted oceans. Their actions, according to these nay-sayers, contributed nothing to the ill-health of their planet, the terminal illness of their world. All of these animals – those that acknowledged their blameworthiness and those who denied any role in their crimes – continued, ceaselessly, with the assault against their home-world despite being fully aware, totally cognisant, that the planet could not survive as a life-sustaining organism, a viable ecosystem, for very much longer.

They persisted in excavating and burning fossil fuels, persisted in breeding beings of other species in their billions to destroy and consume, persisted in procreating in their multiple-millions every year and indoctrinated those offspring with illogical, supernatural concepts and notions of their own superiority and invulnerability which would allow them to live on after their deaths; after their world's death. Their incessant greed for power and material wealth also blinded them to their failings. To them, everything had to have a monetary value and produce profit, or it was worthless. Fossil fuels had such value, the dead children of other species of animal, reared to be tortured and devoured, had such value and the children of their own species, bred to toil and abuse, also had such value. The abuses committed against the planet, those other life-forms and against themselves could all be traced back to their self-serving political and nonsensical religious power systems, which, in themselves, were synonymous with each other. All of these follies had multitudinous adverse consequences and each contributed to the murder of their planet.

But it would not be some planet-splitting death, not some smashed-to-smithereens type destruction – as a rock, it would still float in the void of space, orbiting its star. That rock, as barren as the other rocky planets in the solar-system, would, without question, remain. Where once there had been a world with millions of life-form types and multiple billions of individual plants and animals, all that would remain would be, more than likely, just that orbiting stony lump with an atmosphere asphyxiated by a noxious chemical mixture or, maybe, no atmosphere to speak of whatsoever.

There had been numerous warnings for these animals over the preceding decades; their own scientists had, albeit weakly, alerted their species, many times, to the catastrophic effects of the constant burning of fossil fuels, yet mere lip-service was paid to these distress signals. Having said that, it was the view of the aliens that had been witnessing this self-inflicted annihilation from afar that the warnings issued by these scientists were, to say the least, optimistic in the extreme. The constant references to a perceived, so-called "Tipping Point" at some time in the near future – though when that would be was never properly elucidated – were thought to be mere delaying tactics by their academics, no doubt monetarily encouraged by their political and economic masters, so as not to frighten the rest of the planet's population of their species into even more of a destructive, frenzied mob than they were under, what they considered, *normal* circumstances.

Tipping Point?

In the opinion of most ap-Vanda, Vatta and Obiah

scientists, that particular milestone had been passed, at least, fifteen years before they would arrive at the hell world; and even after the offending species had been culled to near extinction, there would be nothing the aliens could do to reverse the deterioration of the atmosphere, ice-caps and oceans, other than stop the abuse of these realms and wait. As for the land, they had processes that could cleanse the relatively small areas they would utilise for growing food crops, but the rest...

Again, time would, hopefully, heal the wounds.

Even their successful cultivation of foodstuffs would depend on the pollination of some of those plants by certain invertebrates – at that time, perilously close to extinction on the hell world because of the wanton use of toxic chemicals formulated to stop other invertebrates from eating the crops, but that were, also, poisonous to the pollinators. It was posited by some of the hell world's academics that, should those pollinating invertebrates be caused to go extinct, it would be just a matter of two or three years before they and the rest of their own species would follow them into extinction. However, there was much too much wealth to be gained, by those selfish and already wealthy animals, from the desecration of the planet to concern themselves with their world, their own species and mere invertebrates – what was the eventual death of themselves and all of their fellow animals at some point in the near future compared to their own personal wealth and power at that particular time in the present? It was clear that it meant nothing to them.

And what of the rest of their species, the billions without wealth and power? They all yearned to be one of those rich and powerful animals; they said and did nothing about any of the current or impending carnage. They were passive bystanders, blinded by envy and eager, merely, to increase their own wealth and power.

Stupid, stupid animals, all.

Their corrupt, power-obsessed notional rulers, the

politicians – made wealthy by their pay-masters, the very animals that profited most from the exploitation of the planet and its life-forms – also did little or nothing to try to alleviate the dire situation they faced, except pay lip-service to the warnings. These rulers were fond of saying that technology would save their planet, implying that, until that time came and these magic devices were invented, all was well with their world. The leaders of their unintelligible religions, of course, peddled their messages of salvation *after* death for their species – but only if the acolytes followed their particular brand of illogicality.

So, all was well with their world.

It was not.

It was too late for this species; it was, almost, too late for the planet. Soon the violence would stop.

***

The ap-Vanda were not a violent species of animal; neither were their two allies, the Vatta and Obiah peoples. They all had a strict moral code and nothing other than exceptional circumstances could have swayed them from these paths. They did not, normally, kill other animals of any other species for any reason.

On discovery of that hell world, so far away, these three species of alien animals determined to end the misery that all of the planet's inhabitants suffered by culling the perpetrators of that world-wide wretchedness and begin a new phase in the evolution of the planet and all of the varied life-forms it supported. It had taken many years of preparation; building spacecraft and amassing the paraphernalia of extermination, educating the participants and devising the schedule of death and renewal, but, eventually, over one-thousand craft from each planet, with five-hundred thousand animals of each species, departed their home-worlds for their long journeys to save that most rare entity in the galaxy – a planet capable of nurturing, nourishing and sustaining precious life. The invaders could have been described as animal husbandry practitioners, culling the planet of a large infestation of destructive vermin and dealing with the consequences of that animal's actions. Though that was not how the three species viewed it. They saw themselves as, first and foremost, educators – it was unfortunate that, to succeed in their task, they also had to extinguish up to thirty billion lives.

Soon they would arrive.

chapter two

And then there they were.

At last.

Hundreds of them, parked in the void; motionless and unnoticed.

The spacecraft were floating in the almost empty vastness of this alien vacuum, this foreign solar-system. Biding their time, awaiting their companions.

The star creating this gravitational well could not be described as either large or extraordinary – far from it, on both counts. Comparatively speaking it was, within the enormity of the galaxy, an unremarkable entity; as was, it could be said, the galaxy itself in the theoretically infinite vastness of the universe and its multiple billions of other such galaxies.

But there they were.

Despite the relative anonymity of this unpretentious, medium-sized yellow star, they were in a special, almost unimaginably rare, place in that galaxy, perhaps, even, in the entire universe. They were in the very near vicinity of that most precious of stellar entities – a life-sustaining planet, teeming with millions of unique species of animal, vegetable, fungal and protist life. They were not here to gawk in awe at the wonders of this uncommon rock orbiting that mundane star, though at first they would. They were not even here to study the multifarious live species growing, flying, crawling, walking, slithering and swimming within the world's atmospheric confines, though they had studied them from a distance and would continue to so do at some stage in the future.

They were here because one of the species of animal on that beautiful, perhaps unique, planet was determined to annihilate all life upon it.

And that should never be allowed to happen.

It would not be allowed to happen.

These mammalian-type animals, billions of them, were blithely and unbelievably, destroying the very ecosystems they and every other species of life on the planet depended upon for their very existence. Soon, very soon, these billions of delusional, destructive animals would not be in a position to harm other species of animal, vegetable, fungal or protist life; to pollute and besmirch the planet.

Soon, they would all be dead.

chapter three

Over the preceding twenty or so years, a mass of information had been gathered about this world and all of its inhabitants. The probe that had first discovered the planet had been, and was still, channelling its own scan and tele-visual information, plus the communications data from military, governmental and private sources of those animals, the primary target species, back to its home-world and, for the past seven years, back to the spacecraft in the fleet sent to liberate the planet. Those primary target animals were the Kaahu. From all of that data, and, perhaps, as a parody of the Kaahu's illogical ideas, the aliens designated the planet, from one of the soon-to-be-dead Kaahu languages, the *hell world.* The term, *Kaahu,* came from a now-defunct ap-Vanda language and meant *Fool.*

***

Even with all their individual and combined mass and all their numbers, the invaders were invisible to those billions of Kaahu animals on the target planet below, just half a million kilometres or so beneath the alien spacecraft. There were others too; hundreds more vehicles were hurtling to join them, streaming in a regular formation towards that same hell world. At that time, most of those other vessels had zoomed past the outer edge of the asteroid belt that spans the space between the dead, red fourth planet and the large, gaseous fifth planet of this solar-system, sped well beyond that dead planet and were on course to catch up with those craft already in position around the hell world. Some of these vessels, careering through space at just shy of one-million kilometres an hour, were to be utilised for post-invasion support, carrying, as they were, all of the required paraphernalia of renewal, but most of the craft would be integral to the main plan of attack – the cull. This accumulation of conveyances had arrived at the edge of the solar-system just under three years earlier. They had emerged from the Empty Space passage and all had, after just a short yet necessary respite, accelerated towards the distant star some eighteen-billion kilometres ahead of them.

The invasion would begin as soon as all the vessels were in position.

***

Although the Kaahu animals on the planet had been evolving in their present form for around two-hundred thousand or so years and, somewhat less than humbly, considered themselves to be an ultra-evolved, technologically advanced species, they were, in the opinion of all three of the alien species involved in the mission, retarded both in evolutionary and emotional terms or, at the very least, evolutionarily challenged. They were smug, over-confident animals, though for no apparent reason perceivable by the aliens. They were, however, the most intelligent animals on the planet – if intelligence can only be gauged by the complexity of communication processes or tool usage, or whatever. It was a moot point – it still is.

The feeble electronic systems these self-professed, highly intelligent animals had devised and deployed to detect any danger coming from outside the space around their planet was confined to an orbital radius of about five-hundred kilometres. They could not even locate stray asteroids hurtling towards them and, even if they had found such a rock approaching them, they could have done nothing about it. Nothing at all, save, perhaps, attempt to destroy the incoming celestial boulder with one or more of their crude yet horrific ballistic weapons or, maybe, just pray to their imaginary gods.

The latter, no matter how risible, would, more than likely, have been the more successful option.

***

Those inadequate and, to the newly arrived aliens, antiquated systems they employed to detect objects in space were useless against the defensive technologies utilised in all the vessels of the alien fleet, especially as these Kaahu animals did not, nor could they possibly, anticipate an invasion from space. Their cosmologists' theories, whilst sound in some respects, failed to conceptualise the existence of the Empty Space passage which made it possible to travel vast interstellar distances in exponentially less time than it takes to traverse the comparatively tiny space-time of an average solar-system from interstellar space to the star itself. As far as these animals were concerned, except for those amongst them with more vivid imaginations than the norm, or those more delusional – if such a thing could be possible – such voyages through space and time were unimaginable because they had learned or, at least speculated, that matter cannot travel as fast as or faster than the speed of light. As the nearest star to their own was a massive four light years away, what risk could possibly be posed from that distance? They were quite correct, of course, matter cannot travel at such extreme velocities – under normal circumstances, that is. How, therefore, could these animals on the target planet below, by any stretch of their collective and limited imaginations, possibly anticipate that three other species of animal, each from worlds themselves separated by many light years of normal space, could travel yet further huge distances into the galaxy with the sole purpose of annihilating them? Even if the Kaahu could, indeed, anticipate such an attack, the primary target animals would not, nor would they have ever been able to, detect them, despite their close proximity to the planet. The ships were all constructed from a blend of vegetable-based silk, metals and other materials that absorbed all known spectra of light and radio waves making them invisible to both ocular and electronic detection devices. In fact, the primary animal targets, or any other animals for that matter, would need to be in very close, physical proximity to the vessels to know they were there. And, of course, the other vessels were also hidden by the million or so kilometres of distance from the planet and by the velocity at which they were travelling towards it. Even the comparative few spacecraft that had disengaged their high-speed particulate driven engines and detached themselves from the main body of the fleet to set in motion the process of mineral extraction from amongst the floating debris of planetary assemblage and destruction at the asteroid belt, were also hidden by that same mass of asteroids surrounding them. They had stopped there two days before to offload the mining automata and their associated tender vehicles for usage at a later date.

But, of course, the Kaahu could not possibly perceive anything smaller than a whole planet *that* far out into space anyway.

Further evidence of the target species' technical vulnerabilities, if further proof were required, came as one of the spacecraft, designated as the lead ship, had preceded the rest of the fleet vanguard and journeyed towards the planet. The craft had been able to approach and land a team of technicians on the adjacent satellite moon, just over three-hundred and fifty-thousand kilometres above the target world surface, and set-up an observation post. All achieved without detection – which, of course, was the whole point of the exercise.

***

Despite the fact that no individual in any of the three alien species would ever describe themselves as military – far from it in fact – the offensive and defensive technologies they possessed between them would ensure the eventual success of their mission against the primary target animals on the planet below – without question. They would not physically invade the planet; they had wanted to avoid direct animal-to-animal conflict, they had superior offensive capabilities yet they had not wanted to inflict any of the pain and fear on these animals that a surface invasion would, unquestionably, necessitate. There was no need to do so. They could accomplish most of their objectives from space. Most, but not all, of their objectives.

For all of their bluster, as displayed in most, if not all, of their fictions, the majority of the primary targets, the Kaahu, were just like any other animal – desiring of freedom from physical or mental harm and, when confronted by such travails, were scared, individual little creatures. However, a substantial minority, the rest of their species, in fact, were total and utter psychopaths. Given their propensity for instilling dread and terror into, and inflicting almost unspeakable tortures upon, other species of animals that were less capable of defending themselves, before murdering and, in most instances, eating them, it had been determined that the primary target animals were just cowardly oppressors that used their superior technological capabilities to overwhelm and violate their victims. Had the invaders physically assaulted the planet, faced with far greater technologically advanced species, the Kaahu would, undoubtedly, have capitulated without much resistance, as all cowards in such situations inevitably do. But the capitulation of the primary targets was not the purpose of the mission; that purpose was the, almost, total annihilation of the Kaahu.

***

The preferred weapon of choice for the invading aliens, the orbital culler, had been proven to be unreliable on previous occasions when the target species' population density was, in most areas, just far too high for the weapon to efficiently destroy all the animals in those locations. Physical confrontation could well have been necessary. The culler weapon had three distinct components: the targeting equipment, the stream discharge mechanism itself – the part that did all the damage – plus an everyday medical scanner, as used by medics on all three of their home-worlds, built into the targeting system. From the data garnered by these scanners, medics and, admittedly part-time, weapon technicians alike, could discern the species, age, gender and, even, specific genetic malformations of any animal under their scrutiny. They could also detect physical defects or injuries such as broken bones, torn ligaments, viral infections, tumours or ulcerations, though the latter two maladies were comparative rarities amongst members of all their species. Perhaps equally as important, the scanner could discern and report whether an animal was dead or alive. It was, both as a medical tool and an implement of death, a remarkable instrument. However, in the present circumstances, the orbital version of the weapon itself was lacking and inadequate. In the beginning, the culler had been a portable point–and–shoot weapon, either attached to a vehicle of some description or carried and operated by hand in animal-to-animal confrontations. Both of these options were still available to the invaders, though they would have preferred not to take them up. In the past, on similar missions on worlds not quite so burdened by massive overpopulation as the current primary target species, the orbital culler weapon had been specifically formulated to recognise and select the unique genomic characteristics of that species within a given area, usually up to a fifty kilometre radius. Once acquired, the weapon would discharge, transmitting a condensed beam of energy to each recipient with those targeted genetic markers, instantly annihilating the brain stem, instantly nullifying motor, cardiac and respiratory functions, instantly killing all of the selected animals within those designated boundaries. Under ideal conditions, it was also capable of excluding individuals from destruction based on pre-specified genetic criteria. This selective aspect of the orbital culler weapon had always been a vital component in the successes of earlier missions but now, on this particular world, grossly overpopulated by the target Kaahu species, another strategy and, perhaps, other weapons would have to be employed for the *Temuri* collection phase of the mission. The desired level of efficacy for orbital deployment of the weapons for the current mission could not be assured by the culler technicians. They could but speculate – they only had digitally-generated test models to work with rather than actual live animals – that the resulting effects of such an attack may render some, most or, even, all of the primary target animals within the specified area alive, paralysed and in severe pain. Given the sheer number of targets that were known to be crammed into population centres at multiple locations, the culler technical people had also posited the theory that reducing the size of the cull-zone, even to as little as a five kilometre radius, may result in critical injury rather than instantaneous death for some of the animals. In the past, both of these outcomes would have been unacceptable to the alien forces. Throughout all of the long years of planning, preparation and travel, these shortcomings in the orbital culler weapon had been well known to the aliens and, throughout most of that time, the culler technicians had been striving to improve the efficiency of their devices. They believed they had found a solution. However, they had little choice other than to use the main orbital culler weapon in most circumstances. They had to balance the pain and distress suffered by the relatively small number of animals that might not die in an instant against the agonies that many would endure using other weapons, ones which could also, if used indiscriminately, cause massive environmental damage. The orbital version of the culler weapon, therefore, could and would have to be used against the primary target animals and against the vast majority of the secondary target creatures. They *would* be utilised against military and governmental targets.

One of the primary goals of the mission, the extraction of selected Temuri subjects, would be accomplished using the newly-developed, probe-based culler weapons. Planetary transport vehicle-mounted, automaton and hand-held versions of the culler, in conjunction with, where possible, limited use of the cremator and the repeller weapons, both as hand-held devices and assigned to automata, would be utilised in all other situations, if necessary.

The cremator was a heat-pulse device, normally fitted to and used by automata for manufacturing, agricultural and domestic processes such as metal fabrication, land-clearance or refuse disposal, which, even on its lowest setting, would have a very damaging and painful effect on an animal victim. One version of this device, calibrated at a level higher than that used for refuse disposal, was used for cremation of dead animal bodies both back on their home-worlds and, though very rarely, on their spacecraft. A single pulse, at this level, incinerated the entire body, hence the weapon's name. The almost unpalatable truth was that the Temuri collection teams would have to kill any live target animal, any Kaahu, that unexpectedly arrived on the scene during their incursions. Where possible, the portable culler weapon should always be deployed, as using the heat-pulse device, the cremator weapon, against a *live* creature would inflict an unknown amount of agonies upon the victim. A single pulse from the cremator, on the surface impact of its destination, attained a temperature of upwards of two-thousand degrees centigrade, instantly destroying all of whatever flammable object it hit, leaving only ashes. Operatives of the cremator weapons would also have to take into account the fact that the heat-pulse device was a powerful and dangerous implement that, in the inexperienced hands of their people on the Temuri collection teams, would be a threat to other team members, whereas the cull weapon, calibrated to primary target's dna, would not. A heat-pulse device would also be damaging, fatally so, to the Temuri and the aliens themselves should an accidental discharge occur. Although the prospect of using this weapon repulsed the aliens so much, they believed they had little option other than to authorise its use.

The third weaponised option, the repeller, was an energy projection tool mainly used as fixed settlement boundaries, or sometimes during wilderness expeditions on their home-worlds, to discourage other species of possibly dangerous animals from encroaching on their number. Should an animal walk or run into the projected energy, its path would be diverted by the static power field generated by the tool. However, even on the low to middle range calibrations, a directed beam from this implement could seriously injure an animal the size of an adult member of the primary target species, and that animal may die from those injuries. On its middle to high setting it could, quite possibly, blow an animal to pieces whilst not necessarily killing him or her straight away. All of their spacecraft were fitted with these devices, at their highest settings, as they could deflect most asteroids or other space debris encountered during their travels – the larger objects were just plain avoided. This tool was also utilised, when necessary, for defending their home-worlds from marauding asteroids threatening to collide with their planets. On one of their home-worlds there had been two such instances. On both occasions that these potentially catastrophic events had occurred, the combined power of three and four spacecraft, respectively, armed with these tools were required to avert disaster. The use of this weapon would also go contrary to two of the preferred requirements for the mission. Firstly, their strong desire not to cause undue pain to any of the target animals and, secondly, the need to kill them in an instant. The culler weapon mostly fulfilled both of these criteria, not taking into account the possible performance variances in heavily populated areas, and the cremator most probably complied with the second preference. The repeller did neither and so was thought to be the weapon of last resort.

***

Having had unlimited access to all military and governmental communications from all such organisations around the target planet for many, many years, the three alien species were confident they knew the exact locations of all their target's military bases, aircraft installations, aggressive marine vessels and other martial camps; the precise positional coordinates of their, so-called, stealth devices and the whereabouts of the offices and living accommodations of all their political and military leaders. They also knew the locations of all facilities utilising or storing radioactive or other hazardous materials such as power-generating plants and biological or chemical warfare facilities. All of this data had, of course, been classified by the primary target animals as secret, as confidential, and had been heavily encoded – though, with the alien's superior technical abilities, the ciphers used had been broken and disseminated with ease. These military and governmental targets would be attacked, utilising the orbital culler weapons, almost simultaneously and first. This information also included the whereabouts of most, so-called, "terrorist" groups. Apparently, this was a relatively new term that these divisive Kaahu animals had coined to describe anyone or, more usually, any group of their number that they disagreed with. There were, it seemed, many types – religious terrorists, state terrorists, right-wing terrorists, left-wing terrorists, ecological terrorists, animal rights terrorists; if there was a philosophy, there was, inevitably a terrorist or two behind it. And who, on that tortured world, could say they were not the terrorist? Retaliatory atrocity followed retaliatory atrocity. One set of ignorant animals, all indoctrinated by the hatred, lies and greed for power of small-minded males of similar or less intellect than their followers, would kill their purported enemies, other ignorant, indoctrinated creatures, and any animal that, by ill-chance, happened to be in their way – and by any means possible. Yet their political leaders, again, merely paid lip-service to the violations against their fellow animals. In public they would wring their hands and claim empathy with victims of terrorism, yet, behind the scenes, they would obey the will of their masters by increasing the number of weapons they possessed, more military equipment. But not to avenge those victims, only to increase the wealth and power of their masters and, to a lesser extent, themselves. Their indoctrinated military forces would terrorise their perceived adversaries, perhaps those who dared to worship an alternative version of their own made-up chimeras, inadvertently, or perhaps not, creating yet more radicalised foes seeking revenge, either at that time or at some point in the future. It was an endless cycle of stupidity, anguish and death. All of these woes could, in either the short, medium or long term, be traced back to the greed, short-sightedness and cruelty of the Kaahu. Had the wealthy, powerful and vicious animals amongst them not dominated, discriminated and dispossessed their weaker fellow animals for the preceding decades, centuries or millennia, perhaps there would have been no need for them to have coined the word "terrorist" and then to have tarred every other one of their species who somehow dissented from the norm with that scorn. The entire unintelligible species were terrorists as far as the invading aliens were concerned – these monsters murdered hundreds of billions of non-Kaahu animals every year; perhaps as many as one-billion or more creatures were slaughtered every single day on that planet.

chapter four

It was an unfortunate fact that there were many, many more secondary targets on the hell world than there were primary targets, the Kaahu. But all would require culling. The sheer nature of these species' wretched circumstances dictated that many would be located in more bucolic surroundings, forcibly confined in large groups either inside structures or within other impediments or barriers, such as wire fences, stone walls or metal cages. The majority of these secondary targets were those unfortunate creatures that had been born and bred for slaughter and consumption by the primary animal targets and for no other reason. Others, in both rural locations and in areas of dense populations, were kept in permanent confinement in prison-like institutions, for the shameless amusement of the primary target animals, though they had committed no crime nor misdemeanour.

The three invading alien species also knew that the Kaahu on the planet imprisoned, mutilated, tortured and murdered other species of animals, millions of individuals, for, so-called, scientific purposes. The vivisection practitioners of the primary target species who performed these experiments claimed that these practices were undertaken for the benefit and well-being of their own Kaahu species, which nullified any moral or ethical considerations that they or their society may have on the subject. As primarily moral and ethical species, the invading aliens had to question that belief. If the species experimented on are similar to their own species as to be like-to-like comparisons, how can moral and ethical considerations not be relevant? Or, indeed, if the species exploited in this way are genetically or anatomically dissimilar to their own species as to nullify any resultant conclusions, what possible benefits can be derived from the practices? To the aliens, not even taking these questions into account, there could be no possible justification for the target species' actions. Similarity or otherwise of physiology or genetic make-up was irrelevant; inflicting pain and distress on another creature solely for personal gain, as it could only be construed, was nothing less than an atrocity.

One example of the primary target species' unforgivable conduct is that, in some instances, military personnel were known to inflict gun-shot, stab or burn wounds on *suidae* and other species of animal to provide experience of such injuries suffered by their own species, inflicted by their own species, for their medics. There was no morality attached to the concept or application of these acts of intense cruelty, but this was, by no means, the worst instance of such terror.

Yet further examples of secondary targets were the hundreds of millions of companion animals of numerous species living with or amongst, and, of course, for the benefit of, the primary target animals alone. There were other groups of animals, bred for *sport* or *game* – though these descriptions bore no resemblance to any sport or games that the aliens knew – or they were raised for work. All of these unfortunate animals were also designated as secondary targets. The list appeared endless.

None of these creatures, through any fault of their own, could be excluded from the cull; they had to be killed because, due to the sheer number of animals involved – for many species, the rape of artificial insemination was continually increasing their populations – their continued existence would have been incompatible with both the evolutionary and ecological well-being of the planet. Hundreds of millions, perhaps even tens of billions, of herbivores released to graze and roam free in a newly-created wilderness with few, if any, predators would be catastrophic. Loss of habitat for other species of vertebrates and invertebrates would be inevitable, soil quality would be irrevocably eroded and harmful gaseous emissions from the creatures would increase. Although it could have been argued that the dearth of males in these groups of animals, who would be slaughtered at an early age by the primary targets, would very soon ensure that their populations would decrease, that was thought to be too much of a risk to leave to chance. The fact that these animals were, on the whole, the results of unnatural selection procedures and were also, for the whole of their lives, heavily drugged with antibiotic, growth-enhancing and other chemicals, was also a deciding factor.

All *felidae* are an exclusively carnivorous family of mammals and the subspecies, *felis*, kept as companion animals, were no exception to this fact. It had been estimated that there was a worldwide population of half a billion of this subspecies living with or around the Kaahu so, allowing that number of tiny carnivores to roam and decimate avian, smaller mammalian or reptilian species would have been an irresponsible act on the part of the aliens. Similar considerations had to be taken into account for the *canis* subspecies of *canidae*. Of the others, many would be unable to survive without the attentions of the primary targets.

The locations and concentrations of all or most of the secondary target animals made them suitable recipients of the orbital culler weapons' processes. But none of the assaults would begin until all the vessels of the fleet were in their designated positions.

chapter five

Sissonæ was all alone, sat in her windowless, two room accommodation aboard one of the spacecraft orbiting that planet so far away from her home-world. It would take less than a day or so for the rest of the fleet to catch-up with them. For such a long time now, it had been day-to-day routine of invasion training, administration, meetings and maintenance – mixed with their normal studies and plenty of exercise and leisure time, those vital ingredients that had so far kept everyone, as far as she knew, from going completely crazy. They had all got used to this routine over the seven long years of their journey. But it was now almost *that* time. She was, not for the first time, thinking about what they were about to do, the sheer number of animals they were about to destroy and her absolute belief in the rationale of the mission, at that point in time, was under severe strain. She was wavering.

She got up, poured herself a drink of water from the dispenser on the side wall and sat down, again, on the edge of her bed. Her thoughts turned to home – as so often they did these days. She felt stressed. She had learned, a few moments earlier, that her team, with her as leader, had been selected to be part of the first ever group to land on the target planet to collect Temuri subjects – an exciting yet, at the same time, profoundly terrifying prospect. Along with five Vatta and five Obiah, she and her four closest friends would be the first of all three of their species to land and explore, albeit for a very short time, the target planet, the hell world; the same planet that would, more than likely, be her home for the next twenty or more years, perhaps for all of her life. So, was it not natural that now, more than ever, she was missing her own home-world, her own family? She wondered what her parents and sibling would be doing at that particular time. She looked up and behind her at the time displayed on the back wall of her room, and then back to her water, watching the bubbles fizz busily in the receptacle. She smiled to herself. It would be the middle of the night back at the settlement, so they probably would not be doing much of anything other than sleeping. Last she heard, though it *was* two weeks ago – she really ought to make more of an effort to keep in touch – her mother was in good health. She was still researching her particle physics theories plus designing and building new and improved automata, those components so vital to their society in agriculture, manufacturing – well everything, in reality. Her father was also well. Still obsessively focussed on his engineering projects, now, apparently, enthusiastically assisted by her younger sister. She was particularly proud of her mother, her sister and, though mildly begrudgingly, of her father.

Her female parent was dabbling with finding improvements to the antimatter components of the particle drive engines used in their spacecraft though, at that time, with little or no success. Sissonæ's mother had told her that her father and sister were working on a few interesting projects, all with a singular emphasis on mobility. Her species had already done much work on external, automated servo-assisted systems, but her father and sister were concentrating on ways to integrate micro-systems into animal tissue to facilitate movement without the need to rely on clumsy and unsightly, externally-worn machinery. It was an accepted fact that their society had, in most instances, eliminated genetically-derived forms of physical disability in their own species, though there were still problems with accidental incidences of paralysis or restricted movement from sports injuries or other causes that required solutions. Up until that present time, people injured this way had had to put up with those clumsy and unsightly, externally-worn aids to movement and her father and sister wanted to remedy this. The last she heard, they were not quite there yet.

Not for the first time during this long, often mind-numbingly boring journey, she wished she had refused to undertake this damned mission. She wished they had never learned of this damned hell world and the damned Kaahu, the target animals, all those years ago; wished she had not been so eager to please when they invited her to join the project; wished she had not gotten so involved with the whole ethos of the mission and, if none of those things had occurred, she could have stayed at home with her beloved mother and sister. She really missed them. Her father, she could take or leave.

The sort of traditional family units typically found on the target planet were not such a fixed, or particularly required, concept on her home-world. The whole relationship thing on that strange, little planet below them was bizarre – part superstitious, part political and part emotional, but in no way animal. How can that ever hope to work? How can you legalise emotions? Other than if you were a parent speaking of one of your children, how can you promise, or even suggest, that you will love someone for the rest of your life, no matter what? It may well be the case, it may occasionally happen – though how can you possibly know that as factual at the point of commitment? And why would their gods or legal authorities be involved with an individual's private relationships, anyway? She knew the answer to her last question, of course: that insatiable lust of the primary target species for power over one another – to her species, as with most of the motivations and actions of those Kaahu animals, totally inexplicable. Her species had no delusions of gods, demons or afterlives in eternal ecstasy to enforce their compliance or deter them from curiosity; no threats of eternal torment as deterrents to misbehaviour in life. Nor did they have all-powerful governments or prejudiced legal systems to control their lives and loves, unlike on the hell world below. And what benefit has been accrued to that world and all of its inhabitant species of life from the machinations of those self-obsessed, small-minded Kaahu animals? She could think of none. She was glad that such irrational customs, traditions and laws were unthinkable on her own planet; she liked to think that the norm there was more *natural*. On her home-world, males would often play little or no meaningful role in their children's upbringing after the child was weaned off its mother's milk. They would be attentive during the pregnancy and assist the female during the first year or so of the child's life though, more often than not, would only have a peripheral role in the child's upbringing from that point onwards. The traditional roles of males as would be, no doubt, defined by some other species, was to protect and provide for their offspring for many years to come, but neither responsibility particularly applied on her home-world. Other than the very remote possibility of an attack by another species of animal, there were no physical threats against their children and, even if there were, males were no more adept at averting danger than females – even in the highly improbable instance of assault by another of their own species. Some males, albeit the younger animals, would yet still preen and strut and bluster to attract females. That innate, compulsive behaviour, that urge to win the affections of a potential mate, was deeply ingrained into the psyche of the male of the species and, despite the centuries of a different evolutionary path, was certainly not an easy emotional directive to deny. Most females, though not, by any means, all of them, whilst recognising the reasons behind these males' actions, would discourage such conspicuous displays of aggressive masculinity – they had no need of such archaic exhibitions of swagger. But these instances of what could have been described as retrogressive behaviour by these few males were rare and diminishing each year. They had not, nor had they ever, descended into situations that could be called violent – yes, these males would puff out their chests and talk big, but that was as heated as it ever got. There was also no longer the requirement for a male to provide sustenance or shelter for his family as there was at earlier stages of the ap-Vanda species evolution. All the necessities of life, as well as all the luxuries of life, were available to all at no cost. The male evolutionary imperative to protect and provide for their offspring was still burned deep into their dna though, and that requirement was, or appeared to be, fulfilled during the first year, but the need to continue with that level of commitment for an extended period was negated by the favourable circumstances of their lives. After that first year, females tended to raise and nurture their children alone or, sometimes, in conjunction with other, related females such as their sisters or both the maternal and paternal grandmothers or aunts. Males tended to concentrate on their academic work – that work often taking them to other settlements or to off-planet stations or expeditions – or on their artistic and sporting pastimes. That was not to say that the work and play of the mothers suffered conversely, as there were no social or other barriers to their continuing both their work and leisure activities. All of this seemed, to Sissonæ, to be in keeping with the natural orderliness of other animal species' lives, of life itself. However, although generally the most accepted method of child-rearing, this lifestyle was by no means universally adopted by all parents on her home-world. Some males did live with their children and their mothers on a permanent basis or within very close proximity to them, dependent on their work circumstances. Unless they were on an orbital station, an orbiting moon or on some trip out in the middle of the solar-system, none of the planet's settlements were more than an hour away from each other thanks to the speed and efficiency of the planetary transport systems. It was even possible to commute to and from the orbiting off-planet stations on a twice-daily basis – but it was very inconvenient and tiring. And, of course, there were also both all-male and all-female households that the Kaahu would describe as *homosexual,* though there was no such specific term in their species' language that differentiated between these and any other type of relationships on her home-world or those of their allied planets.

Another aspect of their society, stemming from the preferred, non-monogamous nature of their species' relationships was for females to have children with more than one partner. Her father was not the father of her sister. Technically, that would make them half-sisters, but this term was never used either – they were sisters and that was that! Strangely, perhaps, her sister had developed more of an affinity with Sissonæ's father rather than her own male parent and had decided to study biology, bionics, micro-engineering and general engineering because she had so much respect for him. Back on the spacecraft, the female alien animal smiled to herself as she thought of her sister's admiration for the old male – especially the old male who, in her experience, was only interested in his work! She had never had that kind of relationship with him, or anywhere near that amount of respect. Her father, as much as she loved him – and she *did* love him – had not played a huge part in her upbringing, less than the norm she thought, because he spent so much time engrossed in his work, so his not being around did not generate the same sense of longing as those for her mother and sister. These longings, however, seemed more deeply felt at this particular moment; more, perhaps, than she had felt these past seven years since leaving home. She was, as if from nowhere, feeling remorse for a species that she, and probably all of the people of the three invading worlds, had grown to despise over the years. Yes, that disgust was tempered by a certain amount of pity for the primary targets and their circumstances, most of whom lacked the intelligence to question their actions, but she did not think that *that* particular emotion, compassion, would have surfaced with such a debilitating effect. Not for these merciless, moronic Kaahu animals, surely? She had not even considered she would be *so* negatively affected by the mere thought of killing them.

She looked up from her drink and watched the live feed from the moon orbiting the planet. The images of the hell world were displayed on one wall of her windowless room and, although, apparently, quite a bit smaller than her planet – it did not look smaller to her – it reminded her of home. She stared at the image for a few moments. It looked a beautiful planet. Looks, however, were deceiving in this instance – this was, indeed, a hell world.

***

The female creature, missing her home planet and sipping her drink of water, was having palpable doubts about the ethics of their mission. She did not want future generations to judge them harshly for what they were about to do. They were not here as conquerors. They had not come to enslave the planet – far from it. They were there to preserve a thing of beauty, a tiny paradise in the vast, cold, empty void that was space; that self-same planet she was, at that moment, staring at by way of visi-sensors on an orbiting planetary satellite. They were there to rescue all of the wonderful and amazing biodiversity that this particular paradise contained. They could have been described as, she supposed, what the primary target animals would have called *pest controllers*. What an ugly phrase that was, she thought; if some other creature annoys you or is, in some other way, an inconvenience – destroy it! So typical of the Kaahu to consider only themselves! Perhaps that was not the right phrase for her to use? Although she had learned to read, understand and speak a few of the languages spoken on the target planet – that was part of her job – the nuances, perhaps, still eluded her slightly. Soon nobody would be speaking, reading or writing any of the Kaahu's languages – not for quite some time, at least. So, no matter.

She began to rally herself. She brought to mind a quotation that, surprisingly, was attributed to a leader of one of those absurd superstition-based groups that abounded amongst the primary target animals on the planet below. Admittedly, this group was not normally as dogmatic, and, unusually, less violent, in their beliefs than most of the other delusional doctrines on the hell world yet, nonetheless, it was still an absurdity – and they were only less dogmatic and less violent when it suited them. At the time she first read the quotation, she did not think the mission needed any justification, certainly not from such an irrational source, but now, at this low point in the journey, in her life, it seemed quite apt. She could not recall the passage word-for-word but, in essence, it could be paraphrased as:

If someone is in a position to prevent further violence – strike first, strike hard and strike fast.

And there was oh, so much violence on the hell world – violence against all of the life forms on the planet and, incredulously, against the planet itself – and her species and their friends were in an ideal position to stop all the pain once and for all. They will strike quickly, they will strike first, they will strike with extreme violence.

She knew their task was an awesome responsibility – however it was defined or categorised – and she knew they were doing a *good thing*!

***

Sissonæ got up from her seat on the bed and walked over to the desk in the corner of the room.

She leant over the metal table, said, 'communication link, please' and listed four names.

Almost immediately the image of one of her colleagues, a male, appeared on the wall in front of her desk, followed, a couple of seconds later, by the image of a female face. They all smiled and waved a greeting to each other. Her female friend was about to speak when two other faces, one male, one female, also popped-up on her wall. The background view from both of their images, and the fact that those images were orientated in that familiar, from the knee position, suggested they were both at the same location and were using their personal communication devices. They, too, smiled and waved a greeting.

'Hello, all', said Sissonæ. 'Tufu, Tsaan – are you both in the First?' she asked.

The *First* was one of the four recreation rooms on the first accommodation level, the one nearest the front of the spacecraft and one of four such rooms on each of the two passenger floors. The occupants of each level ate, drank, socialised and, sometimes, studied in these rooms, though they all, sometimes, would visit the other recreation spaces at that level or those on the second accommodation floor, just for a change.

'Yes,' replied Tsaan, the male ap-Vanda, looking and sounding somewhat guilty. 'We did not ask you all to come because we thought you would not want to... not today.'

'We did not want to be alone,' Tufu, the female with

him, added.

Tufu and Tsaan were, at that time, seeing each other, not just as the friends they had always been, but engaging in a romantic-sexual relationship.

'Sorry, friends,' Tsaan belatedly added.

'It is not of concern to me, I *did* want to be alone earlier,' said Sissonæ, now sat behind her desk.

'And I am working,' said Loopolz, the other male participant, anticipating where the conversation was heading, 'and will soon have a session in a simulator to attend.'

Loopolz, or Loops, as his friends insisted on calling him, much to his annoyance, was quite an insular, serious-minded young male who, it often seemed, preferred to translate the primary target communication documentation or work on his academic studies rather than socialise with his friends and colleagues. But, when he did socialise, he was always an interesting companion and, occasionally, could be quite amusing. His friends forgave his little quirks.

'What are you working on, Loops?' asked the previously silent female, Hentanayre. 'Perhaps we could assist you?'

'Thank you, but I do not believe you can help – it is not translation this time, I am still working on those modification to the crusher-bot code I mentioned to you all the other day. It is... taxing, to say the least.'

'Fine – I withdraw our offer of assistance, Loops,' Hentanayre replied with a smile.

'Why did you connect, Sissonæ – to go to the First?'

'Yes. As I said, I thought I wanted to be alone but, having tried that for the past half an hour or so I realise now that I really do need the company of my close friends. Although I feel pleased our team has been selected, I am also troubled... so I think I need to talk this through with you all.'

'What do you think, Loops?' Asked Tsaan. 'Will you

be coming?'

'No, I apologise, I would like to but I must finish this work. Time is short and I really, really cannot come. Then there is the pilot simulation...' replied Loopolz with some disappointment in his voice.

'You know where we will be, Loops,' Sissonæ said, not wishing to push him.

'I was about to connect,' interrupted Hentanayre. 'I have just had a shower – we had a game, *I* was very subdued, can you all believe that? Very strange – but, anyway, I was going to see if you all wanted to meet or not. I consider my friends,' she added.

She smiled and pushed her tongue out so as to be slightly visible between her lips – an amicable rebuke to her two friends already at the recreation room. The images of both Tufu and Tsaan skewed-off to one side and lost focus as they held out their arms in mock protest. The images auto-readjusted themselves to sharpness as they resumed their earlier positions.

All five friends were smiling.

'I will call for you on my way there, Hentanayre. Loops, if you change your mind...' said Sissonæ, letting the sentiment hang.

'I know,' Loopolz replied, 'perhaps after the simulation.'

'We will see you both shortly,' said Tsaan. 'Take care, Loops.'

Without another word, they all disconnected.

Sissonæ got to her feet and said 'mirror, please' out loud. She checked her appearance against the full length digital image that displayed on the wall in front of her. Satisfied, she headed for the door but stopped just shy of it. She decided to go to the bathroom and relieve herself first, before she left. There were lavatories in the recreation rooms but she disliked using them, though she did not know why, it was just that she preferred the privacy of her own toilet. She urinated, washed her hands, checked she had her communication device with her and left her room.

***

The walk to her friend's room and on to the first recreation room on the first accommodation level of the spacecraft took less than fifteen minutes. Hentanayre had been ready and waiting for Sissonæ when she arrived at her room and they were soon both ordering drinks from the automated dispenser in the First. They had seen their other two friends, Tufu and Tsaan, more or less as soon as they had entered, and, after the usual greeting pleasantries, the four of them were soon sat together discussing the upcoming incursions, the invasion proper and their feelings about it all. These four friends, and the missing Loopolz, had all grown-up together, both on their home-world and on this spacecraft. They were all sixteen years old, bar Sissonæ who had turned seventeen a couple of months earlier. Like most of the passengers of the spacecraft fleet, of all three species, it could have been noted that they had all been young and immature when their mission to the hell world began. But that would have been a comparison with the seven, eight or nine year old children of the primary target species and that analogy would have been unfair.

The children of the ap-Vanda, Vatta and Obiah were not like those of the Kaahu. Their formal education began at a much earlier age and there were none of the distractions so common on the hell world – no sexual, physical or mental abuse, no indoctrination of illogical superstitious beliefs, no instilling of difference, no gender stereotyping or division. They were taught, almost from birth, not only the basics of language and mathematics, but also, as they grew, the sciences, history and art of their species, about other species of life and about the planet they all shared. In contrast, the offspring of the primary target animals appear to have always been sexually abused, physically beaten and coerced by intimidation. They had been conditioned to have faith in ethereal philosophies with no demonstrable basis in fact. The many prejudices of their parents were inevitably passed on to the children of the primary targets, their biases against any trait, anything they disliked or were ignorant of. These offspring were not taught to embrace difference – rather, they were actively encouraged to fight against it. Millions of female primary target children, those that survived infanticide by their parents, were denied any education at all based on their gender. Millions more, both male and female, though mainly the latter, were actively discouraged from studying subjects of their choice as those areas were deemed inappropriate for their gender. The children of the three alien species, in effect the entire force of invaders themselves, suffered no such burdens and, it seemed, could better assimilate the knowledge that had been passed on to them by their parents or teachers, and appeared to be more mature than their primary target counterparts.

***

The four friends, conversing in one of the recreation rooms of one of the thousands of spacecraft surrounding or approaching the hell world, had similar emotions about their roles in the upcoming operation.

'And it is not going to get any easier,' Tsaan was saying. 'We are going to kill seven-billion of these animals plus billions of other creatures of multiple other species – if we are doubtful before anything has occurred, which we obviously are, how will we feel when upwards of twenty-billion bodies, perhaps thirty-billion, are littering the planet surface? Also,' he added, 'I do not want to kill *any* other animal.'

Tsaan was not usually quite as serious-minded as their other male friend, Loopolz, yet that evening he had, perhaps unwittingly, adopted his friend's mantle. He had been so glad when Tufu had suggested they go for a drink, he would not have been able to sit in his own room, all night long, all on his own. He, too, was excited when he first learned about their inclusion in the first ever landing on the target planet, but, on reflection, he could not decide whether that was good excitement or bad excitement. He had been alone when he read of the mission decision on his static communication device in his room and, just like his good friend, Sissonæ, had sat on his bed, deep in thought. He had decided it was bad excitement – fear. He had been wondering if their allies, the other two species who had experienced similar attacks in their histories, were feeling as he did. Then came Tufu's call and invitation to the recreation room, minutes after he had received the news; it had broken his thoughts and he had accepted with relief.

He broached the subject with his friends.

'Both the Obiah and Vatta have been through similar experiences, should they not be advising us on how to handle these feelings?' he asked.

'The last invasion was over four centuries ago,' responded Sissonæ. 'They will be feeling the same as we are, I think.'

'I suppose that is true,' he replied, somewhat sullenly.

Tufu squeezed his hand to comfort him.

'Try not to worry, Tsaan,' she said. 'We all have these emotions – us, the Obiah, the Vatta – it is who we are. We would be no better than the Kaahu if we felt no remorse, no compassion.'

Sissonæ, despite her earlier misgivings, was now championing the cause – she had no idea why. She wondered to herself that, perhaps, in reassuring her friend, was she also trying to convince herself?

'And we were advised on what to expect, Tsaan,' she said, adding, 'Yes, we all told ourselves that it would not be this bad, though each one of us, in a way, knew, deep down, it could be.'

'I know, but...' said Tsaan.

'And remember why we are doing this, why we are here, billions of kilometres from home,' Sissonæ interrupted him.

'I know, but...' repeated Tsaan.

'The Kaahu we are about to kill, they deserve it, my friend, you know that is correct, you know what they have done.'

Tufu re-joined the conversation.

'Sissonæ is right – we have known about the awful things that these animals have done for all of our lives. We grew up with this knowledge. We grew up knowing we had to stop them.'

Hentanayre, as usual when their conversations touched on serious matters, remained silent yet attentive, she took a sip of her tea and carried on listening to her friends.

'Look around, Tsaan,' Sissonæ was saying. 'There is Naanich, she is Vatta. They will be doing most of the unpleasant work. Look at her face. Ask her how she is feeling.'

The male looked across the room in the direction that his friend had indicated and saw the named female Vatta in question. Naanich was in conversation with two other members of her species and an Obiah. None of the four appeared to be particularly happy – though, with the Obiah, that was never an easy emotion to discern anyway. Naanich was one of, approximately, one-hundred of her species on board the spacecraft. There were also around one-hundred Obiah. All of the remaining three-hundred or so passengers were ap-Vanda, the species that first discovered the hell world, and the species to which Sissonæ and her three conversing friends belonged.

'It is over four-hundred years since her species and the Obiah were involved in such a mission as this, yet they are now expected to go face-to-face with the Kaahu and obliterate them with cremator weapons and the like. We are here, mostly, to collect and nurture the Temuri. How do you think Naanich is feeling?' continued Sissonæ, with just a hint of exaggeration.

'It does not make me feel any better to know that you and everybody else on this vessel, perhaps the entire fleet, are experiencing similar emotions, Sissonæ,' Tsaan replied. 'And, although I realise that this is something we just *have* to do, I do not like these feelings.'

'None of us do, my friend, none of us,' replied Sissonæ.

There was no resolution – how could there be? The conversation continued along this vein for a couple more hours before the four close friends decided to retire to their respective rooms, though, in fact, Tsaan and Tufu went back to his accommodation.

Loopolz had not shown-up.

***

There had been others, many others, in the recreation room at that same time, groups of friends and colleagues of all three species, sitting or standing around, supporting, consoling or just being with each other, just as they four had been. As Tsaan had speculated, similar conversations had taken place in every other passenger-carrying spacecraft in the alien fleet. They were all feeling exactly the same kind of guilt as Sissonæ and her friends were – it may be a morally questionable thing they were about to do but they all knew it was a necessity. Nobody amongst them was in the slightest bit comforted by this conclusion.

chapter six

Except, perhaps, Hentanayre.

She was not feeling particularly guilty – well, maybe a little bit, but not a lot.

Hentanayre did not take things as seriously as her friends, not when it came to the Kaahu anyway. She did not care about those animals at all; not their ridiculously delusional beliefs, not their unintelligible power-control systems, not the way they treated others of their own species. She did, however, care deeply about the other species of animal both on her home-world and on the target planet. Hentanayre was disgusted by the Kaahu and their abuse of those other animals.

Hentanayre was, first of all, an engineer – she just loved to design machines or structures and watch as her ideas took shape, after the manufacture-bots had produced the components and the build-bots had put them all together. She was not, however, so good at coding the contraptions she designed so, maybe, she would not go down in the annals of her species history as a great engineer – but she was unconcerned about that. She was a competent engineer and a good teacher of elementary engineering. She was happy enough with that. She was not keen on intra-atmospheric flight. She was not terrified of heights so much as falling from high places or crashing and burning when flying in an atmosphere, Unlike almost everybody else that she knew, she was not a planetary transport vehicle pilot – even being in the control room of a flight simulator made her feel dizzy and unwell. Once out in the vacuum of space, she was fine – there was no chance of plummeting anywhere out there, after all. She was an adept biologist, again, qualified enough for teaching younger members of their society, but she had let her research into the general areas of study lapse and so she rarely taught it these days.

Hentanayre was, however, making a name for herself as quite the expert on the atrocities committed by the Kaahu on other animal species on their hell world. The fact of these atrocities was, of course, well known amongst all the spacecraft populations, but the precise details of, for example, the conditions in which animals were kept before slaughter were less well disseminated across the fleet – for years the mere fact of the mass torture and slaughter of other species of animals had been sufficient knowledge, along with all the other failings of the Kaahu, for action to be taken. For eight years now, Hentanayre had not only been studying the biological life on the target planet but also, in her spare time, researching the methods, motivations and locations of the Kaahu's theatres of exploitation of other animal species on that target world. Ever since she had been very young she had been fascinated by animals, plants, buildings and machines, so biology and engineering were obvious choices for study and research as she grew. The year before the fleet left the orbit of their home-world, her mother and father, who, unlike all of her friends' parents, lived together, took her and her older brother on a wilderness vacation for the first time ever in their young lives. She had barely turned eight years old. In the past, for breaks, they would have visited one of the science or art sites around the globe, with Hentanayre, inevitably, sat between her parents with her hands over her eyes throughout the entire airborne journey. This time, though, they had flown to the middle of nowhere, Hentanayre's eyes shut tight behind her hands all the way from home, and were staying for a couple of nights in a tree-house in a large ank tree overlooking a watering hole; just the four of them. Surmounting the ladder to the tree-house was difficult enough for Hentanayre and, when her parents had ascended with the luggage and provisions for their stay, they found her hugging the trunk of the tree, unwilling to move. Despite her mother saying that their arrival would have frightened away any animals at the drinking space, after a quarter of an hour or so, her brother was whispering her name as loudly as he dared and pointing towards the pool of water. Curiosity got the better of her phobia and she edged towards the viewing window to see close-up, in the flesh and for the first time in her life, species of mammals and birds she had only ever seen digital images of before. Morans, caliperia, doos and huge maraa were all in groups of up to twelve family or herd members around the small lake, lapping-up the water; long-legged garas were wading and hunting for fish or invertebrates a few metres from the shore line whilst a single, larger and much longer-legged paramanata was watching them, suspiciously, from some high water-grass on the far side of the pool. Her fear had dissolved in a flash and, anyway, they were not *that* far off the ground after all – maybe a couple of metres. No problem. That night, after they had eaten, the four of them had sat for hours, as the blackness of night had enveloped them, listening in silence to the calls and movements, the roars and shrieks, the lives and deaths of wilderness animals carrying on all around them.

The whole of the next day, from very early in the morning till sunset, Hentanayre and her family had stared in awe at all the wondrous animals that came to that nondescript place by a large ank tree in the middle of the wilderness for water. That evening and night was spent, as the previous evening and night had been, enjoying the sounds of the wild.

From that point in time, at eight years of age, after

she had torn herself away from the comforting trunk of the ank tree to watch the animals drinking at the small lake, she realised that generic biology was no longer of particular interest to her – though engineering still was – and she wanted to concentrate her studies solely on other species of animals rather than botany, micro-organisms or other related subjects.

By this time she and her family all knew she would soon be traversing the galaxy towards the target planet, and it had been her father that had suggested that she study the animal species of that distant world rather than those of her home planet. Over the following year, before all the spacecraft had departed, she had gathered together as much data as was available to her on the non-primary animal species of the target planet and, after the fleet had begun its four year journey to the Empty Space passage, she refined her area of research to those unfortunate species bred for food, vivisection, companionship and so-called sport. Hentanayre hated what she discovered.

When she had returned to her accommodation from the recreation room on that vessel so far away from the wildernesses of her home-world she undressed, placed her personal communication device on the small bedside shelf, and laid down on the bed itself to reflect on the evening's conversation.

She was feeling drowsy, it had been another long day of work and exercise and, of course, the shit tea always took the edge off any nervous tension she may have felt.

Shit tea. She spoke, read and understood three of the target planet's languages. In one of those soon-to-be dead languages, the word *shit* was not associated with a delicious tasting, aromatic infusion derived from the dried leaves of a small shrub-plant; it meant effluence, faeces or, more colloquially, a bad or tainted thing. When she had learned of this, many years past now, she had, at first, avoided her favourite beverage – it had been a strange reaction, even for her. But soon the wonderful aroma of the tea, as she entered any room where it was available or was being drunk, overpowered her earlier, inexplicable, queasiness about it and she recaptured the deliciousness of it all again. She had enjoyed two cups of her favoured beverage that evening, sat listening to her friends worrying over their future actions and those of their colleagues and allied species. She had sympathised and consoled, of course, but her conscience was virtually clear; how could one feel remorse for these Kaahu? Her friend, Sissonæ, had been quite correct – they all deserve to die; not only those who perpetrated and condoned the crimes committed on the planet, but those who, by their ignorance, apathy, or inaction, allowed the continuance of those crimes. These Kaahu kill more in any one minute of any one day than any single culler weapon could do in an hour. She wondered what kind of minds could conceive of the obscenities, the atrocities that the Kaahu perpetrated. It was bad enough that they kill each other in huge numbers for their unbelievably stupid theologies (and how dare they make them out to be scientific?) or their selfish economic reasons – which she would never understand. What do the Kaahu doing the killing, or those being killed, gain from the exercise? As far as she could tell, absolutely nothing – but to subject other species of animals to such things was abhorrent. Force-feeding a creature by driving a metal pipe down their throat to create a food from one of their organs; or to insert an electrode into the anus or vagina of an animal to electrocute him or her so as to create a garment; or, unbelievably, to forcefully remove a baby from his mother, confine him in a crate to prevent basic movement, feed him only non-mother's milk laced with drugs and slaughtering him at around fourteen weeks old – how does one formulate such tortures? What kind of person would one need to be to even consider such actions? And it was not as though these were isolated incidents – similar disgusting behaviours were being undertaken non-stop on the hell world by these Kaahu.

She recalled a quotation she had read a few days earlier. A Vatta colleague, Synaerun, one of the many of all three species working on translation of the Kaahu mass communication nexus, had posted it to her and a few other people she knew across the fleet. Surprisingly, the phrase was written by a primary target animal, obviously not one of the billions of evolutionarily challenged Kaahu on the target planet. She picked up her communication device, found the quote and read it out aloud:

'Your meat did not die happy. It died kicking and screaming, fighting for its life, confused and terrified. *You* were the reason.'

Hentanayre knew, of course, that the word *meat* referred to the dead body of an animal, a non-primary animal, and she was impressed by the individual who had written or said this. However, she also knew that the number of Kaahu who thought this way was so few as to be negligible in comparison with those with contrary views.

No, these Kaahu deserved all they were about to get.

She noticed that Synaerun had sent another translated communiqué entitled *The Ten Ugliest Animals on the Planet* and had sarcastically noted that – surprise, surprise – there were no Kaahu in the list, when she could think of, oh, seven-billion or so. Hentanayre smiled, even though she had seen this document before or, at least, one very much like it.

Hentanayre returned her communication device to its former position by her bed, slipped herself under the covers, asked for the lights to be turned off, rolled over on her side and began drifting into a deep, guilt-free sleep.

chapter seven

Even as Sissonæ, Hentanayre, Tsaan, Tufu and Loopolz were enjoying a good night's sleep, or otherwise, more and more alien vessels of the three invading species were arriving at their pre-designated tethering locations in their massive spacecraft.

If any of the primary target animals below them were, in their wildest dreams, expecting any alien invasion fleet to arrive in massive, shiny metallic craft, concave or saucer-shaped and with a myriad of bright, multi-coloured lights flashing at them from their undersides, they would have been sorely disappointed had they been capable of seeing the reality that had turned up. They were very large vehicles, though. Each vessel was, more or less, identical; long, black, nondescript cuboids. Each one was five-thousand metres long, one-thousand metres high and five-hundred metres wide. Each was the matt black colour of particulate-coated, hardened vegetable silk. None displayed external illumination nor brash, decorative insignia of any kind. None had apertures other than the five space-tight doors on their lowest levels to enable entrance and egress for smaller vessels. Incorporating any kind of window or other type of door was both impractical and unsafe as the insulated skins of the craft had to be, and were, much too thick for such openings, and, of course, would also be significant weak-spots in the infrastructure of the vessel. All of the real-time external displays on the spacecraft were supplied by a series of sensors uniformly placed at ten metre intervals across the height, width and length of the entire craft – any image created from any of these sensors could be displayed, in isolation or in combination, in the main control room or in any room in the vessel. Alternatively, should the room occupant wish it, a view from one of their home-worlds or, perhaps, from the moon or probe orbiting the target planet, as well as images from the electronic archives, still or motion, could be displayed. Visi-communication, both inter-craft and inter-fleet, could also be fed to each room. To initiate a display, the potential viewer need only specify the dimensions of the required image by touching the upper and lower axis on a wall, any wall, of their room, or by specifying the measurements verbally and, in either instance, state the desired view. The any-view facility from the processor archives was always popular during the time spent in the total nothingness of the Empty Space passage. Of course, should the room occupant not desire a view or virtual window, and not everyone did, no images need be displayed. The view-screens in the main control rooms of all the craft were, however, in permanent use and always displayed images from the exterior of the vessels – even throughout the two long months of total blackness in the Empty Space. All of the craft were intrinsically and inherently linked – every one of them knew exactly where the others were at all times – any significant change in course by the designated lead vessel would be instantly followed by the rest, unless that order to do so was specifically overridden by those persons overseeing the vessel. All of these passenger-carrying spacecraft had one-hundred and thirty-two levels, of which over half – sixty-eight – were used to grow their food supplies and store and recycle their water. Each of these vessels had two floors of passenger accommodation, one entire floor housed the mainframe processing apparatus to manage the running of the craft, three floors for propulsion engineering – one complete level was required for the particulate drive engines alone – two floors each for vehicle storage, sports, academy and manufacture plus fifty floors containing cargo for the mission and beyond. Every craft in the fleet was powered by a single fusion reactor which, in turn, powered both the fusion drive and particulate drive engines. The former was capable of propelling a vessel up to two-hundred and seventy-thousand kilometres an hour, and was used mainly for manoeuvring and to get the craft up to the required speed to engage the latter to enable a velocity of slightly over nine-hundred and ninety-nine thousand kilometres an hour. The particulate drive allows the vessel passage through a solar-system within a relatively reasonable time frame; in the current instance, in less than three years as opposed to the eight and a half years it would take under fusion power alone. Most of the vessels were capable of carrying over five-hundred passengers, but not all did. Of the three-thousand, four-hundred and eighty-four craft in the fleet, three-hundred and eighty-five carried no passengers at all, only cargo. These cargo vessels, which included fifty containing only dormant silk plants, were automated craft, with no animal involvement whatsoever in their operation, and had much different internal configurations. Of the remaining three-thousand and ninety-nine craft, most had the full complement of five-hundred passengers, some less and a few slightly more. All-in-all, the animal population of the invading fleet from the three associated species was in excess of one and a half million persons.

Their journey through this solar-system had begun almost three years ago on their exit from the Empty Space passage and, after experiencing two months of the complete nothingness of that shortcut through time and space, the sight of the galaxy was a relief for all of the passengers in all of the alien spacecraft. Seventeen days passed on the brink of interstellar space and the gravitational pull of the medium-sized yellow star at the system's centre before the craft began their journey inwards towards that star. During that period, a probe support vehicle was unloaded from one of the ap-Vanda spacecraft so as to, at this early stage of the mission, boost the transmission power of the radio signal between the probe orbiting the target planet and their home-world. A similar vehicle had been launched at their end of the Empty Space passage which also assisted the signal boost. Later, if everything went to plan, this craft would be utilised for future exploration of the galaxy. Those seventeen days were also spent exchanging passengers between vessels – some from ap-Vanda craft to Vatta and Obiah craft with reciprocal movement of members of the latter two species to ap-Vanda vessels. These exchanges marked the first time that any members of the three species had met each other, in the flesh, for almost four-hundred years. They had kept in touch by electronic media and they had passed on technological and scientific advances that any of them may have discovered, up and down the line, but, in all that time, none of the three species had travelled to the others' home-worlds – mainly because of the length of time such journeys would take. But, despite their isolation in terms of distance, the three species were as one. Physically and, in many ways, culturally, they were different from each other; however, they all spoke the same language, the universal language as they called it, and they all held the same principles, ethics and morals. Once aboard their respective new berths on the various spacecraft, the different alien species settled into their new surroundings and met with their new travelling companions. As the journey progressed, the three groups of aliens would find that, in work on the invasion planning, training for that assault, and in areas of sport, they worked and played well together and that the ap-Vanda and Vatta contingents socialised with each other with ease.

***

The Vatta and the ap-Vanda were quite similar, both in terms of physical appearance and general demeanour. Both were quite a gregarious people, appreciative of the company of other, like-minded beings in a social surrounding, no matter the size of those groups. The Obiah, however, were somewhat less convivial animals, preferring smaller gatherings of close friends or, perhaps even more preferable to them, their own company. That was not to say that the Obiah did not participate in such crowded functions as enjoyed by their two alien companion species; they did but were, obviously, a bit uncomfortable at them. This social discomfort was noted throughout the fleet but it caused no issues; all passengers, of all species, recognised the differences between themselves and their colleagues and accepted the situation. Anyway, after an initial burst of inter-species bonding, albeit mainly amongst the ap-Vanda and the Vatta, everybody on-board all the vessels in the fleet reverted back to, predominantly, socialising with their own close friends of their own species, though that is not to say that there were no long-lasting bonds of inter-species friendship formed during that period of travel from the outer edge of the solar-system to the hell world. And, when it came to their studies, all of the three species tended to go it alone – except where the Obiah tutored the Vatta or the Vatta taught the ap-Vanda. There was that whole knowledge-gap procedure thing that they had to follow.

***

The aliens all knew the risks and consequences associated with unfettered over-population of worlds by immature species of animals; the inevitability of self-destruction by those, evolutionarily-retarded, species and the dire ramifications that awaited them, other forms of life and the planets they inhabited. In this particular instance, all the aliens were all deeply shocked and dismayed by the sheer number of the primary target animals on the planet, their environmental recklessness, their diverse yet oddly identical superstitious beliefs and their predilection towards, and delight in, inflicting extreme savagery upon other species of life, including their own. Both the Vatta and the Obiah had previously encountered alien animals with large populations that held strange, illogical beliefs and had maltreated both their own and other species of life, but never had they come across a hell world such as the one they were about to invade.

And they had to get there in a timely manner.

The massive armada of spacecraft at the very edge of interstellar space, more or less twenty-billion kilometres away from the target planet, began their journey towards that world on the eighteenth day after they arrived at that position in space. All personnel were advised to retire to their protective cocoons within three hours and the required instructions were entered into the ships' processors to enable automatic flight until the desired cruise speed was reached. Not that the crew actually, physically *flew* the spacecraft – even when not in their protective cocoons – they just oversaw the automated processes, ready to intervene in the event of technical failure or other such mishap. Not that one had ever occurred. Once released from the cocoons, the personnel resumed their preparations for the mission, due to commence as soon as they arrived at their destination.

***

The very worst aspect of space travel was that most necessary of evils – space/time speeds. It was bad enough being stuck in the confines of a spacecraft for many years on end, the constant claustrophobia, the breathing of mostly recycled air, eating, in some instances, reconstituted food and drinking recovered water, but having to spend multiple hours at a time strapped into a protective yet restrictive cocoon-like contraption really was the limit. In order to reach the target planet from the outskirts of the solar-system in a relatively reasonable time-frame, all the spacecraft had to engage their particulate drive engines to attain the required speed but, to achieve that, the initial gravitational forces created by the acceleration to that cruising speed were enough to splatter anything against the back walls of wherever it was on the ship if it was not secured, leaving just embedded remains and, in the case of an unsecured animal, a bloody stain. It would take over two and a half years to traverse the required distance, but the first two days were spent accelerating up to just short of one-million kilometres an hour and, for these two days, all the occupants of all the spacecraft had to be secured into their individual protective cocoons. It was not only the animal occupants that had to be secured – everything that was not fixed to the bulkhead had to be stored away or locked down somehow. And it was not just a sudden spurt of speed that did the damage. As the craft accelerated, whatever object was unsecured at the time would gradually find itself pressed against a wall that was situated conversely from the forward motion direction of the vessel. Eventually, as the velocity increased, the previously unrestrained object would be forcing its way deep into whatever barrier it had encountered.

In order to feed their occupants, each ship had sixty-eight dedicated decks of edible vegetable matter growth which was constantly cultivated. For many years the problem of protecting these plants during the initial phase of particulate drive travel had vexed them

– so much so that, for many years, the craft on their long distance excursions carried preserved food with them in vast storage areas. Eventually, they redesigned the entire agricultural levels in such a way that made both the growth process and gravitational protection possible, but only with the assistance of automatons – none of these levels were accessible by members of their species. The structural design of the ships containing the silk plants also had this unique feature, but on a much larger scale. These plants, unlike the food plants, were not required as part of everyday life, and all were kept in cool, near-vacuum conditions which would render them dormant until the fleet arrived at the target planet.

All flight controls during these cocoon-based periods were, of course, fully automated, as was the emergency shut-down procedure which would self-engage at the first sign of a fatal technical failure. This latter program would not be disengaged until cruise speed had been reached. Only when that safe level of momentum had been achieved would the restraints inside the cocoons be released and the covers opened. This was a proven safety system for all three species which, to their knowledge, had never failed, but it was agreed by all who travelled this way that it was the most uncomfortable and disconcerting part of the journey. The best way to endure the time was to sleep; but, in most instances, it was such a weird, indescribably awkward-feeling experience that sleep was difficult to achieve and, truth be told, many people could not achieve a *natural* sleep until they were released from the confines of the cocoon.

chapter eight

Sissonæ was one such animal. The cocoons were ingenious devices but she hated them with a passion. Every passenger room on every vessel was equipped with a cocoon. They spent the majority of their time unused and unnoticed beneath the floor under each bed, but as soon as possible after notification of the three hour limit of the speed and power increase, everyone on board returned to their rooms to ensure everything was locked down fast and safe. Once the passenger was wearing their full space-tight environmental suit, and on vocal command, the bed would retract into a secure niche and the cocoon would rise from its resting place in the floor, open its covers and await the occupant. When the occupant was installed into the device and had attached the relevant connections to their suit, the cover closed and the interior material tightly enveloped every bodily contour of its user, and the whole machine dropped back down to be fully integrated into the floor of the craft. The spacecraft was aware, by way of its processors, when everybody aboard was securely ensconced in their cocoons. As such, the entire fleet was aware, by way of their processors, when everybody was securely ensconced in their cocoons in every vessel in that fleet. As power was increased by pre-programmed increments to the fusion and particle drive engines and, in turn, the velocity of the vessel increased, other currently unessential and unused systems such as the internal atmospheric filters, artificial gravity generators and illumination were disengaged.

Lying in her personal cocoon, trying to ignore the awful sensations, the intense claustrophobia, the all-over straining, that gripped her body, Sissonæ had been attempting to force her thoughts to things more pleasant but, as usual in these contraptions, it was proving impossible. There were tremendous pressures on her muscles, her skeletal structure, her brain, her whole being. She was certain that there was not an atom in her entire body that did not feel stretched to breaking point. The sounds in her ears suggested that her blood was pumping around her vital organs at the speed of light and there were bright, flashing multi-coloured lights in front of her eyes despite the fact her eyelids were scrunched up tightly, an unavoidable facial muscular reaction under these conditions. For the first twenty or so minutes, she was not capable of any movement whatsoever, as was always the case, and this was the same for all of her colleagues, so she knew she had to bear the discomfort until she could even begin to contemplate struggling to find the whereabouts of the *off* button. After about ten minutes the cacophony in her head had subsided to a sufficient extent, and her mind had settled down enough for her to return to more lucid thoughts. She was still incapable of actual physical movement, however. They were getting closer to their target now so she allowed herself to dream of the future. Although the circumstances surrounding their arrival would be far from satisfactory, and there was another two and a half years to go, she longed for her first steps on the solid surface of the planet which the fleet was now racing towards. Seven years in space was much too long a time; or it would be by the time they got there. She had, for an age now it seemed, missed the demarcation point between night and day, dawn and sunset and the wind in her hair, the sun on her face, the taste of cold, sweet, fresh water and the sounds of other species living their every-day, every-night lives in the wildernesses of her home-world. In a few years, she would experience similar emotions on the alien planet ahead of them. She realised, of course, that the air would perhaps not be as pure as she had been used to on the ap-Vanda home-world, nor the water as clean, but it had been oh, so long since experiencing anything like that, she was certain she would not even notice the differences. She daydreamed of what she would do on the planet.

She imagined herself swimming in some ocean or other, laughing with her friends and colleagues whilst splashing through the surf as the warm sun beat down on them. Or strolling through the rain to one destination or another – she had forgotten about rain... and snow. How could she forget rain and snow? Especially snow. She remembered all the enjoyment she had had snowboarding in the mountains near to their settlement – perhaps the most fun she had ever had – and all of those wonderful, beautiful views over the planet that the landscape had afforded her. All of her child companions from that time were now with her on the mission, though not all aboard the same spacecraft. One of them, the male Loopolz, was aboard and had, recently, but only for a short time, become her lover whilst on the journey here, and her thoughts turned to him. She imagined them walking together through the wilderness, perhaps through an area of tall grasslands or in a wooded glade. She mentally added her other friends, Tufu, Tsaan and Hentanayre to the scene – although she and Loops, as everybody called him, were no longer together, they were much too different, personality-wise, they were still good friends. As were the others. Tsaan and Tufu would be, as usual these days, hand-in-hand in her little daydream, whilst Loops would be fretting about something or other, as usual, and Hentanayre would be mocking him – in a good-natured way, but mocking nonetheless – again, as usual. She tried to smile but the gravitational forces on her face would still not allow it and, instead, she continued grimacing.

Her mind returned to the hell world – all of the televisual content they had received over the years showed a planet of rain, snow, mountains, plains, vegetation and multiple species of wild animals – so much like her own home-world. She was unsurprised by the similarities between her home planet and the hell world – it was no coincidence that, if the circumstances of a planet's position in conjunction with a particular type of star, are so similar, as these two worlds were, that their geographical conditions, if not the life forms they sustain, would be very much alike. Of course, at that time, the target planet had acid rain and acid snow due to massive air pollution, melting snow caps on mountains because of global warming, less and less wild vegetation each day due to the over-population of Kaahu animals and their over-exploitation of land and forests, leading to desertification and an ever-decreasing number of wild animal species because of encroachment into their natural habitats and hunting or poaching of those species perilously close to extinction by those primary target animals. Those oceans she had just been dreaming about were also a lethal cocktail of heavy metals, Kaahu excreta, oils and multiple other pollutants. It always seemed to return to the Kaahu and their selfish, short-sighted stupidity. From what she had learned growing up and, more recently, from reports she had read from the teams monitoring the target planet's mass communication systems, whilst they were aware of the devastation they were causing, though many, inexplicably, denied it, the Kaahu did nothing to change their ways. They continued to pump billions of tonnes of carbon dioxide and other toxic wastes into their atmosphere every year whilst destroying millions of hectares of forests at the same time. The water they were not wasting on non-essential things, they were heavily polluting. Sissonæ was not feeling great to start with due to being stuck in this awful constricting contraption, but these thoughts ruined her mood.

She forced open her eyes to look at the current speed projected onto the visor in her helmet just above her eyes, and a sigh, inaudible above the cacophony of the discordant white noise in her mind, passed through her mouth – another thirty-eight hours, at least, before the cocoon release kicked in. Although just about everyone hated to use it, there was, in each cocoon, a device that released a fast-acting, sleep-inducing chemical into the oxygen supply of the environmental suit that, after the recipient awoke, caused a mild, short-lived but irritating headache. The *off* button. Reluctantly she struggled against the gravitational forces to find the relevant button on the control panel next to her right hand, hit it with her finger and, almost in an instant, drifted-off into a deep sleep.

chapter nine

It would take the fleet of spacecraft over two and a half years at just below one-million kilometres or so an hour to reach their designated positions around the target planet, so everybody had plenty of time to practice their manoeuvres or refine their plans of action. For the target-specific communication monitoring teams on all the spacecraft, there was no change in routine. They continued to source, analyse and classify a huge mass of data on a round-the-clock basis. They were solely interested in military and governmental communiqués emanating from the planet and from those sources they were almost certain they had located most, if not all, military bases, positions of stealth submarines, launch sites for the primary target animals odious nuclear weapons and the locations of storage facilities for other, equally as abhorrent, genocidal weapons across the planet. Monitoring these Kaahu organisations would alert them should their presence be discovered at any point and data from the governmental category should, in the near future especially, inform them of the primary target species' responses to their presence, if, in the highly unlikely event they were sighted before the mission proper had started – but that was so, so improbable! Although most of the spacecraft populations had some down-time after the rigours of their time in the cocoons, because the data from the probe continued to be received and had yet to be analysed, this group of aliens, one section on each ship, were always kept very busy. These teams were, as the amount of data received increased, augmented by teams charged with monitoring the Kaahu's electronic popular communication traffic and were also constantly employed around the clock. On their long journey to the target planet, the data from the probe orbiting the hell world was streamed back to the fleet by way of the second probe tethered at the Empty Space passage access point at the edge of the solar-system, on its way back to their home-worlds. All of that data required analysis and categorisation, though, as the journey progressed, they discovered that it was mostly junk. As the time passed, the quality of the data, in technical terms, improved even if the content it conveyed did not. After they had exited the Empty Space passage and began their long trek through the local system, they noted the emergence of much more of that type of electronic traffic, the almost unintelligible type, and concluded that improved communication technology had become more widely available to more of the primary target population. The vast majority of this new traffic was chatter – inane and unimportant – and very rarely caught in the specific taxonomic search criteria compared to the mass of encrypted documents from military and governmental sources. They also noted the gradual increase in this type of traffic as they progressed through the solar-system towards the target planet and the currency of some of the messages were often conveyed well before the official or more established news platforms. Although their resource planning had not quite predicted this development in terms of such an abundance of new data, they decided it was important enough to assign small, dedicated teams on each vessel to monitor and translate this content on a full-time basis over two years before they were scheduled to reach their destination. All their disseminations were later transmitted back to the ap-Vanda, Vatta and Obiah home-worlds.

The rest of the fleet populations continued to busy

themselves with their studies, their sporting activities, their invasion training routines and the day-to-day maintenance and management of themselves and their spacecraft.

chapter ten

Sissonæ was lying on the bed in her windowless room.

She had showered after a two-hour session in one of the many fitness rooms on the lower decks of her ship. It was part of her normal daily routine but, as far as anything could be in their society, it was almost mandatory for everyone in every craft to spend time exercising – if not mandatory it was certainly smart. Studying or teaching one academic subject or another, painting, writing or training in flight-simulators or other mock-ups was all well and good, but tough, physical exercise was essential to rid oneself of the boredom and the claustrophobia associated with the incessant nature of long-distance space travel. She played quite a bit of football, too – at least twice a week for the past seven years on board and for a few years before that at her home settlement. She was considered quite talented or, at least, she had been when she was younger.

For some reason, that day she was in particularly good mood. And, for now, she had ten minutes to just lie down and relax before she got ready to attend a concert. She contemplated on the incongruity of it all. They were less than twelve hours away from killing millions of Kaahu and here she was, a soon-to-be killer, about to go and listen and dance to music played by friends and colleagues, soon-to-be killers all, whilst their victims, blissfully unaware, continue with their lives, albeit warped and evil, below. It would not be a celebration of what they were about to do – more a team-bonding session to reassure everyone that they were together and that they were doing the right thing; a good thing. An ethical thing. And it was not the personnel on her spacecraft alone holding a concert – every ship in the fleet with passengers, was holding a similar get-together and everybody, save those considered vital to the smooth running of the vessels, had been asked to attend.

Before she had been in the fitness room, she had attended a meeting on visi-link. At seventeen years, she was the second youngest member of the organising panel, having been asked to join when one of the original members died whilst they were traversing Empty Space. The original member was quite old at one-hundred and fourteen years of age and was very highly respected both at home and with all the fleet population – she was also universally well-liked. She had been a fine administrator, though her first loves were cosmology and physiology – two of the subjects she had taught to her successor, Sissonæ, during the latter's youth on their home-world and aboard the spacecraft. Sissonæ had been assisting the elder female with her duties on the panel since before the fleet had set off for the journey and, the panel had decided, she was the obvious choice to replace the elder ap-Vanda. It was an honour for Sissonæ to accept the role, though her decision was tinged with the obvious regret of it being preceded by the death of someone she had known and loved for so long. She had considered the elder female a member of her immediate family, so her death was particularly upsetting – especially as all of her real immediate family were all back at the home-world. Having said she was the second youngest member of the panel, she was, in fact, one of the older members of the general population of her species out here in space, in percentage terms. Around eighty per cent of their number were under the age of seven when the fleet left their planet seven years ago. She thought of the Kaahu; from all she had learned about them over the years, they would consider that fact as strange, unbelievable even, she had no doubt, but, at seven years old, the members of her species were far, far better educated than Kaahu children of a comparable age – actually, the differences were beyond comparison. On her planet, children were not shackled with unintelligible nonsense or downright lies from birth and they started their formal education at a much younger age. As far as they could tell, it was not the fact that the children from her home-world were more intelligent than primary target children – they more than likely were not – the truth of the matter was that the parents on her world were far more intelligent than their Kaahu counterparts. Children start life as blank sheets of paper and their entire lives, and consequently the lives of their own children, are coloured by the example set by their parents. If, for countless generations, primary target children had been indoctrinated from birth with not only superstitious garbage such as being *created* in the image of some mythical, all-powerful being and, therefore, being superior to all other species of life, but also with concepts such as *greed is good* or *might is right,* or other such ridiculous platitudes which appear to have permeated all layers of all the Kaahu societies for millennia, how can a child's development and outlook on life *not* be irreparably warped? Couple these perversities with all the other mental, physical and sexual abuses that all primary target children would seem to have suffered over time, is it any wonder that there is a whole planet full of very sick primary animals down there?

She checked the time and tut-tutted softly to herself – she had been lost in those thoughts and now she was going to be late meeting up with her friends for the concert. Damn those Kaahu! She quickly dressed and looked at herself in the projected mirror on the nearest wall. She wore a pair of black trousers, a white casual top and a pair of flat shoes – all made of a plant-based, cotton-like material. Not for her species that disgusting, habitual use of the skins of other species – dead animal skin, just think of it! – to clothe themselves, so loved by the Kaahu. Still admiring her own dress-sense in the mirror, she laughed quietly to herself as she imagined what the Kaahu would think of her and her companions. As much as she had enjoyed their science fiction visi-entertainments and writing forms, their ideas about other extra-terrestrial species were, to say the least, ridiculous – or maybe that is *why* she enjoyed them? No identical uniforms with massive shoulder padding, no hairstyles indistinguishable from every other member of her species regardless of gender; no tattooed faces and no obligatory ray-gun slung from the hip for this bunch of aliens, and not a single one of them *ever* wore long, flowing robes with huge hoods – unless it was raining, of course! She would not be seen dead in a figure-hugging one piece jumpsuit or in a skirt so tiny that her underwear was on permanent display. Neither would any of her female friends – well, except maybe Hentanayre... There was, for these extra-terrestrials, no over-decorous jewellery hanging from their ears, necks or noses – no jewellery anywhere on their bodies at all, in fact. Her people could not truly understand the Kaahu fascination with adorning themselves with shiny metals and polished minerals. Such things had no special value on her world and, to their eyes, certainly were not at all attractive draped around any animal of any species. The Kaahu female obsession with plastering their faces with coloured mineral extracts and other such materials to cover their skin, although a strange concept to Sissonæ and all the other aliens, was slightly less incomprehensible – all the animal products the Kaahu ate and drank, the other poisons they introduced to their own bodies by multiple means, the polluted air they breathed and the stresses of living such miserable lives on the hell world, had a deleterious effect on the condition of Kaahu skin. None of the three alien species, be they male or female, needed to hide blemishes or premature wrinkles with such materials – their diets, their atmospheres and their ethea ensured their complexions and consciences were clear. For these species, age-related lines were to be respected, not obscured by muds and minerals.

Sissonæ was still contemplating the Kaahu fictitious interpretations of alien life-forms. *Nor did the ap-Vanda possess special powers*, she was thinking; they could not communicate telepathically nor could they heal wounds by a mere touch of a digit, they would be unable to fly, unassisted by machines, in the hell world's atmosphere, and neither could they read an animal's mind by the careful placing of hands onto that animal's face – nor any other such nonsense. Neither could the Vatta nor the Obiah. Nor had any of these species ever, ever heard of other animal species with such, so-called, evolved attributes. None of them had ever travelled in time to the past nor to the future, unless time spent in the Empty Space passage could qualify as such a form of travel – a moot question still hotly debated by their academics.

Sissonæ tried to push to the back of her brain the ridiculous images she had, inadvertently, called to mind of her friends, heavily armed and with strange haircuts, gaudy clothing, too much make-up and in independent flight over fleeing Kaahu animals, zapping them with beams of energy radiating from their eyes. She laughed out loud for a couple of moments but stopped herself – she had an important event to attend. Still laughing quietly to herself, she turned from the mirror, picked-up her personal communication device and left the room. The mirror display and the lights in the room switched-off automatically the instant the room realised it was now empty.

***

By the time the female alien had arrived, albeit slightly late, at the meeting-cum-concert and, later, finished dancing the night away with her friends and colleagues, most of the fleet of spacecraft were busily manoeuvring themselves into their pre-arranged positions in geosynchronous orbit around the hell world at a distance corresponding, more or less, to the distance from the planet surface to its orbiting moon of approximately three-hundred and seventy-five thousand kilometres. The remainder of ships, mainly support vessels, were still arriving or yet to finally position themselves at their designated locations. These support vessels carried equipment not necessarily required for the journey from their home-world but essential for the mission proper. Some carried the component minerals to build, in conjunction with the silk, other types of craft or other machines, and still others contained automatons so necessary for all of their structural requirements, all their manufacturing processes and all their agricultural tasks.

***

On the planet below, every minute that the three distinct populations of aliens on all the spacecraft with animal passengers spent discussing the coming events or dancing to music or sat, listening to either, multifarious atrocities were being committed by the Kaahu. In various locations across the planet, upwards of one-hundred and fifty-thousand non-Kaahu animals were being slaughtered for consumption by the dominant species at a rate of two and a half thousand every second, equating to nine-million every hour. Multiple thousands of marine creatures of numerous species were being dragged from the safety of their undersea world to suffocate in the gases above the water surface, whilst oceanic and freshwater mammals and reptiles were also perishing, trapped in the same paraphernalia of death utilised to capture the animals with gills, every minute. Every minute, multiple thousands of feathered aves of various species were being held upside down by their more than likely already broken legs, in contraptions designed by the Kaahu to slit the throats of the unfortunate animals before releasing them, still very much alive, into scalding hot water to facilitate the removal of their feathers. Thousands of land mammals of various species would also be held upside down and have their throats cut to slowly bleed to death, whilst Kaahu animals would cut and pull and strip the dying creature of his or her skin for use in unnecessary and absurd items, such as shoes or seats. Yet others would be shot in the head with a metal bolt, often not killing the animal but merely badly injuring him or her, leading to the creature being skinned and butchered whilst still alive. These methods of slaughter were used for both commercial gain and inane religious purposes – it made no difference, the outcomes were the same. Even those non-Kaahu species considered so-called *pets* in most areas of the planet, those felines and canines, were not safe from slaughter and consumption by many Kaahu in different locations. They would be killed in their hundreds after spending hours crammed together in tiny cages before being processed, which could mean being thrown alive into boiling water, beaten with sticks or being skinned alive before being killed – this was happening every single minute of the day somewhere on the planet. This caused great consternation amongst those *pet-owning* Kaahu who knew of this practice – as if the particular species of a tortured and slaughtered animal mattered. The Kaahu, it would appear, had a particular penchant for skinning animals alive. Again, these thousands of deaths occurred every minute on the hell world. Animals of other species were not only massacred for food. As a single example of such cruel activity, the largest land mammals on the planet were being murdered by their thousands every year for their tusks – that they be made into ornaments to adorn the homes and bodies of wealthy Kaahu. These magnificent animals were, at that time, on the very brink of extinction. Thousands of other individual animals would be murdered or die in Kaahu experiments, zoo-prisons and their so-called sporting activities. Every single minute on that hell world also brought death and misery to many hundreds of the Kaahu inhabitants who would be murdered by members of their own species for little or no reason, left to starve to death or freeze to death or die of some curable disease, all because of the greed or neglect or indifference of their fellow animal species.

***

By the time the female alien awoke from the sleep of someone who had danced the night away, the whole fleet was in position and ready for the task in hand.

chapter eleven

There were, more or less, sixteen-thousand artificial satellites orbiting the hell world at various altitudes. Most were former working machines of some description or other, but were now just lumps of useless metal, cluttering-up the space around the planet. Everything on, around or above the hell world, it seemed, was polluted. Despoiled by the Kaahu.

At a pre-arranged time, all of the required spacecraft, at a sedate three-hundred thousand kilometres an hour, began the short, hour-long journey to attain an altitude of forty-thousand kilometres above the target planet and, once they were all in a position to cover the entire globe, the vessels started to emit a combination of ultra-high-powered microwave and electromagnetic pulses towards the planet surface, ensuring that all of the primary target's working satellites were also in their line of pulse-projection. After a few minutes of such exposure, the immediate effect of the dual radiation attack on the planet was to instantly and permanently disable all independently powered electric or electronic systems anywhere and everywhere on the hell world. This meant all power generating operations, all electronic communications, including all military and all governmental communications, and all modes of motorised transport in whatever form was fatally crippled, save, perhaps, for those powered by the labour of the Kaahu or of other species. This meant no electric lights, no heating, none of their computers would ever calculate again, no electronic communication, no launching of weapons of mass destruction. This meant that in-flight airborne transportation vehicles would stall and crash to the ground, whilst those already on the ground would never again reach for the skies. This meant that all of the primary targets' motorised wheeled land-based vehicles, all powered ocean or sub-oceanic vehicles and all non-primary-target-propelled river craft would cease to function. The land vehicles would now be unusable save for free-wheeling and the water vehicles would be capable only of drifting aimlessly in the currents. This meant that the capacity of society on the planet to properly function or mindlessly destroy was disabled and would now never recover.

All of the satellites were instantly and permanently disabled. One of those satellites was larger than most of the others and contained five animals, all members of the primary target species. The data analysis teams back on the spacecraft watched as, console by console, all of the monitored traffic on the social, governmental and military channels stopped and their visi-screens, for the first time in decades, seemed to freeze. Their task of analysing current data from the hell world had ended and they could relax, for a short time at least. The orbital scan and culler weapons were activated on-board all of the vessels still proceeding towards the target planet. The overall coverage of each scanner was set to a twenty-five kilometre radius. The weapons were fully charged and ready to go. The first members of the primary target species to die from the cull weapons in this stage of the project were those five animals orbiting the planet inside the large, artificial satellite, when the nearest craft activated a short burst from its weapon lasting less than half a second. They would have been dead shortly afterwards, anyway – all of the life-supporting systems on-board the satellite had been destroyed by the earlier electromagnetic and microwave pulse attack and, at the point of their deaths, the animals would probably have been already gasping for breath attempting to access the oxygen in their previously discarded space suits; which, being governed electronically, would not have worked, anyway.

On the planet below, even as airborne transport vehicles were still dropping from the skies as their engines and vital electronic systems seemed to give up and ceased to function, in all areas of military and governmental importance to the primary targets, hundreds of thousands of their species were dropping dead where they stood, sat and walked. Those still sleeping would never again awaken. From a military point of view, the first to die were in those areas deemed by the organising panel to be the most dangerous to the outcome of the mission, those in control of nuclear weapons and other such abominations. These systems should all have already been made inactive but the aliens did not like to take unnecessary risks. Each deployment of the orbital cull weapon lasted for around thirty seconds and, immediately after one area had been culled, the next area was targeted and the weapons discharged. After fifteen minutes, over twenty-thousand targets had been accessed and the area culled, leaving perhaps ten- to twenty-million dead animals in military camps, on board sea-going vessels, in deep, supposedly impenetrable mountain range bunkers, far beneath the oceans, far above sea level, in capital cities, wilderness or rural retreats and legislative buildings, plus any animals within a twenty-five kilometre radius of the centre of these targets. This, effectively, wiped-out the military capabilities and political leadership of the entire planet – particularly those with the means of potential mass destruction – just in case.

On the spacecraft directing the attacks, attention was then given to the next set of targets.

chapter twelve

After those short minutes of high intensity radiation bombardment, even as the spacecraft began their orbital assault, one-thousand dull, black, rectangular probes were launched from the same number of vessels. A few minutes later, these new probes, complete with scan and culler weapon components, were heading towards the target planet. It had been estimated that these one-thousand machines would be more than sufficient to carry-out the Temuri extraction phase of the mission. On the designated lead ship, still tethered in space near to the moon orbiting the hell world, much work had already been undertaken to identify Temuri extraction targets for this essential stage of the project. Scanner operatives had examined detailed electronic maps of the planet to find isolated areas of primary target habitation and had identified a small cluster of structures on the largest island land mass in the lower hemisphere of the planet – lower based on the Kaahu perception of how their world was orientated in the universe. They had earlier employed their medical scanners to ensure that there were, indeed, Temuri at the site.

Once the affirmative decision to proceed with this phase was received from the organising panel, the relevant data was entered into the scanner parameter program and the extraction teams were briefed on the details of their mission. The extraction teams would be the first members of any of their three species to step foot on the target planet and the teams were all extremely nervous about the prospect of coming face-to-face with the primary targets, alive or dead, for the first time after learning so much about them whilst growing up on their home-worlds and on the long journey here. They knew well that the first Kaahu they would encounter would, more than likely, be dead, but there was always the possibility that either the weapon component on the probe failed to work to the required specifications, or that one or more Kaahu, not in range of the weapons when activated, would appear on the scene, perhaps on the back of some species of animal classified by the Kaahu as a *working-animal*. They also knew that, if either of those events occurred, they would have to kill any primary target they met – and that was the terrifying part.

The planetary transport vehicles that the extraction teams would use were two of many thousands of similar vehicles of various sizes that the three alien species had transported from their home-worlds. Each powered by fusion drive engines and, as all of their craft, constructed from the silk compound materials, the version they were about to fly was fast, strong, agile and streamlined for intra-atmospheric flight. The pilots were all well versed in flying the vehicles – but only in simulators. It had been many years since any of their number had actually flown any kind of vehicle in space or entered an atmosphere, so this was also a source of some trepidation on all of their parts – pilots, passengers and the panel. Flight simulation was all well and good but recent experience of the operation would have been the preferred option for all of them. It did not help that there were so few of the aliens of an age that had *any* experience of such intra-atmospheric flights. In any event, though, all the craft were capable of fully automated flight; should any mishap occur in-flight or, perhaps, during atmospheric entry or escape, a simple voice command would enable that facility and the auto-systems would take control. Eventually travelling at a speed of around seventy-five kilometres a second, it would take the two planetary transport vehicles less than half an hour to cover the distance from their home ship approaching the very edge of the atmosphere to the planet surface itself. Once there, the plan called for a maximum of half an hour on the surface to locate and secure the Temuri subjects before returning to their ship with them. The first planetary transport vehicle would carry the sixteen members of the primary extraction team; five from each of the three alien species and a pilot, whilst the second vehicle, also carrying fifteen passengers plus the pilot, would act as a contingency in case of unforeseen circumstances, protecting the scene and visually recording and transmitting the effort back to their home ship and the rest of the fleet. The first planetary transport vehicle would, after discharging the teams, also go airborne to both illuminate the area and, if necessary, deploy their on-board cull weapon to quell any unexpected primary target intrusion in conjunction with their colleagues in the secondary vehicle. They had practised the manoeuvres many times but only in the confines of their home ship's spacious hangar in a mock-up of several three-storey primary target-type homes, complete with stairs and replicas of the furniture the teams would be likely to encounter and have to navigate to reach their target subjects. Much like the space flight and atmospheric entry concerns of the pilots, the extraction teams were apprehensive about their lack of practical experience. All they could do, however, was keep practising in the hangar and to check and double-check their equipment whilst the pilots, in the simulators, went through the flight procedures until they were given the go-ahead for the mission.

In another part of their ship, and on two-hundred or more others, an area was being prepared for the extracted Temuri subjects. The first extraction team's planetary transport vehicles were launched from the ship within fifteen minutes of the deployment of the probes, as the initial orbital culler assault was drawing to a close, and they quickly attained their optimum cruising speed of almost two-hundred and seventy-thousand kilometres an hour. On the lead ship, the scan team had chosen a small group of buildings in the designated area that, in total, contained twelve animals of the primary target species – ten were to be culled and two to be extracted. This particular site had been chosen because of the opportunity to extract two animals that matched their criteria in such an isolated area. Most of the sparsely populated areas they had scanned had no such prospective extraction targets, and a few contained only one Temuri – this area was ideal for their purposes. The necessary location coordinates, dna and cellular data were fed into their processors and transmitted to the probe nearest that location, and this, in turn, positioned itself, hovering three-hundred metres above the specified zone. The probe auto-adjusted its scan and weapon facilities to home in on the target area and opened its aperture to widen the scope of operation to a radius of two kilometres, with the structures containing the primary targets squarely in the centre of its aiming mechanism. Both of the extraction teams' planetary transport vehicles had, in the meantime, arrived at and successfully surmounted the atmospheric barrier that surrounded the planet, albeit with some accompanying gut-wrenching turbulence. They continued with their flight and, on arrival at a predetermined point, contacted the lead ship to inform them of their location. On receipt of the message from the extraction teams, the scanner operator on board the lead ship activated the necessary command to initiate the cull weapon. The probe altered its orientation from a vertical to a horizontal bearing, engaged the scanner and began to slowly spin on its central axis. On acquiring the required rotational speed, the culler component on the probe was discharged.

The probe had been designed by a Vatta male named Anawanaouitu, and many people questioned his creation, saying that its axis-spinning was unnecessary, that the task could be performed without such rotation and that it was only for show. Anawanaouitu vehemently denied such allegations – but always with a slight grin and with an obvious twinkle in his eye.

The culling process lasted less than a second and there was no loss of power in the probe noticeable to the eye of the operator back on the orbiting lead spacecraft. He immediately checked the read-out from the scanner and confirmed to himself that the test, from his point of view, had been successfully completed. He relayed this knowledge to both extraction teams who were, at this point, also hovering above the test site at an altitude approximately parallel to the rotating probe. The first planetary transport vehicle began its descent to the surface as soon as the confirmation was received from the lead ship whilst, at the same time, the second vehicle was scanning a radius of one kilometre around the test site for any sign of primary target life – none was found. It was a warm night towards the middle of the planet's summer season in the lower hemisphere and particularly dark on the outskirts of the area with the buildings containing the targets. The area was, in fact, in total darkness. As the first vehicle settled on the surface of the planet, the pilot of the back-up craft illuminated the area around the buildings with powerful lamps embedded in the underside of her vehicle. The fifteen members of the extraction team exited the first vehicle as soon as it had landed and the air-locking doors, closed to prevent any contamination from this alien world, had been opened. As soon as they alighted, the pilot closed the outer doors and raised the vehicle to the same hovering height as the companion vehicle to assist in scanning the area and add some more illumination. The extraction team stood motionless for a few moments to allow the debris, agitated by the transport vehicle's fusion engines, to settle and, in truth, just to marvel that they were actually standing on solid ground for the first time in over seven years. One or two even stamped their feet up and down as if making sure it was physically solid. In silence, they glanced at each other, smiled and looked around the site. What they assumed to be the frantic barking of a canine was heard coming, it seemed, from one of the smaller buildings at the edge of the area; obviously aware of their presence even though their mode of travel was virtually silent – though the glaring lights from the two hovering craft may also have given them away and alerted the animal. From a large nearby structure came the sounds of shuffling hooves and characteristic lowing of bovine animals. Other than these sounds, the incursion site was silent and still.

The team were all wearing their black extra-vehicular vacuum protection suits which were mainly constructed from their silk-based materials, as were their spacecraft and planetary transport vehicles, but also had an outer layer of reinforced graphene for added protection from the explosive metal projectiles so loved by the Kaahu. Although not particularly required on this mission, the protective suits were motion-assisted by small servo-motors at the relevant, corresponding movement points of their bodies but may be useful should they need to lift any heavy objects – such as animal corpses. The outfits were also fully self-contained, environmentally controlled bio-suits keeping the wearer at their ideal body temperature, either in the deepest cold of space or here, in this hot, dry desert of an alien world. Embedded within the headgear, and already activated, were powerful lights and visi-sensors which, as opposed to similar sensors on the planetary transport vehicles, were designed for recording events only and not transmission. The constant movements of the wearer often distorted transmissions, especially over great distances, so the more static vehicular sensors were deemed more suitable for this purpose. The atmosphere surrounding the team was not thought to be harmful to them, not out there in the middle of a desert, hundreds of kilometres from large towns or cities; it was, after all, constituted of more or less the same gases they would have breathed on their own planets. But the organising panel had decided at the outset of the mission proper that none of their number should remove any part of their protective gear whilst on the surface of the hell world – not yet, at least – as there may be bacteria or pollutants in the air or on surfaces they may touch that could be harmful to their species that they were unaware of and, at later stages, there would be harmful bacteria flying around as lifeless organic materials began to decay. Judging by their facial expressions, even though they were separated from the environment by their protective clothing, they all seemed to agree that it felt good to stand on solid ground once again.

The five Obiah and five Vatta were each armed with either culler, cremator or repeller portable weapons, whilst two of the ap-Vanda team members, Loopolz and Hentanayre, were carrying hand-held culler weapons. Two others, Tufu and Tsaan, were carrying two large boxes. The final member of the ap-Vanda team, Sissonæ, carried a portable medical scanner and it was this team member that led all the others to the first building which, as shown on the instrument she carried, contained the first extraction target. Three other, dead, Kaahu should also be there – the data from the test ship had suggested that the targets would be grouped together in two buildings; four, including the first extraction target, would be in one building and the other eight in or around a second structure, fifty or less metres away. Hentanayre, carrying a portable cull weapon, led the way into the first building, with Sissonæ and the other ap-Vanda following closely behind. The cull weapon was pre-set with generic primary target specifications so any unexpected encounter with any member of the primary target species could be instantly resolved. The Obiah and the Vatta took up defensive positions outside of the structure. Their research suggested that, if a dwelling was more than one storey in height, the occupants tended to sleep on an upper storey and, as it was in the middle of the night, they expected all of the Kaahu in the area to be in their beds. This was a two-storey building so all five ap-Vanda members of the team climbed the stairs in single file, the lights on their helmets illuminating the way.

They stopped at the first door, which was ajar, and Sissonæ pushed it further open. She moved into the room, watching her scanner for any sign of life. On a small bed, covered by a blanket and sheet, lay a small, unmoving form. The instrument was also unmoving. She believed the body to be that of a young female, but it was difficult to tell as the body was on its side, fully covered by the bedclothes and the head partially obscured by a combination of the bedclothes and the animal's long, fair hair covering its face. She turned and left the room to join her colleagues. As they proceeded down the narrow corridor, each of the other team members looked in turn at the dead body as they passed the doorway – their first sight of a primary in the flesh, albeit dead and mostly hidden from view. It was, at the same time, both horrific and fascinating. In the next room down they found their extraction target sleeping peacefully. The scanner readings confirmed life, gender and age. Sissonæ and Hentanayre stepped aside as a third member of the team, Tsaan, entered the room and approached the sleeping target. He put his box on the floor, opened the lid, stood and reached down to pull back the bed-covers and pick up the target. This final action provoked a response and the animal struggled in his arms. Tsaan was, however, much stronger than the much smaller

animal and it was subdued without difficulty, though
it screamed loudly and, as Tsaan placed the animal in
his box, persistently. Sissonæ communicated a short
message to the transport vehicle pilot, an ap-Vanda
named Ofnu, as Tsaan, with his container of screaming
Temuri headed down the narrow corridor for the steps.
As he and his charge returned to the landing site, the
transport vehicle was, as they approached, setting down;
and, as target number one was being secured in one of
the specially designed, separate isolation compartments
adjacent to the airlock, the rest of the team were stood
in a third room in the dwelling looking over the bodies
of two adult animals – one male, the other female –
lying on a bed, larger than those in the other rooms,
covered only with a single fabric sheet. The scanner was
unmoving. The team remained motionless and silent
for almost twenty seconds looking, staring even, at the
dead animals, until Sissonæ turned and left the room.
All the others followed immediately, except for Loopolz
– he leant over one of the bodies and nudged it with his
gloved hand, perhaps expecting a response. There was
none. He, too, turned and left the room and, shortly
afterwards, the dwelling itself.

The four of them, with their ten covering sentinels
in close proximity, moved towards a long, narrow
single-storey building from where the second life signs
were emanating some fifty metres in front of them. As
they neared the building, the barks and growls from
the canine grew louder, more strident. He or she, they
could not tell from where they were, was situated a
few metres past the door they were heading towards.
The four were all looking towards the animal as they
approached their next destination, anticipating an
attack. It did not happen. By the door of the structure
sat a body slumped in a wooden chair; a dark, slender
male Kaahu animal holding some form of weapon with
double barrels. Sissonæ checked his life signs against

her medical scanner – no indication of life. The Vatta and Obiah contingents, one by one, all went over to have their first glimpse of such a creature before resuming their defensive positions. He had, perhaps, been tasked with guarding the area after the power failed. Each of the extraction team peered at the corpse with interest as they passed it. The ap-Vanda entered the single storey building, their helmet lights showing them a room with eight beds, four at each side and four of which were occupied. They walked through the middle of the room towards the back where they could see a door and, again, each of them glanced down at the four beds in which lay the four dead animals. Once through the door, they were in another narrow corridor with four doors, two on each side, with the life signs being generated from the farthest door on the right which, like the other three doors in the corridor, was closed. Sissonæ turned the handle and opened the door to its widest extent and entered the room. There were two beds; one, larger than the other, holding two prostrate forms under its sheets, was illuminated. In the harsh light they saw a small, open mouthed but silent face staring back at them from the smaller bed, the hands with clenched knuckles tightly gripping a wooden horizontal rail atop numerous vertical slats of wood surrounding its bed. Loopolz, by the door, was startled by the sudden sight of the aware creature in the harsh light and, on impulse, the culler weapon was raised. Tufu and Hentanayre instinctively placed their hands on his shoulders, both to stop him discharging the weapon and to try and calm him down. He lowered the weapon. Tufu removed her hand from her colleague's shoulder and moved towards extraction target number two. As she neared it, she could see tears welling up in its eyes, but it remained quiet. She opened her box, picked up the animal from the bed, laid it in the container and headed out of the building towards the transport vehicle which had stayed on the ground. The others followed her until they reached the outside of the building.

Sissonæ, the team member with the medical scanner, walked towards a small shed where the canine was still barking. He, she now noted, was a large animal with short black and brown hair and, as she approached, he growled menacingly, baring his teeth, and strained against the chain attached to the collar around his neck and also tethered to a metal post in the ground two or so metres away. Keeping her distance so as not to upset the animal further, and for her own protection, she activated the scanner and recorded his dna sequence. She returned to her colleagues and, between them, they entered the data into the portable cull weapon controls and a Vatta culler weapon operator targeted the canine and discharged the weapon. The body of the canine glowed slightly for an instant and the animal immediately died.

After the unfortunate killing of the canine, they moved to the much larger, barn-like edifice. All three team leaders, one of each species, entered the building and found up to forty bovine animals shut inside. Also in the structure were eight equines, tethered in wooden cubicle spaces – their whinnying had been drowned-out by the lowing of the bovines so their presence came as somewhat of a surprise to the aliens. Sissonæ scanned both species of animal, recorded their data, took images and turned to leave. On her way out, she transmitted the details to the transport vehicle's data-processor and spoke briefly, directed at one of the two pilots, though all aboard both vehicles could hear. All of them, the ap-Vanda, the Vatta and the Obiah, retreated to their transport vehicle. On their return they found that the two extraction targets were secured into their seats in the isolation areas and both were now screaming and crying simultaneously and incoherently, though they were barely audible through the dividing transparent barrier. The returning team members settled into their own seats, strapped themselves in and Sissonæ signalled to the pilot that they were ready for departure.

The pilot, Ofnu, asked the data-processor to shut the inner airlock doors and directed the vehicle into the air. During their ascent the second vehicle, armed with the data received from the barn containing the bovine and equine animals, utilised the on-board culler weapon towards the building, instantly killing all of those species within the building. Both planetary transport vehicles headed towards the upper atmosphere, through that barrier to open space and, eventually, back to their home ship. The whole operation, from landing to take-off, had been completed within fifteen minutes and had been a total success. Most, if not all, of the fleet's occupants were following the extraction team's exploits on the planet as relayed from the visi-sensors on the second planetary transport vehicle hovering above the scene and, audibly, though little was actually said, from the team on the ground.

At its conclusion, almost everyone was extremely satisfied with both the execution of the mission and the outcome – it could not have gone better. It was obviously distressing that other species had had to be culled during the mission but, from the outset, they had known that, because of the primary target's savage practices, billions of such individuals of other species would also have to be killed so as not to upset the balance of the ecological and evolutionary processes of the planet. These other species, bred in their billions purely for slaughter as food for the Kaahu, would, for the most part, be detrimental to the environment and to wild species if they were allowed to roam freely in such vast numbers. Other sub-species domesticated over time as companion animals to the primary targets, such as the canine just culled, would probably be unable to survive on their own and if they did, once again, there would be vast numbers of them wandering around the planet, many of them carnivorous, destroying habitats and, in all probability, decimating other species. Of course, great care would be needed when culling these animals, as similar species, non-food and non-companion, were also living on the planet, many of them in danger of extinction. Generally, though, the test mission was thought to have been hugely successful. It had shown both the robustness and stealth capabilities of their planetary transport vehicles and the steadfastness and bravery of the extraction teams. Plus, and perhaps most importantly, it had proven the theory behind the probes with selective scanning and cull technology.

Throughout their journey through the atmosphere of the hell world, both there and back, Hentanayre had sat, much like when she was a young child on her home-world, with her hands covering her face.

chapter thirteen

On their return from the extraction mission, the two planetary transport vehicles, their thirty-two ap-Vanda, Obiah and Vatta passengers and the two extracted Temuri were all kept in quarantine until the possibility of harmful bacteria or other such threats – either airborne, on the exposed surfaces of either of the vehicles or the team's protective suits or from anywhere on or in the extracted animals – could be eliminated. The sixteen members of the secondary team felt slightly aggrieved that, despite the fact they had not even landed on the planet surface or been in contact with the planetary atmosphere, let alone been in contact with the Temuri or any dead Kaahu, they too had to be quarantined for a short time. They got over it.

In the isolation room, Loopolz sat apart from the rest of his colleagues from the two extraction teams. Although there was a great sense of exhilaration surrounding the successes of their mission and huge satisfaction with their joint achievements, emotions he shared with all the other members of the teams, he was also feeling a contradictory emotion of deep disappointment in his own actions. He had been one of the culler weapon carriers on the mission and had almost discharged that weapon towards the second Temuri extraction target; if it had not been for the quick, soothing responses of Tufu and Hentanayre, two of the other team members, he could have killed the animal. They had trained for this operation for months. Several hours every day over that period had been spent practising for every eventuality that they could foresee but, in the end, all it took to spook him were those two wide, moist eyes, illuminated in the darkness, staring straight at him. The cull weapon was not calibrated for a specific primary target's genetic make-up, unlike the weapon used on the probe, so, had he used it on the Temuri, the animal would have been destroyed. His colleagues had attempted to console him. They said he was not a military, none of them were, and it was a perfectly normal reaction during such a stressful mission. They said that they had been the first of their species to walk on that alien planet and said that he had been charged with protecting the extraction team on the ground. They said that it was a massive responsibility and his senses must have been heightened to such an extent that his reaction to the situation was understandable. They said they probably would have reacted in exactly the same way had they been similarly charged with such an obligation. He knew they were right in most they had said to him, but it did not quieten the doubts in his mind. Hentanayre, his friend, had also been present and she also was armed with a culler. She had not reacted the way he had done. But they were correct, he was not a military. He was many, varied things; first and foremost, a mathematician, plus he dabbled with geophysics and he was a planetary transport vehicle pilot, despite never actually having flown a real vehicle; a designer of dwellings and data-processor software; a linguist – he spoke and read four of the most popular target planet languages; a musician and an athlete, albeit not a particularly good one. But he was not a military.

He had spent a good part of his life in space. He was nine years old when the fleet of spacecraft had left the orbit of their home planet to begin the journey to the hell world. For over seven years before that time and ever since, his had been a life of study, creation and recreation. On departure from the home-world, he was already fluent in three of the alien languages and had always shown great proficiency in mathematics and basic physics. He was particularly enthralled by mathematics and, as with all members of his species, he was encouraged to pursue the academic subjects and creative paths he most enjoyed and to practice and research those areas, interspersed with acquiring skills in other fields of study or activity such as piloting and music. He chose to specialise in mathematics because, in his opinion, it was the basis of everything in the universe. He loved to create music and played percussion and a wind instrument, both with a few other friends for the former and as a soloist for the latter. He and his musician friends had often performed concerts for their fellow travellers in the recreation rooms on the ship over the long years of the journey. He also loved to play football, though he knew he was a less than average player. He loved the mixture of exercise, friendly competition and banter. He loved that very, very rare feeling he got when he scored a point for his team. Football was, by far, the most popular sport amongst his species, both on the home-world and out in the vastness of the galaxy. Every spacecraft organised internal leagues of ten or more teams that ran, for all intents and purposes, throughout the year and games were played almost every night of every week.

For the past six months or so, though, the music and football had had to take back seats as work took centre stage. Because of his linguistic skills, he had been working as a data analyst with the tele-visual tracking team for some time but only for a few hours a week; watching news or current affairs transmissions from the target planet, in some instances translating the verbal communications to their own language, writing and presenting analyses to on-board logicians and administrators and, by visi-link, to members of the organising panel on other spacecraft. He had also volunteered to assist the translation and analysis of the mainly textual electronic shared nexus of the target planet as they increased in volume.

He had grown up with his good friends Sissonæ, Hentanayre, Tufu and Tsaan – they all had lived in the same settlement – and was proud to be part of a team with them. Except for football, none of them shared his interests – Hentanayre had never even *attempted* to play a musical instrument – but they were all very loyal and supportive. Even so, he often felt alone and isolated from even these close friends. He wanted to be popular and he wanted to be successful in everything he did, but in his own mind he had failed, spectacularly, at every turn. And here he was, again, a failure.

He had not dared to believe that *they* would be members of the first ever landing party to the hell world and, when that call came, it involved hours of daily training – a task he undertook happily and with some pride. And then came his inappropriate reaction to the primary extraction target and this feeling of overwhelming self-disappointment. He would definitely need to speak to his designated analyst.

All of the passengers aboard all of the spacecraft were encouraged to communicate their feelings in one way or another. A visi-record, perhaps, or a textual document or, generally, chatting with friends, relatives, if aboard, and colleagues. But each person had a designated analyst. They were not all fully-trained psychologists or psychoanalysts, but many of the passengers had a grasp of the basics – the ap-Vanda, especially, would need such skills when caring for the Temuri. Loopolz, himself had taken the training and was a designated analyst to three ap-Vanda – but he would need to discuss this episode with someone other than himself.

***

The extraction team members were released from isolation after two hours and a shower. Neither of the planetary transport vehicles nor any of the team's extra-vehicular vacuum protection suits were found to have been contaminated by unwanted bacteria, but they were also sent to be thoroughly sanitised – just in case. The Temuri extraction targets, however, were still in quarantine and under observation by teams of suitably clad medics and bacteriologists. Samples of various bodily fluids and solids had been elicited from them and they were being tested and scrutinised. It would be a further three hours before they were transferred to an area of the spacecraft especially modified for these and future *guests*. The testing would not finish there, however, as once settled into their new environment, teams of geneticists would start sequencing each individual animal's genomes for defects not discernible from their normal medical scanners.

The organising panel later held a visi-link conference reviewing the data from the extraction team's helmet-mounted cameras to ascertain whether or not any useful information could be gleaned from their experiences on the surface. The unfortunate incident with the second extraction target and the cull weapon carrier was noted, but it was decided that the blame must lie with their training methods rather than with the individual himself, and perhaps in future, weapon operatives should not physically accompany extraction team members into dark, enclosed areas where target life signs are detected. It was also thought to be prudent, in light of this incident, to limit night extractions to occasions where there were no alternatives. All-in-all, the culler weapon operator's negative experience had turned out to be a valuable lesson for the future and this, in turn, was part of the feedback he and the other members of the extraction teams received from the panel, and it was specifically stated that both extraction teams must be highly commended for their actions during the mission.

chapter fourteen

It was mid to late winter on that auspicious day in the upper hemisphere of the hell world.

It was on a day that was not normally spent at their usual places of employment or study, as was traditional for the primary target species. The Kaahu called it the *weekend*.

It was a day where, in one area of the planet and across a particular time span, up to three-million or more animals would congregate in specific locations to watch their favourite sports. Millions more of them engaged in personal, commercial activities and other non-employment or non-educational related pursuits.

Utilising the standard time system used on the planet, it was slightly after the fifteenth hour at the precise point from where the Kaahu had arbitrarily deemed that those calculations began. That area was a densely populated, relative to its size, peninsula at the western end of the largest continental land mass in the upper hemisphere. Some Kaahu considered this area to consist of two separate continents, but this was a political rather than a geological demarcation.

Moving to the east from that geographic position, the time measurement increased until, at the farthest edge of the continental land mass, it was eleven or more hours ahead of that time.

At the same time, a few thousands kilometres even further to the west, across an ocean from that peninsula on the coast of the upper continental land mass, the primary target inhabitants had started their day a few hours earlier. On the far side of that continent, however, the animals would be, mostly, either still asleep or beginning to wake up from their nocturnal rest.

In the lower hemisphere it was mid-to-late summer.

At the site of the test extraction, on that large, continental island, it was nine hours later, already into a new day and most of the primary target animals would, more likely than not, also be sleeping, as the Kaahu culled in the test extraction had been before their deaths.

It was beginning to get darker in the sports arenas towards the western edge of the largest landmass in the upper hemisphere.

Although the primary target species could not have possibly known it at the time, all of their devices that utilised electronic and electric processes, from power generation to their mobile communication equipment, would have been fatally compromised during that previous fifteen or so minutes as the electromagnetic and microwave pulse beams saturated the their home-world. However, taking the apparent ubiquity of those personal communication devices, many of the animals, if not most at that point, must have suspected that something was amiss, though it was doubtful they could have foreseen their imminent deaths as a consequence.

Some of the alien invaders, out in the periphery of the planet's atmosphere, imagined that the audiences must be getting impatient for the lights to come back on and the spectaculars to begin. From what they knew of them, however, the Kaahu would not leave, they had paid their currency – nothing was more important to them than their currencies – and power cuts were not particularly unusual to the animals attending such events. Somewhat bizarrely though, the aliens had also learned, these power outages were sometimes deliberately caused so that some other Kaahu, somewhere, would benefit monetarily from gambling and engineered such instances for their own profit – it beggared belief.

Some aboard the vessels had surmised that many of the animals attending the games, however, must have been in positions in the various stadia, those in or near large cities, to watch, probably horrified, as distant air-borne passenger vehicles, seemingly dropped from the skies; the enclosed design of the arenas, perhaps, denying these sights to the rest of the audiences.

Those that did witness the sight of plummeting craft may, they supposed, have attempted to leave and, in doing so, must have relayed their reasoning for their departures to others who had not seen the catastrophic happenings. They imagined that, soon after, rumours of the events in the skies around them would have circulated to many of the sports fans inside the stadia. This, coupled with the ever-increasing darkness, may have fuelled distress and panic.

But that was all pure conjecture.

The aliens would never know exactly what actually happened – they were all very glad of that.

The panel had recognised that having so many animals confined in such close proximity to each other at, more or less, the same time, albeit in different locations separated by thousands of kilometres, was too good an opportunity to pass up – if *good* was an apt adjective in this context.

At around the fifteenth hour plus sixteen minutes, some of the orbiting spacecraft turned their focus onto these arenas and the surrounding areas, again, to a radius of twenty-five kilometres. By the fifteenth hour plus seventeen minutes, and after the discharging of the culler weapon components, another seventeen-million of the primary target species were dead. Two and a half million or so of them were conveniently stored together for ease of retrieval or disposal at some later stage.

Whilst around one-hundred spacecraft were utilised for processing the sporting arenas, the remaining vessels started to concentrate their culler weapons on the planet's largest cities.

Working in groups of four, each craft self-adjusted their focus to target a combined radius of one-hundred square kilometres of prime real estate in the middle of cities with a population of one-million or more primary target inhabitants.

By the fifteenth hour plus thirty minutes, at least two-thousand of these teeming settlements had been attacked.

At this point the scan and weapon facilities aboard the spacecraft were shut down to allow a short time to recharge the equipment, study the resulting data and, if required, for recalibration.

chapter fifteen

'Where are all of their super-heroes and gods now?'

The question resounded around every populated room across the fleet. Sissonæ had been sat in a chair in the isolation room of the ship with the other members of the two extraction teams, trying to console her friend Loopolz and recover her own composure after the excitement of their recent incursion onto the hell world. She had also been half-listening to the chatter between the main control rooms of the attacking ships. Chatter, perhaps, was too strong a word for it – the silence had, up until that point, only occasionally been broken. She had found it difficult to take her eyes from the visi-screens on the wall, displaying graphical representations of all the areas being attacked on the planet below that had changed locations every thirty seconds or so and the numeric counters on each screen, as the estimated number of dead primary targets were calculated, kept ever-increasing. As has been noted, however, there had been little conversation between the people in the many control rooms of the vessels. They had been monitoring the performance of the weapons and feedback from the scanners. The data they had received suggested that, at that point in time, the fatalities amongst the primary target animals were in the region of three-hundred million – once the combined fire-power of three-thousand spacecraft concentrated their weapons against densely populated areas, the death count increased dramatically and swiftly. And there was still a long way to go. The largest of the cities they had attacked had a primary target species population of upwards of seventeen-million, spread over an area of two and a half thousand square kilometres, whilst the smallest contained under two-million or so in an area of almost one-hundred and fifteen square kilometres. As each of the cull weapons were, at that moment, limited to a radius of a mere twenty-five square kilometres, they could only cull a relatively small percentage of the animal populations at these locations at any one time, given the sheer number of primary targets on the planet. They could have extended their combined radius but were concerned that the effectiveness of the weapons would be even more compromised than they had anticipated, perhaps leaving more individual animals alive, scattered over large areas of the planet and, although this would not have been too huge a logistical problem, they had not planned for the extra time and resources they would require to locate and cull these individuals. Ethically, however, having large numbers of injured animals lying around the place, probably in great pain, was not acceptable. Otherwise, everything was going according to plan.

As she sat in that isolation room, striving to take it all in, Sissonæ had been trying to imagine what those animals still alive must have been feeling at that point in time. She guessed that, in many areas of the planet, it would be very cold, very dark and, because the Kaahu would have no idea what was happening to them, very frightening. However, she also realised that, in many instances, being cold, in the dark and being fearful would not be a unique experience for these animals. Many millions of the creatures had lived like that for generations – according to her research, at least. Also from her studies, she could, she thought, have predicted with confidence that there would be mass panic turning into violent confrontations between diverse groups of Kaahu, looking, as usual, for someone else to blame for their problems – someone other than themselves. There would, she also guessed, be multiple murders, widespread looting and the gratuitous destruction of homes and other buildings. On the plus side, if her conjectures were correct, there would now be slightly fewer animals to cull and, perhaps, a few less structures to raze. All-in-all, she experienced a weird, mixed emotion of deep, deep remorse for the deaths they had caused coupled with a strange sense of quiet satisfaction with their success. Very, very strange.

***

It also has to be said that this first half-hour of the mission proper had a profound and long-lasting effect on the entire population of the fleet. A few months earlier, as the craft were traversing the solar-system towards the target planet, someone, somewhere – perhaps in homage to the science fiction literary form of the primary target species or, perhaps, in contempt – started to refer to the cull weapon as a *death-ray*, the portable version as a *ray-gun* and the heat-pulse weapon as a *phaser*. These terms soon became very popular synonyms throughout the fleet, more amongst the younger members, and it even gained currency with certain people on the organising panel. After that first half an hour of what would become known as Day One of the New Era, these terms, whether originally meant as reverential or derisory, were never heard or read again.

***

And then, out of the ether, one young male data monitor in one of the control rooms somewhere within the fleet had, during that initial period of carnage, wondered out loud:

'Where are all of their super-heroes and gods now?'

It was not meant maliciously, there was no cruelty in his voice, no smile or sneer as he uttered the words – only an ironic question, tinged with sadness. His query was shared over the electronic communication network to all of the other tactical rooms on all of the other spacecraft in the fleet. Nobody commented or laughed and there was silence in all of the rooms and over the communication network for the remainder of the session.

***

Hentanayre had also been sat in a chair in the isolation room of the ship with the other members of the two extraction teams, quietly sipping tea and watching the unfolding events on the hell world below by way of the visi-screens and their informative graphics. As she watched, there was no sign of remorse on her face, no real regret tugging at her conscience. The estimated death toll was continually rising on the screens and all she could think was how apt it was that these spacecraft, crewed on the whole by animals who were little more than children of fourteen, fifteen or sixteen years of age, were raining death down upon those perennial child abusers, those serial killers of children of many, many species. Hentanayre was more gratified than contrite.

chapter sixteen

As the scan and weapon apparatus on board all of the three-thousand plus offensive spacecraft were recharging, preparations were being made to launch four-hundred or so other planetary transport vehicles from the vessels designated as the home craft of the remaining extraction targets. Though by no means the largest, all of these vehicles were significantly bigger than those used during the test extractions with an original, normal passenger capacity of up to fifty-four people and a flight crew of two. All of these particular vehicles had been built or adapted to carry up to twenty passengers in total isolation from the rest of the occupants. At that time, on each of these vehicles, were twenty-four extraction team members, eight of each species, and two pilots – all environmentally-suited-up and ready for take-off. Each planetary transport vehicle had been pre-programmed with the specific coordinates of areas on the planet where extraction targets had been, initially, identified. Those locations were to be confirmed, in-flight, after the deployment of the many cull weapon probes that were floating around the planet's atmosphere at an altitude of two-hundred or so metres, heading for the identified target areas. On all of the three-thousand plus spacecraft, complex commands had been fed into the scan and probe controlling technology whereby five units combined and harmonised with each other; the probes selecting a pre-designated location containing extraction targets and utilising the selective cull option whilst the other four orbital weapons targeted the surrounding areas on full primary target cull mode. As the planetary transport vehicles were preparing for launch, almost seven-hundred and fifty different, specially designed and constructed automated probes were heading for the planet surface from some of the numerous support ships tethered further out in space. These probes were to land on the surface at locations where there may be dangerous processes continuing despite there being no animal contribution to the effort; in particular, nuclear reactors at power generating plants, military facilities and other sites around the planet. Each probe was carrying automata that would enter these facilities and their mission, upon entry, was to shut down or make safe these processes before any irreparable damage could occur. In many instances the lack of power to the reactor systems would, indeed, shut the processes down, but there were many installations that would have required further attention from their animal engineers to cool the heat from the radioactive materials in any normal, potentially disastrous, course of events. Water would be required to be pumped in to cool the process down and, afterwards, filtered to prevent excessive radiation damage. This cooling process was governed by electromechanical or electronic equipment which, by that point in time, had been destroyed and would not function even if any of the primary target species were present. The automata, with their in-built power cells, were programmed to ensure that these cooling-down processes were activated. The organising panel was well aware of the dangers of these primitive sources of power generation. They had studied the consequences of previous nuclear accidents on the planet, in particular, the incident on the large continental land mass in the upper hemisphere that had significantly and disastrously affected an area of at least thirty square kilometres – an area which will be uninhabitable to many species of animal life for the next twenty-thousand years – and the adverse consequences of the accident that spread well beyond those limits. They had no intention of allowing this sort of thing to happen on this planet ever again. It had been determined by the panel that weaponry armed with nuclear or biological capabilities would have to be dealt with on an individual basis and at a later date.

At the same time that these automated probes were deployed, two-hundred and fifty of the largest versions of the planetary transport vehicle were also departing from a similar number of the spacecraft at the vanguard of the assault. Compared to the transport vehicles that were about to undertake the extraction missions and the two used during the test procedure, these machines were massive – though, by no means, the largest vehicles carried by the fleet. These passenger conveyance machines could carry up to one-hundred and seventy-five people, plus two flight crew and, indeed, each of the vehicles now leaving the support craft all contained their full complement of passengers. Their role on the planet was considered, by both the panel and the participants themselves, to be amongst the most challenging and distasteful that any of the invading aliens would have to undertake. The role of two-hundred of the craft was to cull those animals that were confined to the prisons that the primary targets, euphemistically, had called zoos, aquaria or animal parks. There could have been no doubt that these unnatural institutions' sole purpose was for the ugly amusement of the primary targets, despite their protestations of the need for species conservation at the latter stage of their use; conservation required only because of Kaahu activity. Whether the occupants of these places were born in captivity or unwillingly snatched from the wilderness, they had been subjected to unnecessary and unwarranted abuse by their captors and now, innocent as they may have been, they would have to be killed. It would have been impractical to relocate each and every species to their own natural habitats, where they would probably not have the skills required to prosper, and neither would they have been able to survive once the animals that had incarcerated them were all dead; some of those Kaahu were, at that point, all dead and, as the culling mission continued, even more of these imprisoned animals would have to be, however unfortunately, culled. There were known to be over one-thousand such institutions spread across the target planet; some holding a few hundred individual animals and others holding several thousands. It was the role of those members of the fleet aboard these larger planetary transport vehicles to carry out the distasteful task of killing these unfortunate creatures. Having said that, it could be argued that there was an upside to the mission – however tenuous. From the scans that would need to be taken in order to program their portable cull weapons, they would be able to isolate the specific genomes of each imprisoned species. In the course of the cull, they knew they would have to kill so-called companion animals; indeed, those members of the fleet involved with the extractions had been asked to scan any such creatures they encountered during their missions. It had been estimated by the primary target species themselves that there were, more or less, two-hundred and twenty-million felines and one-hundred and seventy-million canines kept as companion animals across the planet. The Kaahu, in their arrogance of course, considered themselves the *owners* of these animals and all other *pets*, just as they *owned* species that were bred for slaughter and consumption or to be used in experiments. Unlike those non-primary target animals in the prison-like zoos, aquaria and animal parks, the panel had thought it more prudent to cull these companion animals, as with the Kaahu, in large numbers utilising the cull and weapon probes in space. However, in areas where subspecies of the same genus had their natural habitats, this could prove disastrous to the wild, non-captive branches of that family of creature. In the scientific terms of the primary target species, *felidæ* is the biological name for the feline family of animals, or cats, and, according to that same terminology, all such animals are *felids*. There are two distinct subgroups of *felids*; they are *pantherinæ* and *felinæ*. The most popular domesticated companion animal on the hell world was one of five subspecies of the *felinæ* genus and all five subspecies were known as *felis*. The other four subspecies of *felis* were, and still are, comparatively rare yet widespread across the upper hemisphere of the planet. *Canidæ*, or canine, companion animals have a slightly less complex family of subspecies but, nevertheless, their entire family genome, or as much as possible, would have to be recorded to effectively carry-out the mission. By acquiring the genomes of as many of these subspecies as possible, fine-tuning of the scanners was feasible, so that rare, wild animals, it was thought, would be kept safe from the cull weapons when they were discharged over a wide area to destroy the primary-target-dependent companion animals.

Most of the zoo-prisons were located in, or very near to, the larger cities of the planet and the two-hundred and fifty large planetary transport vehicles and their passengers each landed, all within the space of ten minutes, at a separate location. The teams exited by way of the airlocks of the vehicles, and began their gruesome tasks. At most of the locations it was either dusk or night time; only a few of the groups were able to undertake their tasks in daylight. At most of the locations there were bodies of primary animals strewn across the paths, over walls or railings surrounding the captive animal enclosures or, often, scattered randomly about the place, inside structures and out in the open air. For the crews of the remaining fifty planetary transport vehicles, their task was, to them, even more distasteful.

Their role was to record and cull those animals held for experimentation by the Kaahu in research facilities of academic, military and commercial institutions. From what they had learned of these atrocities, over one-hundred million individual vertebrate animals, such as primates, felines, canines and rodents, were the subject of experimentation and killed, every year. An unknown, perhaps incalculable, number of invertebrate animals, arthropods, various worm-like species and crustaceans, were also subjected to these horrors. All the teams moved steadily and systematically through the premises of the zoo-prisons and research facilities, recording the genomes and images of the incarcerated animals as they went and they killed them with their cull weapons. Their final assignment would be to raze the premises, those structures that had contained these torture and death chambers, to the ground. These zoo-prisons, these centres of experimentation, torture, and all the facilities of non-Kaahu animal abuse were abhorrent beyond the telling to all the aliens. The personnel aboard those craft would be further utilised for this unsavoury task as more areas of the target planet were freed from the clutches of the tormentors as the orbital culler weapons, in conjunction with the hovering probes, destroyed more and more Kaahu across the world. It was a matter of deep regret that the alleviation of the suffering of these individual creatures in the prison-zoos and the like would be so swiftly followed by their own deaths.

As those unfortunate animals were dying in their unnaturally tiny cages, enclosures and pools of water, the orbital culler weapons and the numerous mobile probes were discharging their fatally efficient particulate beams of energy towards yet still more primary targets in yet still more towns and cities on the planet, leaving only the required Temuri animals alive and ready for collection by the occupants of the four-hundred or so planetary transport vehicles designated for that task.

Those hundreds of planetary transport vehicles had been standing by at their pre-arranged positions spread around the planet, each at an altitude of approximately ten-thousand metres above the surface of the hell world and each in close proximity to a weapon probe, as they and the now power-replenished orbital scan and weapon probes were, once again, activated. Working in pairs, the vehicles travelled to the pre-programmed and auto-confirmed destinations where the first would land whilst the second hovered above the area, protecting the other. On completion of their mission at the first location, the two craft would fly to a secondary destination, at least fifty kilometres distant, and reverse their roles. When both planetary transport vehicles had completed their assignments, they returned to their designated home spacecraft. When all of the pre-selected targets for each iteration of Temuri collection had been successfully retrieved, the scan and weapon probes continued their mission on full-primary-target mode for a further twenty-two minutes before falling dormant for power recovery.

This process continued for many days without a break, day and night on the hell world, until, firstly, the required number of extraction Temuri had been transferred to the spacecraft and, secondly, until most, if not all, primary target animals left on the planet were dead.

chapter seventeen

It had been a horrific few days. From that point on, the number of primary target animals still alive could have been counted in thousands, or possibly hundreds, as opposed to the billions as was. Despite the horror of it all, despite the number of deaths they had brought about and despite the fact that they would still have to cull billions of other animals, Hentanayre was still resolute in her belief in the morality of their actions. So, it would appear, was everyone else in the fleet. Yes, all their leisure activities had changed, football matches, concerts and the like cancelled, but work had to come first and this was something that all of them had worked all their lives for. They all knew the facts; they all knew what was at stake. She was, in fact, more concerned about the others, those billions of innocent creatures specifically bred for slaughter and consumption. They had had no choice in any of this and it mattered not to her that they would have died soon at the hands of the Kaahu anyway. Then there were those domesticated, companion animals that totally relied on their primary target masters – they had no choice, either. Neither did those that were cruelly imprisoned by the Kaahu for their entertainment in their zoos and their amusement parks, to be stared at and ridiculed by the cold, insensitive Kaahu; nor did those who were tortured by vivisectors have a choice. These unfortunate others were the animals that deserved her respect and sympathy – not the monsters that had put them in those positions to begin with. That incarnation of animal life, the Kaahu, would not be at all missed in this universe.

chapter eighteen

Sissonæ was with a group of around twenty or so of her colleagues, including Hentanayre, from the three invading species who were making their way through the debris of some street in some large town or city at the eastern end of the large continent in the upper hemisphere. Others, mainly Vatta but with a sprinkling of Obiah, were forming a moving perimeter ahead, behind and to the sides of the main group. It was the first ever visit to the planet surface for some of the group, and more or less four minutes since this particular area had been culled of Kaahu animals. They all had to tread carefully to avoid stepping on the many carcasses that littered the ground, twisted and befouled in the gutters. It was a cold, grey morning with a flurry of small snowflakes swirling around in the strong wind that blew over and between the structures on either side of the street. All the exposed surfaces, the ground, the windowsills, the flat roofs and the animal corpses, were already lightly glazed with layers of icy, white frost and fine snow. So, as well as stepping with care so as not to be tripped up by the many corpses, it was also required to avoid slipping over because of the frozen surfaces that surrounded them.

Except for the numerous *corvidae* sat noisily on the roofs and some, tentatively, on the numerous ropes and wires criss-crossing a few metres above the lifeless bodies on the ground, a few canines hanging around looking, Sissonæ thought, slightly bemused and confused, and the odd glimpse of small brown rodents scurrying between areas of cover, there was no movement. The corpses were not yet stiff, either from the rigours of death or the near-freezing temperature, as testified by all of their party that, unintentionally, kicked against them as they negotiated the obstacle-course of cadavers. As she neatly avoided the outstretched leg of one of their cull weapon victims, Sissonæ imagined that, even with the cold weather, the stink would soon be utterly unbearable. The aliens were all immune to the smell and the cold, of course, because they were all safely attired in their environmental protection suits with their built-in breathing apparatus and thermal regulation. Looking around, she predicted they would be needing these suits for a very long time if this was typical of the mess they would find across the planet.

Others within the group would, occasionally, point this or that sight of interest out to their colleagues but, generally, they were very quiet, engrossed in their own thoughts and emotions.

Sissonæ stopped walking and, slowly – partly due to the restrictions of her attire and partly because of the ice – turned full circle inspecting the buildings on either side of the road, looking at the mainly one-storey buildings which, she assumed, were dwellings. They were constructed of concrete blocks, wood and what looked like anything else the occupants could find to hand at the time of construction or repair. Some of the buildings had small disks attached to their exterior walls which she, correctly, assumed were some kind of communication devices, and there was a tangle of overhead electrical wires and fibre cords haphazardly slung across the space above her head.

Stepping over the body of an elderly female Kaahu, Sissonæ walked towards an open door a few metres to her left and, on entering the dwelling, illuminated the dark space by turning on the lamp integrated within her head-gear. It was a sparsely furnished single room that, for some reason, looked surprisingly tidy to her. The first thing she noticed was a small metal stove in the far corner to her left with a couple of cooking vessels on the top, a metal chimney leading from it to the ceiling above, with the space between the pipe and material forming that ceiling stuffed with fabric, no doubt to prevent draughts. The wall besides the stove had some shelves carrying plastic packets and tins that must have contained some kind of food – dead animal, she presumed. Underneath the shelves was a large plastic bottle containing a clear liquid – she guessed water – and a bright red, oblong plastic bowl with a few ceramic dishes waiting, no doubt, to be washed – it would never happen now.

Then she noticed the body. It was difficult to tell, it was face-down to the floor and she was not going to touch it, but she assumed it was an older male Kaahu, perhaps the mate of the female lying just outside of the property, the one she had stepped over. Besides the body, to the left, there was a mattress of sorts with numerous blankets and two cushions where the Kaahu obviously slept. To the right, against the adjoining wall, were a wooden table and two chairs. To the right of the only door, the one through which she had entered, was a metal container that must have been used as a commode – there did not appear to be anywhere else for the occupants to relieve themselves. She could not see an access point for a fresh water supply anywhere and, again, she guessed the Kaahu that had lived here must have had to collect it from somewhere else, somewhere outside, hence the large, plastic bottle in the opposite corner of the room, Sissonæ assumed. Neither did there appear to be any form of power connected to the dwelling – how had these animals lived to such an old age in such conditions, she wondered. To the left of the only door, a heavy looking sheet of fabric was hanging from almost all the way up to the ceiling, down to the floor. She pulled it to one side and looked out of the cracked, single-glazed, dirt-encrusted – on the outside – pane of glass or transparent plastic and saw her colleagues, through the grime, wandering further down the street. She did not need to be with them, they could carry out the Temuri retrieval mission without her and, in fact, she had pre-arranged this diversion with the others during the journey from their home craft.

She noticed, just below and to the side of the window, a small shelf with a statue of some kind surrounded by unlit candles, garishly coloured images, some form of jewellery and dead flowers. Sissonæ shook her head slowly and sighed quietly to herself.

She turned to face the centre of the room once more. Unexpectedly, movement down on the floor in front of her caught her eye. Standing there, his or her back arched into an almost perfect little semi-circle with a spindly, tiny tail high in the air, bending towards his head, was a very young *feline* mammal, head down and presenting a sideways-on posture towards her. The animal's hair was spiky down the arc of the spine and his sparsely covered little tail. He was obviously trying to make himself appear as large as possible; his ears were pressed back against his head which, in turn, was pressed back into his shoulders and the young animal was both hissing and spitting at the same time whilst performing short, on his toes, back and forth hopping movements. She recognised it as a purely defensive posture – the poor little creature was positively terrified. And who could blame him? She had difficulty in determining if the little feline was male or female, so, pretty quickly, she had arbitrarily chosen the masculine pronoun for no other reason than, because of the posturing, she thought he must be male. *Wow,* she thought, *my first live, non-Kaahu, alien encounter!* Oh sure, there were other creatures alive just outside the door, but they had not engaged and she did not consider her experience with the canine animal at the test extraction site as an encounter – more a confrontation, she thought. This one, though, was trying to communicate with her, face to face – well, face to protective headgear with heavily tinted face mask. This tiny ball of fluff was telling her that he was a huge, vicious killing machine and, with one wrong move from her, he would pounce and rip her throat out. Well, maybe this was a confrontation too – but this baby animal was so cute!

Sissonæ scrunched herself down to a crouch to be on more of a level basis with the youngster and held out her gloved hand towards him. The young feline was not at all pleased with these movements and leapt backwards in a, relative to his size, high sideways jump and hissed and spat some more. He then ran off towards the wall to the right, but was back almost immediately to resume his stance. Sissonæ stood up and the small animal again began dancing and running around, occasionally threatening to attack her. She laughed out loud – not exactly an appropriate thing to do considering the events of the past few minutes, the past few hours or the past few days. In her headset, over the communication channel, she heard Tufu, the acting extraction team leader, ask if she was in trouble. Sissonæ apologised for her outburst and confirmed she was in no difficulty.

In a way she was elated yet disappointed – she would have liked some form of physical contact with this tiny alien creature, even though the term contact, considering the fact she was completely isolated from it, was relative thanks to her suit, helmet and gloves. What must she look like to that tiny creature? At that moment, nothing would have given her more pleasure than to take hold of this little animal, take him back to the spacecraft and save him from his inevitable death. Of course, that would be frowned upon by all of her colleagues and, besides, if she remembered correctly, felines were, congenitally, totally carnivorous – what would she have fed him on? She sighed sadly to herself yet again. As the animal continued to dance excitedly around in front of her, she removed a scanner from her belt, pressed the on button, pointed it towards the youngster and, almost immediately, looked at the image of the animal and the various readings, both displayed on the small screen. In that instant she had gathered as much data on the creature as she required and she, regretfully, selected the *Secondary Target* setting on the scanner.

She left the structure and stood by the old female's body, looking up and down the street for a few moments. Something strange had occurred to her. She looked out into the distance beyond their current location as though searching for something; around and beyond the planetary transport vehicle sitting stationary a couple of hundred metres away, over the buildings as much as she could, as far as she could see in all directions. Nothing.

She commented, to whoever might have been listening on the communications channel:

'There is no vegetation whatsoever anywhere in sight. How had these animals lived like this?'

Nobody responded. Those that heard her assumed, perhaps correctly, that the question she had asked was rhetorical. She sighed yet again and walked hurriedly to catch-up with her companions. They were nearing the location where the extraction targets were awaiting collection, though the Temuri did not yet know this.

The extraction mission was carried out by her colleagues without incident and they all returned to the planetary transport vehicle, completed the task of covering their companions from the second vehicle as they carried out their part in the extraction mission, and then both vehicles returned to their spacecraft base.

Sissonæ missed the young feline.

chapter nineteen

A regrettable but unavoidable four days passed before the specific cull of the other species of animal, the secondary targets, could begin. These targets included those bred for slaughter and consumption and those companion animals apparently so loved by Kaahu. They had had to wait until the aliens had enough data about the various species they were about to kill before they could begin the process.

Because of the delay, they knew that millions of these animals would soon die or have already died of hunger and neglect, because they would have been confined to some structure or other, unable to access nourishment. There would be others that could not be separated from the same species living wild locally, such as various rodent species, or because the species were, comparably, so exotic that the spacecraft occupants could not possibly identify them as being held captive. These probably included numerous species of *aves*, *reptilia* and many, varied aquatic animals. They also knew that in some areas of the target planet, there would be primates from the seven species of *hominidæ* or large felines such as *pantheræ* or, even, huge *proboscidæ* being held captive against their will, somewhere the aliens were not aware of nor would ever find until it was too late and the animals had died. They had mostly pinpointed the locations of both fresh and brine water so-called fish farms but could not be certain they had found them all, leading to the possibility of millions of other creatures suffering long, drawn-out deaths. This entire state of affairs disappointed them deeply but there was absolutely nothing they could do about it.

The scan and cull weapons were programmed to operate to their optimum range of fifty square kilometres, and the operation began. Former locations of mass primary target population, as well as vast areas of what was considered agricultural land, were scanned and millions, if not billions, of feline, canine, bovine, ovis, sus and equus mammalian animals were culled each day over a ten day period. During that same time span, billions of animals of various avian species, reared for consumption of their flesh and ova, and even further billions of oceanic and freshwater creatures artificially bred in those so-called fish farms were also killed. One species of avian had no significant differences in dna between those born in the wilderness and those bred for slaughter and, in one particular continental area of the hell world, necessitated a less remote form of culling. As with those animals culled at the zoo-prisons and torture-laboratories created by the Kaahu, multiple members of the fleet were dispatched to undertake the distasteful task at close quarters.

Six days into the operation to cull those creatures bred for consumption and companionship, it was estimated that the planet-wide population of the primary target species was less than one-thousand individual animals. Despite the fact that, less than two weeks earlier, there had been upwards of seven-billion of these overly-aggressive and heavily-armed animals on the planet, there had been no instances of violent confrontation between the invading aliens and the indigenous primary targets. And, as the invading aliens had doubted the efficacy of their orbital scan and cull weapons, those same implements, albeit in conjunction with the culler probes hovering above the planet surface, had performed well and it was estimated that fewer than point-zero-zero-one percent of the targeted animals were still alive after exposure to the particulate beams. Of course, that had still left the possibility of almost seventy-thousand barely alive Kaahu in multiple locations, but they could not easily remedy that situation; just as they could not cull all of the many individual companion animals. It was highly doubtful that any of those injured primary targets would have survived for too long – the damage they had suffered would have left them almost totally paralysed and severely brain-damaged, so much so that it would, most likely, be extremely difficult to determine their status without the use of a medical scanner, and that, unfortunately, would be too time consuming and resource-heavy an undertaking for the aliens to carry out.

chapter twenty

The organising panel had thought it would be important for every one of their number to see what they all had done on the planet before the clean-up work began in earnest. Not everyone was particularly eager to do so, having more than a good idea of what they would see, but all agreed that it probably would be for the best. It was a tenet of their societies that everyone should face up to the consequences of their own actions and accept responsibility for them, even if those actions were *so* terrible and, in the ap-Vanda history, unheard of.

That day, across the planet, thousands of aliens were wandering through the aftermath of those awful actions – only the time zones, locations and, in most instances, the climatic conditions were different. Many of their number were witnessing the accelerated putrefaction associated with the mixture of lifeless organic matter, the culled species, and the hot, dank weather of tropical zones. Still others were struggling to see any consequences they may have caused because of the sheer amount of snow that had fallen or was falling at that time.

Although she had visited the surface once before, Naanich, from the Vatta home-world and one of the defensive weapon carriers from the very first extraction mission, was again on the planet surface. In fact, all members of that first incursion mission from both planetary transport vehicles were in this group of fifty-four alien visitors. On the journey down from their home ship, someone had asked the pilot their destination.

When he replied that they were heading for a continent in the lower hemisphere, one of their party, another Vatta female, had said they had been there, done that – a comment that certainly lightened the mood of this particular planetary transport vehicle's passengers. The pilot, with a smile in his voice as he knew of the accomplishments of some of his charges, retorted that this time, the destination was *another* continent in the lower hemisphere. The environment they found themselves in was very different from the desert-like conditions of their first visit. For a start, it was daylight and, yes, it was hot, but it was also wet. Very wet. The planetary transport vehicle had delivered the alien sightseers to one of the rainforests of the hell world.

It was around thirty-two degrees centigrade and pouring with rain – according to the data they had, this particular region of the planet averaged about three-hundred and thirty centimetres of rain per month at this time of year. It felt to them all that the whole quota for that month was now cascading down upon them – the aliens loved it. Wearing their environmental protection suits, they could not, however, experience that wondrous feeling first hand, of water to skin, as they might have done on their own home-worlds, but nonetheless, it was so, so good to see rain again after so many years. For the others, those not on the team that had extracted the two Temuri in the test – that is the two planetary transport vehicle pilots, the fifteen members of the back-up team from the second craft and all the other passengers aboard – the joy was doubled. They not only experienced the wonderful rain, they also had the added pleasure of walking on solid ground for the first time in years.

They were about to view a settlement that had housed around half a million Kaahu which was meant to be surrounded by an area of lush rainforest. Only, it was not surrounded by such vegetation. Not anymore. Not really.

Naanich had had prior knowledge of their destination that day from the pilot, whom she knew, and had researched the area beforehand and during the journey from the home ship down to the planet surface. Once covering an area of seven-million square kilometres, over the preceding twenty or so years the region had been cleared for wood, agriculture, mining, oil and settlement by the Kaahu. It had been cleared of upwards of twenty per cent; a full one-fifth of vital vegetation replaced by crops grown to, mainly, feed bovine animals destined for slaughter and the plates of other Kaahu across the planet. There were also mass clearances in other rainforests to allow the cultivation of a plant that, allegedly, would help the environment by extraction of the oil contained within that plant and processing it as a, so-called, *bio-fuel* to propel the Kaahu's seemingly indispensable internal combustion propelled vehicles; those same vehicles that had so efficiently helped to heavily pollute the planet's atmosphere in the first place. Judging from the data the aliens had gleaned from the Kaahu's shared electronic media, the irony of this was completely lost on most of the Kaahu.

These remarkable arboreal areas, these lungs of the planet, so quickly and so gleefully, ravaged by greed and stupidity – albeit driven by their overpopulation, the Kaahu infestation – were, and still are, vital to the health of the planet because of their carbon dioxide absorption properties, a substance so readily pumped into the air by the Kaahu. Well over twenty years or more ago, these plants had cooled the atmosphere and would have regulated the extreme, adverse weather conditions that had blighted the planet in the recent past, and would continue to do so for many years to come – perhaps many centuries. Wherever the deforestation occurred, it not only had adverse effects from an atmospheric and meteorological point of view, but the harm it did to the indigenous species was massive. It did not do a lot for the land itself, either.

As the alien sightseers were flying towards their eventual destination, they noticed on the view-screens that the lush greens of the forest were suddenly replaced by kilometre after kilometre of vast fields of neat, unnaturally straight-lined rows of plants or large, rectangular areas surrounded by fences. Naanich had read that most, if not all, of the crops growing below her, as the planetary transport vehicle sped above this unnatural landscape, would have been fed to bovine and other species of animals to fatten them up. These same species would be slaughtered and eaten by rich, fat Kaahu living in the area of this continent across the equator in the upper hemisphere. She had also learned that most of the land and, therefore, the crops growing in it, had been *owned* by rich, fat Kaahu living in the area of this continent across the equator in the upper hemisphere. She mouthed that word, *owned,* to herself in an almost silent whisper. The word in this context was, or had been, alien to her species. So much so, she whispered it in one of the popular languages once spoken on the hell world – there was no real equivalent word in her native tongue, the universal language. She could understand the basic concept behind it but not the actual fact of the matter. How could one *own* land, and why would one want to? It was clearly insane. Even crazier? *Owning* another animal!

The planetary transport vehicle they had travelled on from the home ship had landed to the side of a three-storey structure near the centre of the settlement. After a few short moments of enjoying the rain or stamping their feet, their attention was drawn by a colleague excitedly calling and beckoning them over to join her. They all hurried to her position, looking out on the settlement, and each and every one of them caught their breaths as they saw the carnage their species had caused displayed before them. There seemed to be hundreds of half-floating, bloated and putrefied bodies of dead primary targets littering their entire line of sight, in every direction they looked. Some of the structures they saw were little more than burned-out shells and four-wheeled vehicles were concertinaed into long lines giving the appearance of multiple, metallic serpentine creatures that had drowned in the torrential rain that, even now, continued to fall. There looked to be about twenty to twenty-five centimetres of standing water covering most of the settlement, at least most of the parts they could see. One exception was a circular piece of ground, perhaps twenty metres in circumference, in front and slightly to the right of their vantage point at the side of the structure. Here, on another piece of slightly raised ground, were around seven partially consumed primary target cadavers and numerous large avians, primarily black in colour but with white collars and reddish-black feathers, bald necks and heads. They were noisily and, it seemed, ill-temperedly scavenging the bodies of the Kaahu.

Naanich turned her attention to the skies when another colleague pointed upwards. Above them, more avians, possibly of the same species, were gliding effortlessly in circles on the thermal air currents generated, no doubt, by the nearby mountain range; their massive wings spread out wide yet unmoving as the avians soared with the utmost grace. The creatures reminded Naanich of the crutu, a large avian scavenger from her own Vatta home-world, larger than the species she was now watching and with different colouring but, in every other way, so similar, so beautiful.

As Naanich was blithely gazing up at the soaring avians over her head, others had turned their attention to a tall building across the way from their position. The structure must have been fifteen storeys high and, although all of the sightseeing aliens had seen images of such edifices in the data captured from the Kaahu social nexus, none of them had seen one in the flesh, so to speak, built on the surface of a planet. On all three of their home-worlds, the tallest buildings were, at most, three storeys high with the larger structures being housed in space, so most of their number were fascinated at the sight of such an erection. But perhaps it would not be there for too much longer.

Turning her attention back to the corpses of bloated, dead primary target animals littering the area around them, Naanich was quite shocked to realise that she was not particularly overwhelmed with grief at the sight of such carnage. She and most of the other alien animals had grown up viewing images of a myriad of dead creatures of many indigenous species from this hell world on the Kaahu social nexus – perhaps they had inured her to what should have been the horrors in front of her. And the entire population of the invasion fleet had had many a lecture and numerous seminars about the possible personal consequences each individual may experience, plus many face-to-face meetings with their own psychotherapists. The message taken from each of these sessions was one of collective responsibility rather than individual culpability. All three of the alien species, whether a part of the cull there on the target planet or back on their home-worlds, were all equally to blame, if any such burden needed to be so ascribed – any one single animal should feel little or no guilt. Perhaps it was these lectures, seminars and meetings that enabled Naanich to, almost dispassionately, view the remains of what had once been sentient beings now rotting in the humidity of the tropical zone here on the hell world. Or maybe it was the fact that all of them, all of the Vatta, ap-Vanda and Obiah animals, had undertaken the gruesome business of destroying these other animals, the Kaahu, from a distance, far removed from the sights of the animals' deaths? How would they all have felt

– how would *she* have felt – if they had had to kill the Kaahu at closer quarters where their eyes, their facial and bodily expressions, were visible to those culling the animals, rather than from the safe distance of orbit afforded by their technologies? Of course, there was always the possibility that there would be a delayed reaction and, one day, all this would come back to haunt them all.

Naanich shrugged her shoulders. Despite the potential onset of post-traumatic shock sometime in the future and whatever the reason for her current, apparent, indifference to the billions of dead Kaahu, they deserved it, after all. She was mostly content with what she and her alien companions had done.

chapter twenty-one

Even as the female alien was considering her lack of remorse for the deceased Kaahu animals and her colleagues, the other tourists, were capturing images of tall structures, high above them, out in the vacuum of space surrounding the planet on multiple spacecraft, thousands of automata were being made ready to begin the cleansing process that would render many such structures to debris. Some automata were huge; many were tiny.

The larger machines would grind or pulverise, the smaller ones cut, melt or even cause to explode – all with the specific mission to level, as much as possible, the Kaahu temples to avarice, their land-based routes of communication and their abodes. But not all structures were to be destroyed, even if that were even possible; cities of art and science, celebrating the achievements of the Kaahu, would be established across the globe and some structures from antiquity, plus others of aesthetic value from the modern age, would also be preserved for posterity. It was, in a way, ironic that these animals, the primary targets, steeped in the blood and cruelty of other species as well as their own, befuddled by nonsensical, superstitious beliefs and blinded by perverse self-love, could create beautiful artworks, compose breath-taking music and build awe-inspiring structures – the irony being in the fact that the vast majority of their creative works were inspired by those very nonsensical superstitions that so hindered their intellectual evolution and development.

And even as those thousands of automata were being prepared for structural demolition, thousands more were being auto-manufactured, by other machines, for a myriad of other tasks: lifting, digging, transporting, dismantling, disconnecting, cremating. And yet more so-called construction-bots were to be utilised in orbit to build habitat platforms, laboratories, academies, processing plants and the solar disposal structures.

Even as those alien tourists were visiting the planet surface, locator-bots were undertaking the task of finding the remains of primary and secondary targets in the open-air, in areas chosen by the aliens for future settlements and for arts and science cities. Other carcasses, those confined to structures within the designated zones, would be buried during demolition. At every other site on the planet, bodies would be left untouched to rot where they lay, perhaps to be rediscovered and researched by later generations. The sites of those remains found by these machines would be logged and transmitted to the main central data-processor for later deployment by, mainly Vatta and Obiah, personnel on cremation duties, though some ap-Vanda would also be utilised for this task.

Cremation of all the accessible dead animals littering these areas would be no easy task, even ignoring the sheer magnitude of it. It was dangerous to the operatives and, also, quite upsetting. The preferred method of disposal was from the detached comfort of a planetary transport vehicle, but this method could only be utilised in areas of the planet where the animal remains were not surrounded by flammable materials because the amount of heat generated by a cremator weapon discharged without discrimination. It was acceptable, for instance, to cremate a group of cadavers that were discovered in the urban areas where they were surrounded by asphalt, concrete, glass and other not so combustible materials, providing that the heat-burst was not sustained for more than a couple of seconds. It was also considered that the disposal of those millions of Kaahu culled at sports stadia could be undertaken by this method because these structures were, more often than not, sufficiently distant from other buildings so as to be of little environmental consequence should they catch fire. On the other hand, utilising this disposal procedure from the air in heavily built-up or rural areas could pose a huge ecological threat. Most of the primary targets' abodes on the planet were constructed using a great deal of wood and, should the cremator weapon be discharged in these areas of habitation, there would be little or nothing the aliens could do to stop any resulting conflagration from spreading throughout the area and beyond, save spending valuable time trying to douse the flames with water. A similar scenario would, undoubtedly, occur in rural areas.

Where aerial deployment of the cremator was impossible, therefore, the aliens were forced to burn the bodies of primary and secondary targets on the ground – a task undertaken with much distaste by all who participated. The cremation itself was quick and relatively clean, environmentally speaking. Perhaps unsurprisingly, given the chemical composition of animal bodies, much water vapour was expelled during the cremation process and dispersed into the atmosphere. The remaining ash residue would be reabsorbed, at some point, into the very fabric of the planet. The operator merely aimed the weapon at the corpse and quickly pressed and released a button. A beam of heat was propelled toward the target and, on contact, immediately burned up anything combustible connected to that initial contact point; that is, the rest of the body, any garments or anything else flammable in contact, such as other bodies, until the heat waned. If, for example, the weapon was fired at a body with six others in contact with the first, depending on the size of the cadavers, it was likely that four and a half of those bodies would be turned to ash before the heat subsided. The sight of the half-charred remains of one and a half dead animal bodies, taking the above example, would have been, however, quite unpleasant for the operatives. A more sustained burst of the weapon would, undoubtedly, have disintegrated the entire group of corpses to ash, and in many circumstances such actions were taken, but in other instances the surrounding factors had to be taken into account. The organising panel of the mission, no less than those members of the alien fleet operating the cremator weapons, would have preferred that automata could have been designed and constructed to undertake this unsavoury task unsupervised but, although it was technically possible, they had no way of testing such machines prior to the invasion. Supervised deployment of cremator-bots was, however, very feasible, but still distasteful to those overseeing the operation. But that is how they proceeded.

In multiple groups of up to five individuals and one automaton per group, the alien invaders set about clearing vast areas of the selected primary settlements. The procedure was unchanging: planetary transport vehicles carrying both the animal and mechanical contingents would land in a pre-designated area, and the passengers with their machines would spread out in a circular pattern. After checking for primary target life-signs using their medical scanners, they would direct the cremator-bots to destroy any dead bodies they came across. In the event that one or more cadaver was positioned next, or very near, to combustible materials, the body or bodies would be shunted away from the potential fire hazard by use of a repeller weapon which could be handled by one of the teams, but was also a constituent part of the automaton. In some settlements there would be comparatively very few animals to cremate – these would be the areas that were culled during the night and the Kaahu would have taken shelter. In others, however, there would be thousands upon thousands of corpses littering the ground, especially in areas of commerce.

There were additional hazards for the aliens as their automated machines burned the Kaahu corpses to dust, none more so than the primary target species' odd predilection for carrying offensive percussive-explosive projectile implements on their person and the problems associated with such weapons when they come into contact with an extreme heat source – such as the cremator weapon. To mitigate the risk of injury to themselves, the automata supervisors always took cover before their machines ignited the cadavers.

It was tough going, both physically and mentally, for the animal operatives undertaking these tasks and, to alleviate any stress that they may have suffered, the organising panel imposed a three-hour limit on the operation by their compatriot participants. When that time period expired, the aliens would return to their home craft for relaxation or study, but were encouraged to discuss their experiences with their designated analyst or, at the very least, verbalise those experiences in a visi-record or text document and, of course, with their friends and colleagues. They would return the following day to continue their task. Other members of their species would replace them and there would be four shifts per day, every day, for many years.

Interestingly, many years later, as the notes of analysts and the records of participants, both visual and textual, were being studied, it was noticed on numerous occasions that the operatives were exceedingly nervous prior to their first missions to cleanse the hell world of culled Kaahu. Hundreds of their number all envisaged their finding writhing masses of nearly-dead animals in front of their eyes. This common misconception could be explained, it was thought, as a consequence of the initial lack of confidence shown by the culler technicians and the organising panel in the efficacy of the culler weapon before the mission began in earnest.

Even as the alien tourists were marvelling at the new sights around the planet – the tall buildings, the art galleries and museums, the antiquated relics of structures from long past – ap-Vanda, Vatta and Obiah colleagues, along with their automata, were annihilating bodies lying in the streets of selected cities and towns around the world. And as all those thousands of other automata were being built in space or deployed on the planet surface – demolishing buildings, flattening and removing the accumulation of defunct wheeled vehicles, churning-up asphalt and concrete, slicing metals and plastics or disconnecting and sealing oil and gas platforms, both on land and at sea, amongst many other tasks – the two largest automata were being launched from their respective spacecraft. These massive, fully-automated machines, over two kilometres in length and powered with six fusion engines each, had one task to undertake – a task that, no doubt, would also take many, many years to complete. Their role was one of lifting very large objects from the surface of the planet and delivering them to the weightless void of space. Basically, it was an up and down task; descend to the required location at the surface, extend their mighty grasping appendages, secure the required load within those powerful mechanical arms, ascend through the atmosphere and release the consignment to the ministrations of other, tiny by comparison, machines in orbit that would prepare these unwanted materials for solar disposal.

In particular, these largest of alien automata were designed to rid the planet's oceans of those metal sea-going craft, the weaponised monstrosities, the oil, gas and container carrying ships, and the soon to be disconnected drilling platforms dotted around the globe, but of course, they could, and would, be utilised on any object deemed to be too big or too dangerous for pre-processing on the planet surface and to transport those materials into orbit after processing.

These waste materials were not to be merely jettisoned, irresponsibly, into the vastness of space. The automata that took delivery of the unwanted ocean-going vessels were there to assemble all of those disparate pieces of refuse into one or more aggregations to be dispatched to the ultimate disposal. The drilling platforms, nuclear weapons, submarines, warships and other assorted debris of the Kaahu's failed and fetid societies would be cast into the destructive inferno of the nearby star.

chapter twenty-two

Even though there would be hundreds of thousands of Obiah, Vatta and ap-Vanda animals on the planet surface and a similar number, if not even more, automata scurrying or hovering around during the first decade or so, there would be vast areas of the planet, previously occupied by the primary target species, that the invaders or their machines would never visit, would never cleanse. In these places, those not formerly the locations of, for example, military camps, chemical or biological weapon facilities or nuclear power generators, oil and gas drilling areas, seaports or airborne planetary transport terminals, the bodies of dead animals and their infrastructures, the dwellings, manufacturing plants and roads, would be left to the powers of nature to salvage what it could from the resultant chaos of the cull. Soon the corpses of all the species killed would putrefy, disintegrate and be dispersed to the environs of the planet, but not before a multitude of other, perhaps more worthy creatures had feasted upon their remains.

The concrete, baked clay bricks, glass and bitumen aggregates of the structures and roads would soon succumb to the persistence of vegetation and climate with, eventually, their buildings collapsing and their roads, were there any land vehicles to attempt it, becoming impassable.

Over-flying planetary transport vehicles may well, in passing, have discharged their on-board repeller weapons against the larger structures in these areas; at its higher settings this implement could easily destabilise or flatten a building, but it was very unlikely that any of these craft landed to inspect the effectiveness of their actions.

Future generations may well excavate these areas for archaeological research but that would, more than likely, be many centuries hence. In the meantime, much of the planet would be left to its own devices.

***

The three invading alien species were, however, well aware that there may have been individual animals, or even, perhaps, small groups of the primary target species that had, somehow, avoided the cull weapons' deathly gaze. If so, they would possibly be struggling somewhere on the planet; hanging on to their tenuous grip on life. Although they had no definitive proof of their continued existence, they were unconcerned by the possibility. Were the aliens able to locate them, these Kaahu would be suitable animals for observation and research – or they could be destroyed. But the aliens would have to find them first.

Those probes, so vital to the aliens in their Temuri collecting efforts during the cull, were, in conjunction with other similar automata, directed to constantly search for, scan and monitor any animal life signs across the globe. When even a square centimetre of the planet can contain multiple species of life, it was nigh on impossible to distinguish one animal from another without first processing and analysing the data. Had they found such Kaahu animals in, say, a group of fifty or more, they may have tried, once again, to expose them to the culler weapon's lethal power. But they found no such groups, nor groups of fewer numbers, nor any individual Kaahu animals.

***

Over the coming years the Obiah and Vatta contingencies of the alien invaders would oversee the machinations of their automata as they flattened dwellings, dismantled bridges, punched holes through dams or ploughed up highways and demolished those ugly and ridiculously tall, penis-substitute buildings; constructed solely, it would appear, as vanity projects to stroke the egos and libidos of a small number of the Kaahu and all, bar none, were mere temples to their love of power, be it sexual or political, and their monetary wealth. Surely there could be no other reasons for these overtly phallic erections? They could not possibly have claimed that these ultra-high rise edifices were built to combat the Kaahu's dire overpopulation and land-use issues; the members of their societies most affected by those burgeoning problems, those animals without material wealth or political power, were not allowed anywhere near these, and many, many other structures of similar dimensions, unless, of course it was in a janitorial or some other menial task capacity – another of the Kaahu's divisive traits.

Ever-aware of the threat of potentially atmospheric polluting effects of dust particles expelled upwards from large structures being demolished, extra care was taken when demolishing these edifices. All three invading species witnessed, albeit with a time-lag, the miasma of noxious materials created in a singular instance when two similarly tall buildings were assaulted by a pair of the Kaahu's airborne transport vehicles slightly over a decade earlier – a particularly striking example of not only how demolition of these structures can cause atmospheric pollution, but also the total stupidity of these overly-superstitious animals – if citing such an example was required. To alleviate these issues, the destruction of these buildings was carried out gradually.

After scanning the structures to ascertain the mode

of their construction, automata placed explosive charges at locations corresponding to perceived weak spots and, over a period of weeks or months, depending on the size of the structure, detonated the charges individually, allowing time in between explosions for the particulate matter to settle on the planet surface. Buildings of a lesser stature, up to around two-hundred and fifty metres tall, were not demolished – there were far too many of them around the globe. Where they could in these instances, the aliens would direct their automata to blow out all, or as many as possible, of the windows in such structures to allow the elements – the wind, rain, snow, sleet, the summer's heat and winter's cold – to permeate and take their cumulative toll against the buildings and accelerate the deterioration process.

Even as they oversaw the destruction of some parts of the primary target species' settlements, these same aliens were managing the conservation of science museums and art galleries for future study by researchers. Structures adjacent to the galleries and museums would be demolished with the surrounding areas flattened to allow for planetary vehicle access. All of the deceased animal bodies were removed from the interiors and disposed of by cremation. Those preserved bodies of non-Kaahu animals that were already exhibited in museums were, after some debate by the panel, retained – mostly the cadavers had been slaughtered many years earlier and some were those of species since made extinct so, despite the obvious distaste the aliens felt, there was some scientific value to the unfortunate stuffed corpses.

All-in-all, only eight areas were chosen as art and science sites which meant that most of the artistic and scientific physical artefacts from the Kaahu history would, for the time being, be lost to posterity. Images and data of these artefacts would, of course, be available electronically.

***

During the first twelve months or so, actions were taken to transfer fruit, vegetables and, especially, pre-filtered water from the planet surface back to the spacecraft fleet – though the initial reason for these relocations was for testing purposes rather than consumption. The water proved to be drinkable; were they in a desperate situation, none of them would have been particularly poisoned had they drunk the liquid as they had found it – nonetheless, the aliens re-filtered the precious water many times before they imbibed it. The fruit and vegetables were, however, a different proposition. All of the produce was found to contain a multitude of harmful substances – xenobiotic chemicals such as heavy metals, solvents and pesticides. Indeed, had the aliens ingested these foodstuffs, because they were not inured to these toxic substances as the Kaahu obviously were, the ap-Vanda, Vatta and Obiah invaders would, undoubtedly, all be made sick, perhaps in some instances fatally so. But, fortunately, not all such foodstuffs were irredeemably contaminated. Produce reduced down to their more constituent parts, fruit squeezed for its juice or grain ground for flour, for example, could be further processed to remove the offending noxious materials. Soon the Vatta, Obiah and ap-Vanda would experience bread and juices from strange grains and exotic fruits.

Besides these exceptions, much work would need to be done to clear the soil of those noxious substances before food fit for their consumption, and that of the collected Temuri, could be produced on the planet. The aliens had both the experience and technology to make this possible but it would take a number of years. The provision of suitable land to grow their food bore heavily on the choice of semi-permanent settlement sites for the Temuri; that, and protection from the elements, where possible, and areas that would not inconvenience other life forms too unnecessarily. Avoiding the excesses of the weather would prove to be increasingly difficult as the years passed. The wheels had long since been set in motion for deteriorating meteorological conditions; the Kaahu predilection for dumping huge amounts pollutants into the atmosphere for decades had irreversibly affected the weather systems of the planet and there was nothing the invading aliens could do to stop it – even their technological advances had not evolved to the stage where they could tame nature. Neither would their technologies be able to prevent the icecaps at both poles of the planet from, at some point in the near future, partially thawing-out and the resultant rise in sea levels engulfing low-lying lands across the globe. But that was for the future.

However, their technologies *did* enable them to predict where, and to what extent, these inundations would occur, so even though they could do nothing about the tornadoes, typhoons or hurricanes, torrential rain, blinding blizzards, crippling ice-storms or blistering heat-waves, they were confident they could, at least, find sites that were high enough above the current sea-levels to be safe when those levels rose. And so they did.

***

As this was their species' first experience of such an expedition, the ap-Vanda were there, primarily, to observe their colleagues from the other two species and to tend to the needs of the collected Temuri. In all, there had been over eleven-thousand such animals rescued from the planet-wide cull. They were all between twelve and fourteen months old and all had been members of the primary target species; but now no longer. They had been collected from a multitude of locations on the planet and, as far as could be determined, were representative of every colour and so-called racial grouping of the Kaahu. Unfortunately, over five-hundred of the collected Temuri, after more thorough genetic screening, were found to be deficient in one area or another and were returned to the planet surface for eventual culling during the continuing mission proper. Some were found to have incurable, fatal diseases, unknown to any of the three alien species, whilst, in many others, genetic markers suggested they would be susceptible to severe mental illnesses at some point in their future lives. As a consequence, for example, any of the children found to have a dna profile that suggested psychopathy were sent back to the planet. There was evidence that such mutations were natural, a winning mechanism for survival on the hell world, but, the aliens judged, there was no room for such callous animals within the new society they were hoping to create.

No Temuri was rejected as unsuitable because of a physical disability, as the aliens knew that such impairment was no barrier to a full and productive life – this had been shown many times in their own experiences and would not happen on their own planets. A tiny minority of the babies were rejected because they displayed medical evidence of having been sexually or physically abused – the effects of these kinds of abuse could adversely manifest themselves much later in life with their own or other children; a risk the aliens did not want to take.

The other Temuri, for the time being, were being cared for on an individual basis by the ap-Vanda on the populated craft within the fleet orbiting the planet, until there were suitable settlements constructed both in orbit and on the planet surface below. Their education had, however, already begun and would be a life-long commitment for the Temuri.

part two

chapter twenty-three

As days go, this one was either auspicious or ominous – depending on your point of view. Just twenty-four and a half years or so earlier, nobody on that distant planet, the ap-Vanda home-world, had any idea there was life on the planet that would soon be known to them as the hell world. Oh, they knew there were planets orbiting a yellow star in that particular area of the galaxy, that was not remarkable – their long-range imaging instruments had confirmed as much a century or more earlier, though they were not exactly sure just how many planets there were. However, they also knew that the possibilities of finding a life-sustaining world anywhere were very remote, taking into account the three-hundred to four-hundred billion stars in the vastness of this particular galaxy. For many, many decades, however, an automated research ship patrolling the mouth of what had been named, perhaps incorrectly, the Empty Space passage, located on the very edge of interstellar space and their own solar-system, had been sending probes through to investigate a multitude of other systems throughout the galaxy. Up to that point in time, seventy three of these probes, one a year, had been dispatched to search that galaxy and, perhaps, beyond. The research ship, before it launched each probe through the Empty Space passage, moved position along the frontier between the solar-system and interstellar space by a few tiny degrees; they had learned that, by doing so, the probes would scoot off towards different areas of the galaxy each and every time. Most of the probes had sent back valuable data but none signifying current life, past life or even the potential of life of any kind in any of the solar-systems encountered. The search for life on other worlds was a very slow process.

The three-stage probes were manufactured on orbiting factory facilities back at the ap-Vanda home-world and transported to the research ship every three or four years. As it required almost four and a half years to reach interstellar space over a distance of approximately thirty-seven billion kilometres, bulk deliveries of the new probes were the most practical way to proceed – it also allowed for regular maintenance of the research ship's systems and provided invaluable space-travel experience for many of their number. The hoped-for destination coordinates of target systems were fed through to the research ship from the Empty Space passage research unit back on the home-planet – it was not a precise science – and the probes were directed through the entrance of the passage at what had been calculated, or guessed, to be the correct location on the perimeter. As the probe approached the desired coordinates, a beam of graviton particles would be directed towards the membrane separating, so-called, normal space and, so-called, Empty Space, whereupon the probe commences its first split and stages two and three entered the passage. Stage one of the probe would remain tethered at that point in normal space where the main probe had entered the passage, emitting a regular pulse of gravitons, just enough to keep a small tear in the membrane to allow for inter-system radio communication. In the Empty Space passage, the remaining two components of the probe would be propelled at velocities far exceeding the speed of light, though, as yet, nobody had been able to calculate the exact speed, towards the gravity well of some star in the distance. Nor had any academic been able to explain what force it was that propelled the machine through the Empty Space passage despite numerous attempts to classify and identify it. As with the membrane separating that Empty Space from normal space, attempting to pin down the constituent parts had proven, up to that point in time, impossible.

The membrane dividing the two spheres of the void, clearly visible on imaging systems when pierced by graviton particle beams, defied all efforts to collect sample material and was almost invisible to the scanner technology employed against it – though it did register as having mass. Similarly, the energy that propelled the probes and other craft at such incalculable velocities was way beyond their technical expertise and remained a mystery to them. There were theories about the nature of both phenomena, though. However, the mysterious similarities in the duration of the journeys through the passage remained a mystery, defying postulation.

After sixty-five days in Empty Space, the probe reactivated the graviton emissions in the sure knowledge that, on the sixty-sixth day, it would have reached its destination. But the graviton beam was initiated a day earlier – just in case. No matter the distance travelled, one light year or twenty, the time taken to traverse the Empty Space passage was always sixty-six days. This perplexed all of the academics that studied the phenomenon, to say the least. Earlier missions had constant projection of the required graviton particles only for the probes to emerge at a destination on the sixty-sixth day; so, to conserve energy – albeit a tiny, tiny amount – the probes were programmed to desist their graviton emissions until the sixty-fifth day. The graviton particle beam, on that sixty-sixth day, parted the membrane between the Empty Space passage and the unexplored solar system. On exit at its destination, the remaining probe element, containing the two stages, separated once more and finally – one part parking itself by the exit from the Empty Space passage and the other eventually heading out into the adjacent solar-system. Both of the previously conjoined probes, as soon they arrived at their destinations, immediately undertook optical and digital surveys of the particular solar-system they had reached to determine the constituent planetary components of that star's satellites, primarily searching those objects for potential liquid water. At more or less the same time, a general astronomical survey of the galaxy was initiated to confirm the position of the target solar-system in relation to the aliens' home star. By studying the results of those surveys, the positioning of stars from that aspect, for example, the ap-Vanda could establish whereabouts in the galaxy the probe had emerged.

The Empty Space passage was anything but predictable in terms of where a probe would eventually emerge from its total blackness. Of the seventy-three probes sent through the passage, seventy-one, including this latest one, reached a destination solar-system within a radius of fourteen light years of the home star. The remaining two probes, despite entering the passage twenty-one and eight years earlier, respectively, had yet to transmit arrival confirmation messages as was the norm. There were three widely accepted theories for the no-shows of these probes. The first posited technical failure of the machines, perhaps failure of the graviton emitter, whilst the second idea suggested mishaps or collision in the passage resulting in destruction or, thirdly, a combination of both. A less accepted theory, though by no means dismissed entirely by researchers, was that the probes were either still on their way to, or had emerged at, another galaxy or, perhaps, at the gravity well of some orphan, intergalactic star. The former postulation, that the missing probes were still in the passage, would suggest, however, that the standard sixty-six day rule would not apply to intergalactic travel; and the latter, that the probes are actually at another galaxy or at an orphan stellar object, suggested that their communication systems were not capable of operating over such great distances.

When the probes did exit the passage to a star system in their own galaxy, no matter the results of the scans and astronomical surveys, the systems would be investigated by the separated entities. The sentinel section would carry out the required duties as a beacon and transmitter whilst the non-tethered section would explore the system and send back the gathered data via the sentinel.

Despite travel through the Empty Space passage often cutting hundreds of years off interstellar journeys, reducing down to a matter of a mere two months, it still took years for the probes to traverse the target solar systems because of speed restrictions imposed by the limitations of their technology and the physical laws of the universe. The fusion drives utilised by the automated probes were considerably less powerful than those aboard their passenger-carrying spacecraft and could only reach a top speed of around four-hundred thousand kilometres an hour. Neither was this a constant velocity as the probes had to regularly reduce speed to scan any planets or planetoids in the systems which necessitated time consuming, zig-zagging trajectories. All-in-all, traversing this particular solar-system from the Empty Space to the star would have, under normal circumstances, taken over seven and a half years.

In every other mission of exploration and hunt for life originating from the home-world, only data from lifeless planets, gas giants and planetoids was ever sent back. And then everything changed.

Five years after leaving its home solar-system, data from the wandering probe came back through the Empty Space passage, back from the tethered probes at both ends of the passage and the research ship, back to their home-world containing good news, very good news and, less than a few short months later, very disappointing news.

The good news? In this one, nondescript solar-system, past the lifeless, cold or gaseous outer planets and their moons, the scanners on this probe captured the unmistakable chemical signature of liquid water, as opposed to ice, as it approached the so-called habitable zone around the star. There were hints of the possibility of liquid water from the initial survey carried out at the outset of the exploration those five years earlier, but that was all it was – mere hints. This now proved, however, not to be an historic trace; this was actual running, liquid water – and that particular chemical compound was something they had never discovered with any of their many other remote-controlled expeditions to far-off alien solar-systems.

There were also other clues about this alien solar-system. Five years earlier, back on the edge of interstellar space, strange radio signals were picked-up by the probe, with doubtful natural origins, emanating from towards the direction of that distant star at the centre – or relatively close by. These signals got stronger as the automaton neared the centre and, eventually, the academics back on the ap-Vanda home-world identified the third planet as the source of both the liquid water signature and the radio waves. On receipt of this vital information the probe was immediately programmed to proceed non-stop to this apparently water-rich world. As the probe neared the third planet, it also noted a profusion of metallic objects orbiting it. When first reviewing the data, the academics back at the Empty Space passage research institute theorised, incorrectly as it turned out, that the debris must be the remnants of some accident involving spacecraft of some unknown origin – perhaps domestic, perhaps not. It was not until the probe was in orbit around the target world that they could ascertain that the majority of the circulating pieces of metal was junk – carelessly discarded metallic rubbish. It did not bode well.

The distant probe had been, for the first time in the, albeit short, history of their exploration of other systems, remotely programmed to permanently position itself into a high, non-stationary orbit to properly scan the world. On other missions it had always sufficed to merely scan each planet the probes encountered and to collect the relevant data on the star hosting the system. With the discovery of a world with so much potential, the decision was made to also abandon the exploration of the first of the two remaining planets as it was too close to the system's star to be of any immediate interest to them and to postpone exploration of the second world for a later date. Scans showed the first was nothing more than a charred and pock-marked lump of rock whilst the second had little to no potential of being life-sustaining. So, the wandering probe stopped wandering, put itself into that high, non-stationary orbit and began scanning the planet and relaying the data back to its home-world.

And the *very good* news? There was an abundance of life on that watery world in that distant solar-system – millions of different species of animals and plants abounded. Animals that flew over, crawled across, slithered over, walked upon and swam below the surface of a planet with lush, green vegetation and, as expected, great masses of liquid water. This created much excitement, and no small amount of trepidation, amongst the population back at the ap-Vanda home-world.

That same, distant probe, positioned in a high, non-stationary orbit to properly scan the world and transmit the data back to their home-world sent the information containing the *very disappointing*, yet, sadly, not unexpected, bad news. And it came through to the home-world on that auspicious or ominous day – each individual ap-Vanda had to decide for themselves.

The planet, on the closer examination afforded by the proximity of the probe, appeared to be dominated by a single species of mammalian-type animal – quite similar creatures to themselves – and there were billions of them. So many that they were blithely destroying the very ecosystem that they and every other species on the planet depended upon for life. These assumptions could be purported to be fact, even at that early stage, from analysis of the atmosphere and from the, albeit limited, data they were receiving from the communication satellites orbiting the planet. Whilst being very disappointing news, this came as no real surprise to the ap-Vanda. They had always known that, one day, this situation might arise and they would have to deal with it. Now, after all these centuries, they were finally about to undertake the kind of mission that they were warned about so long ago, though nobody on the planet was quite sure whether or not they were pleased with the situation.

The organising panel on the ap-Vanda home-world immediately made contact with their counterparts on the Vatta home-world who, in turn, informed the Obiah home-world of the discovery.

chapter twenty-four

The probe would keep sending back valuable data from the hell world for many, many years to come. But, at the beginning, the information was mainly sourced from analogue televisual and radio broadcasts with, at that time, a sprinkling of military, governmental or academic communiqués sent digitally. This would change as the years passed but, for the time being this data, much of it trivial entertainment, would have to suffice.

It was a relatively simple task for this alien automaton to siphon off all of the electronic information that the ap-Vanda and their alien allies required for their invasion; the machine merely tapped into the nearest Kaahu communications satellite and installed some code that would, initially, permanently and covertly connect the two orbiting mechanisms. Once that installation had been completed, the Kaahu communication implement transmitted that code, firstly to its hub on the planet surface and then to the functioning satellite nearest to it in orbit, where the process would be duplicated until all of the working machines of whatever origin – military, scientific or civilian – and, thus, all of the Kaahu information hubs on the world below, were connected to the Kaahu probe by that embedded code. Every byte of electronic data that had ever been created or would ever be created in the, albeit limited, future of the Kaahu would be sucked up, by way of their own satellites, to the ap-Vanda probe and then re-transmitted by that automaton to its companion probes on either side of the Empty Space passage, then onto the ap-Vanda home-world. The data would also be forwarded on to the Vatta and then the Obiah peoples for translation, dissemination and study by all three alien species. From that point onward, with every new launch of a space-bound vehicle, for whatever purpose, that same code would be embedded into its processing equipment and linked to the alien automaton.

From that point onward, every single mechanical Kaahu device on the hell world that communicated information electronically, verbally, visually or textually, was, by default, surreptitiously supplying data to the aliens to use against the Kaahu; just as, in succeeding years, their own governments would do to suppress any form of opposition to their greed-based and cruel rule. Their attempts, however, would prove to be slightly less stealthy than the aliens.

So, should some conscientious Kaahu technician or programmer, by sheer chance, have happened across this alien code buried deep in their planetary-based processors, they would not, could not, have recognised it as an intrusive, instructive message of betrayal. They would have found what would have been to them some unintelligible gibberish that had no discernible effect on their systems, and which, had they then deleted it, would have been instantly re-written by the renegade satellite concerned in another location within the program without any interruption to the on-going data-siphoning.

This alien probe, and all the others like it exploring the nearby galaxy, initially fell under the aegis of the administrators, scientists and researchers at the Empty Space passage research facility. But now a potential target planet had been identified, the control of the venture would have to be transferred to a new entity who would oversee the whole undertaking right through to the bitter end, despite the length of time it would take. As this was the first time they had had to plan for such an undertaking, the Empty Space passage team were uncertain as to what to call the new body so, provisionally and for convenience, they had named it the organising panel. The name stuck.

***

For all task selection on their world, there was a group of academics specialising in querying the relevant databases, and sometimes utilising their own personal experience, for the best qualified people for whatever task was required at any one time. Who has most experience in agri-automata at this or that settlement? Where can we find someone with a particular interest in this species of animal or plant? Of course, as was ubiquitous across all of the planet's ap-Vanda population, this specialism in data management was not their only area of expertise and, indeed, each was equally or more proficient in other scientific, social, artistic or technical spheres. So much so, some would suggest co-opting themselves onto the panel at a later stage.

The data administrators' first challenge was to select names for the authorising team for the panel. These will be the team leaders of the mission proper, amassing all of the requirements, planning and executing the development structures and hardware manufacturing needed for the main invasion tasks, coordinating it all in a correct and logical manner so everything would be in place when the time came for the departure, journey and implementation of the mission.

There was no military force on the ap-Vanda planet. There was no war nor was there any threat of war from either an internal or external source. Crime, as the Kaahu would understand it, was unheard of, but should some misdemeanour occur, the offender or offenders would be dealt with by a group of their peers – *every one* of their species was a peer – and the relevant punishment, deemed necessary by those same peers, dispensed. There were no prisons. There were no executions. Intentional deprivation of either freedom or life was an abhorrence to the ap-Vanda people of this world and, besides, none of the misdemeanours were ever serious enough to merit such penalties – the were no crimes against property, for example, because there was no *private* property on the planet. Not only was there nothing to steal, there could be no reasons *to* steal. There was no want or need for their species – everything a person could possibly want or need, not only the basic necessities of food, warmth and shelter but, quite literally, everything and anything, was freely available to all. There were no disparities that could cause jealousy or envy between them. A person could see a shiny object in the possession of another person and, if desired, could also possess a similar shiny object by merely ordering it on a data-processor terminal. In reality, there were no such shiny objects. The ap-Vanda, as with all animals on the planet, tended to limit themselves to just the necessities of life. There were no monetary fines because there was no concept of exchangeable currencies – if everything was free, how could there be? The worst crimes anyone could commit would be those against another animal, of any species, or the environment, such as, perhaps, recklessly or neglectfully allowing or causing pain or suffering to another animal or negligently polluting the air, land or water. Those types of offences were, though, so rare as to be almost unheard of. The very worst they had ever had to deal with were the very occasional argument between individuals provoked by the passion of sexual tension or, perhaps, the inconvenience of noisy, high-spirited celebrations of some sort. The most usual punishment for crimes such as these on the planet was a stern talking to by someone the offenders respected – followed by sincerely expressed apologies from the perpetrators.

The structure of any new venture, like the structure

of their society, was instituted along non-hierarchical lines – the team leaders were selected on their merits; the experience, skills and talent they possessed. It was an informal system based on respect. There were no political or personal agendas – there was nothing to gain from either. There was no lust for power, no personal quest for glory. What would be the point? It would, though, be incorrect to describe their society as a meritocracy as there were no elected or otherwise elevated individuals – the ap-Vanda did not seek such power as would be recognised on the hell world. Perhaps the most analogous definition to the primary target political philosophies would be that of an anarchistic community but, even then, the connection would be tenuous.

These same principles used for the adoption of the panel leaders would be used in the selection of the remaining members for the mission proper, as was every role in their society, but that would be years in the future. After many, many days of scouring the relevant databases, lists of suitable specialists were compiled and candidates contacted to determine if they were interested in joining the group. There was never any compulsion. If a candidate did not want to undertake a task – any task – for whatever reason, they did not have to, it was their own personal choice. There was never any coercion. There were never any repercussions. Everyone on the planet knew the uniqueness and importance of this undertaking, however, and, if anything, there was an over-acceptance by volunteers but, nonetheless, all were co-opted onto the program. Some would, by the time the plan was completed, be very old or even, perhaps, dead, but their experience and knowledge right up until that unfortunate time would, nonetheless, be invaluable. A multitude of specialists, including all kinds of cosmologists, planners, engineers, administrators, linguists, astro-dynamicists, botanists, biologists and exobiologists, geologists, exosociologists, mathematicians, metallurgists, all sorts of physicists and many other specialists joined the panel authorising team and, in turn, they suggested possible team members to assist them for each area of specialism.

On the Vatta and Obiah home-worlds, similar arrangements were being undertaken.

chapter twenty-five

Immediately after the planet was found to contain life, further launches of exploratory probes through the Empty Space passage were postponed indefinitely. There were four other probes still exploring four other solar systems, but all evidence pointed to them all being yet more lifeless voids with just floating rocks and gas giants to their, never to be assigned, names.

For the upcoming project, the hell world mission, one of the first tasks was to learn the many languages that were coming through in the data, both written and verbal; though, at first, it was mainly the latter coming back from the target planet. Linguistic teams were assigned to try to distinguish each individual communicative form from the others and assemble supporting teams, including logographers for pictographic text, to translate the languages, analyse the results and, later, educate others that were to be involved in the program. This would be no small undertaking – there were hundreds, if not thousands, of different languages and dialects or regional and social class-based accents with, it would become apparent over the years as more textual information was gathered, a multitude of differing writing systems – ideographic, linear, logographic, syllabic, segmental and so on. The linguists were one of the first sets of experts to be fully mobilised and hundreds were assigned to undertake the task from across the ap-Vanda home-world. Some of the assignments would be difficult and time consuming, but they would have years to accomplish their tasks to an acceptable level. Eventually, algorithms would be written to transform all documents of the numerous Kaahu tongues into the universal language, but first they would all require translation by these linguists.

Translation of the most used languages of the hell world into their own tongue was, initially, relatively simple for the ap-Vanda because the documents that required rendition – scientific, military and governmental data – were usually written formally, the only problems being caused by acronyms, which were never used in their native tongue, the universal language. Time, patience and eventual experience proved invaluable in overcoming that particular issue. However, as work progressed towards less formal data, day to day information, they struggled to translate contractions and abbreviated forms of the languages. The structures and syntax of their own language did not allow for such shortcuts in their speech or writings. Added to that, new abbreviations, contractions and acronyms were almost constantly being created by the Kaahu, whilst others were subtly altered. It was a challenge to the ap-Vanda, but all of their number stood-up, accepted the task and, in due course, became quite adept at translating the textual patois.

At a very early stage of the mission, in fact almost as soon as it was decided what action was going to be required on the hell world, a decision was made to never use the preferred designation of the dominant species but to always refer to them as the *primary target species,* or as the *Kaahu,* an ancient word from one of the dead languages of the ap-Vanda home-world meaning *fool.* It was also decided never to use any of the primary target species' proper nouns when referring to the planet, locations on the planet nor the names of individual organisms living there, other than in the most generic terms: *reptilian, mammalian, vegetable* or *fungi,* for example. All of these words were, more or less, easily translatable or transferable to their own language, whereas the individual names of animals and plants were not.

The gorr species on their home-world may well resemble feline animals on the target planet, but a gorr, whilst mammalian, carnivorous, and although certain subspecies can be the same size as the large felines on the target planet, was certainly not a feline. The ap-Vanda would not refer to any primary target given name unless there was a direct translation of it in their own language. And, of course, there were far too many languages on the target planet to choose but one – would it be cheetah, 猎豹(Lièbào), gepárd, Blettatígur, duma, ghepardo or γατόπαρδος? – there could be hundreds of different variations for the same noun. The ap-Vanda well understood how and why a multitude of different tongues would develop on a planet over time but everything would have been so much easier had these animals spoken the one, single language. Then again, had that been the case, would they still have been living on a hell world at that time?

Some words from the target planet did, however, gain some purchase on the imagination of the ap-Vanda population, usually the younger element within it. One such word, or, more precisely, appendage, was -*bot*, from the Kaahu word *robot* which translated in their own language as *automaton*. The *robot* word, at first, created nary a ripple amongst the ap-Vanda collective consciousness; it was yet another noun from the hell world like any other. Then, in an instant it seemed, people would be saying things like, *cleaner-bot*, *food-bot* or *manufacture-bot*. This suffix, whilst never used in written form, became commonplace in the patois of the ap-Vanda populace. Other than this little word appendage, and despite the occasional, temporary adoption of many alien words and phrases from the target planet, none other entered the ap-

Vanda vocabulary for any great periods of time. The -bot appendage seemed to chime with the universal language, at least on the ap-Vanda home-world. No such adoption of any Kaahu word or phrase took place on the Vatta or Obiah home-worlds. It is still in use on the ap-Vanda home-planet.

The ap-Vanda did not use swear words – why would they? To the ap-Vanda, resorting to anger-based outbursts could only be seen as merely one of the last refuges of the unintelligent animal who cannot properly articulate a counter argument with reason, or as a primal, usually masculine, response to challenges. Unlike the Kaahu, the ap-Vanda conversations were not littered with sentences comprising of mainly obscenities – they could articulate their thoughts and feelings without resorting to anatomical or sexually derived words or insults. That was, after all, just another form of violence. Though having said that, they may, on occasion, utter mild oaths that could be translated as *damn* or the like. Even the ap-Vanda, Vatta and Obiah animals stubbed their toes sometimes!

***

The ap-Vanda had endowed personhood on all species of animal. All creatures had the right to life – if those lives were not conducive to the natural development of the planet, they surely would not have survived the evolutionary process. All life on a world such as theirs and the hell world had a common ancestor, from protozoa to plants, arthropods to mammals and, whilst it was difficult to substantiate without question that vegetable life *feels* in the way that mammalian, avian, aquatic and other more complex life forms do, the lack of neural tissue in plants appeared to suggest they do not. The ap-Vanda, therefore, were strictly vegetarian and all other life forms were sacrosanct – though not in a way that most of the Kaahu would understand that term. These same ethical considerations also applied to the Vatta and Obiah.

Their species did not believe in violence in any form – unlike the primary target species. They did not kill other living creatures for food or for the sick feeling of sheer pleasure the Kaahu seemed to derive from the action, even when perpetrated against each other. The killing or harming of other animals of any species was almost anathema to the ap-Vanda, Vatta and Obiah; only the exceptional circumstances they now found themselves in, or one similar, could have diverted them away from their ethical beliefs. They only took life when, all things taken into account, there was no other alternative. There were no alternatives for the hell world.

The aliens had accepted the fact they would have to kill upwards of fifteen-billion, possibly up to thirty-billion, animals on this mission because of the critical circumstances they had found. This acceptance did not, in any way, shape or form, comfort them.

chapter twenty-six

Regretfully, but not unexpectedly, there were a few oases of bright, questioning minds amongst the vast wastelands of the primary target species' imbecility that inhabited the hell world. These minds belied the accepted ap-Vanda notions of an evolutionarily challenged populous concerned only with short-term pleasure and other, purely self-serving, motives. It was unfortunate, because these shining examples of intelligence were but a tiny minority in a vast desert of apathy and ignorance – perhaps as little as ten percent of the species, though probably even less – as to make no difference to the eventual outcome of the mission. Had those percentages been the opposite way round there would have been no reason for the three alien species to undertake the upcoming cull.

It has to be said, however, that the ap-Vanda were somewhat bemused, if not slightly amused, by the idea of the entire target species taking credit for the work of this tiny minority. The intelligence, the theories, the work of these few appeared to have been co-opted by all of the Kaahu to prove how evolved, how advanced, how wonderful they were as a species – despite this being patently untrue. Having said that, all the evidence of evolution, for example, researched and tested by this small minority of astute individuals was, for the most part, rejected by the insanely superstitious majority and treated for many, many years as heretical across the entirety of the planet and was still treated as such by most of the Kaahu animals even at the time of the alien mission. Surely, the majority argued, an almighty, all-seeing, benevolent yet vengeful, indefinable super-being living somewhere in space, perhaps, had designed every living and, for that matter, every inanimate thing in the universe for their use, for their amusement, for the Kaahu, alone. Not only that, this fabulous being, this cosmological architect, created their planet before all else; with the rest of the universe, with its billions of other galaxies, its multiple trillions of star systems, not created until after the momentous task of creating the Kaahu and their home-world – and only six-thousand or so years before that current time. How dare these radical heretics – these blasphemers – suggest otherwise?

Some, if not most, of the scientific research and subsequent theories undertaken and proposed by some of these brighter than the norm Kaahu, both in the past and at that time, coincided neatly with those of the ap-Vanda. There were, however, fundamental differences in the accepted primary targets' theories about the space-time voids or, as the Kaahu would commonly have it, *wormholes,* and what the ap-Vanda theorised about the nature of the Empty Space passage. Primary target physicists posited the idea, in very general terms, of the wormhole folding time, creating a bridge in space-time. Also, the Kaahu visualised these wormholes as individual, random entities that would be, in most instances, innately unstable. The ap-Vanda studies, undertaken by the Empty Space passage research teams and others before them, appeared to suggest that the Empty Space passage was, more than likely, a contraction of space-time rather than a notional fold and was the underlying foundation of the universe itself. In relatively simple terms, the area, size or mass of Empty Space was considerably less than that of 'normal' space. As far as the Empty Space passage researchers could tell, Empty Space was a permanent, rather than unstable, ephemeral phenomenon and was a universal constant in that, not only does it connect solar-systems within galaxies, it must serve as a bridge or, more likely, short-cut between galaxies throughout the universe – perhaps even a connection to a multi-verse, if such a phenomenon exists.

Their own experiences of traversing the Empty Space passage also showed that, as well as contracting space-time, velocities attained in Empty Space by physical materials, such as spacecraft, appeared to be, had to be, slightly less than what would be considered the speed of light in normal space; but the distances travelled far exceeded those that could possibly be achieved with that velocity limit which, to the aliens, pointed more towards a contraction *of* space rather the a fold *in* space. In essence, Empty Space is considerably smaller than normal space so the distance travelled is substantially less. However, they had not yet discovered a way to prove whether or not this was irrefutably correct and, perhaps, they were in fact travelling at such extreme speeds and, therefore, unfathomable distances that should be impossible, or whether it was just an illusionary consequence of the nature of Empty Space itself – an as yet unknown law of the physical universe.

A few of the primary species' scholars had made a tenuous connection between their wormholes and what they described as *dark matter* and, later, with *dark energy* but, for the most part, these two mysterious substances remained unexplained to the Kaahu scientists. Some theorised that dark matter must be omnipresent throughout the universe as was, by extension, dark energy – those Kaahu scientists had not discovered a way to detect or measure either. Nor would they. The Empty Space passage research team would dispute those theories. What the Kaahu called *dark matter* was, they suggested, the very substance of Empty Space, the membrane between the passage, between interstellar space and a star's gravity-well, whilst the force that drove the expansion of the universe by extending Empty Space was, or appeared to be, analogous to the *dark energy* the Kaahu described.

The Empty Space passage team had also theorised that this source of energy was the same electromagnetic force that propelled matter through Empty Space but it differed fundamentally from the electromagnetic forces in *normal* space. This same Empty Space force also appeared to be anti-gravitational which meant that, rather than dark matter and dark energy being an omnipresent in the *normal* universe, Empty Space was repelled by the combined gravitational forces exerted by stars and their associated stellar materials such as planets, planetoids or asteroid fields, so was only present *under*, or *outside of*, interstellar space. This led them to conclude that the Empty Space lining material or *dark matter* was elastic in nature, as the Empty Space electromagnetic force, or *dark energy,* was constantly stretching Empty Space so as to avoid the gravity in *normal* space, whilst the total mass of the universe remained the same. That force, the mysterious *dark energy* of the Kaahu, was generated by the constant conflict between the gravitational and anti-gravitational mechanisms within the universe. To the Empty Space passage researchers, this theory could explain the primary targets' questions about the absence of eighty-four per cent of matter in the universe and why the universe was expanding.

The Empty Space passage researchers had also theorised that entrances to Empty Space would always be found at the point on the edges between a solar-system and interstellar space, where the greatest amount of gravitational and anti-gravitational forces would be in constant conflict – a kind of gravitational friction – not only generating the energetic force within the passage but also creating an area of potential weakness in the normal space and the Empty Space fabrics or membranes. They had long known that exposure to graviton particles would put enough pressure on those weaknesses to create an entrance to or exit from Empty Space. All of their experience with the probes sent to explore other solar-systems seemed to bear this out.

Although both the anti-gravitational energy and the passage lining, which had been shown to have mass, were ubiquitous in Empty Space, it had proven impossible, up to that point, to either collect samples or analyse the matter lining the passage or the elusive electromagnetic energy as the gravity force exerted by vessels travelling through the passage seemed to be repelled from the material by its anti-gravitational properties. It also defied attempts, up to that point, to be gathered and studied. Alongside this, it appeared that neither the Empty Space matter nor the electromagnetic energy could exist in normal space – neither escaped through the entrance or exit splits – yet matter and energy from *normal* space could both enter and exist in Empty Space, as proven by the ability of their probes and spacecraft to successfully traverse the Empty Space passage. The Empty Space passage researchers had no coherent theories to explain this phenomenon.

The mystery of *black holes*, so-called by the Kaahu, also greatly vexed the ap-Vanda academics. To these scientists, the anomalies were obviously large gashes in the fabric between *normal* space and Empty Space, but how they were created and what precisely they were still required much study, though some academics theorised that these fissures went beyond normal and Empty Space – perhaps to other universes within the multiverse.

chapter twenty-seven

With a planetary population of slightly under four and a half million of the ap-Vanda species – there were, of course, billions of other animals of other species on the planet – there had been little or no use for sociological studies amongst themselves, although some such studies had been undertaken on their ancestors' origins, development, organisations, and their institutions. Over the years, however, a general consensus had emerged of a world, the target planet, where the dominant species had become, in evolutionary terms, a victim of its own success – albeit solely because of the intelligence of a tiny minority of their kind – and because of that success they had, to use one of their superstitions, created a hell world for themselves and all other species of life on the planet. The vast majority of the primary target species did not possess a sufficient amount of intelligence to wisely use the technology at their disposal. Although the target species evolved over a period of between two and a half million to five-million years, the current incarnation had only been inhabiting the planet for around two-hundred thousand or so years. For the vast majority of that time, perhaps up to one-hundred and ninety-nine thousand or so of those years, the Kaahu had little or no impact on those ecosystems so vital to the planet's own evolution, though it does seem clear that they were responsible for the extinction of a number of other species during that time. That being said, they were still in a relatively early stage of their evolution when many of these extinction events occurred.

As the time approached for the ap-Vanda fleet to depart the environs of its home-world to journey to the edge of interstellar space and, before reaching that particular void, plunge into the other, into Empty Space, it was a widely held belief on their home planet that the evolution of the target species had been retarded, by at least five-hundred years, by a combination of those pernicious power structures on the hell world – religious, political and military. In the eyes of the ap-Vanda, all of these systems were one and the same thing, designed to support each other in the retention of power over all of their fellow beings on the planet. But, as all forms of these monolithic institutions varied so considerably in divergent areas of the planet and conflict between these strands of power ever-intensified, it became increasingly difficult to ascertain who actually benefitted from such philosophies other than a very few individuals to whom the retention of power and wealth was paramount – the other Kaahu animals, those that were oppressed by, or died for, these structures, yet actively supported them, gained nothing.

Not that it would matter for too much longer. As the years passed, more and more damning evidence was gathered against the primary target species by the ap-Vanda – damning and extremely disappointing. Amongst other things, they discovered that the overwhelmingly vast majority of the Kaahu, upwards of ninety-five percent of them, appeared to hold those wildly irrational beliefs in supernatural beings and events, all or most based on documents written over a millennia or more before. These irrational belief-systems were based on the benign-sounding concept of *faith* – ostensibly, the belief that something was true simply because, and for no other reason than, one believed it to be true. No empirical evidence was required – no evidence whatsoever, in fact – just the overwhelming desire that it was factual. These continued beliefs stemmed from systematic and multi-generational parental child abuse and a lack of, or inappropriate, education, or, more likely, a combination of both circumstances.

Nearly all of the Kaahu appeared to consider their species to be superior to all other species of animal on the planet. This belief also applied to the planet, everything on or below its surface and, incredibly, the entire universe; everything existed for their pleasure and abuse alone. Their superiority delusions stemmed from their irrational belief-systems – even those very few Kaahu of alleged higher intelligence, those that eschewed the irrationality of the majority based on the evidence of their reason, seemed to still consider themselves superior to all other species and regularly participated, albeit vicariously, in the abuse of those other animal species by dissecting some of them in experiments or eating others. Because of their superiority delusion, the vast majority of the Kaahu wantonly and gleefully partook in, or tacitly condoned, the routine torture, abuse and murder of untold billions of other sentient beings every year.

Throughout their study of the Kaahu, the main words that seemed to crop-up for the ap-Vanda when describing them were; *irrational, illogical, unintelligent, violent, superstitious, apathetic, selfish, avaricious* and *untrustworthy*. Obviously, these were generic observations and the ap-Vanda felt sure that there would be – there *must* be – exceptions. That is to say, not every one of the Kaahu displayed all of these traits – only the overwhelming majority. All of the evidence the aliens acquired and disseminated to assert these judgements had been freely and unashamedly available. Everything that needed to be known about these animals could be viewed or read on any of their media and it could be ascertained from this information that the Kaahu actually took pride in their actions and thought themselves worthy of respect. It became clear that these animals were well aware of what they were doing to other species, to the planet and to themselves.

There was a population of a little under seven-billion primary target animals on the planet – that was fully expected to increase to around seven and a quarter billion or so by the time the alien expedition reached the hell world. It was barely over two-hundred years ago that the first milestone of a population of one-billion Kaahu was reached. A further one-hundred and twenty-five or so years passed before that figure hit two-billion, but only another thirty years for the three-billion mark to be passed. The planet population grew from three-billion to that tad under seven-billion in the space of, approximately, fifty years. It was projected by the Kaahu themselves that their population would further increase to between eight- and eleven-billion within the following forty years – the year twenty-fifty by their calendar. It was believed by the ap-Vanda that those estimates were overly optimistic, to say the least, and would expect the primary target population, even at current rates of reproduction at that time, to exceed twelve-billion within that period. Even if the ap-Vanda were wrong and the Kaahu population of the hell world *only* grew to eleven-billion, that would be eight- or nine-billion more than could be considered safe or sensible for a planetary population by any rational species of animal on a planet of that size. However, due to the socio-economic and political, yet divided, nature of their society or, probably more correctly, societies, it is more likely that one or more catastrophic ecological or self-inflicted disasters would curtail that growth well before it reached that point. Their aggressive tendencies and their failure to protect both the natural resources and defences of their planet over a relatively short period of their history, and yet less than a flash in geological time, would logically point to impending disaster. Obviously, these cataclysmic events would not only be harmful to the Kaahu. Depending on the nature and severity of such catastrophes, all species of animal and plant life on the planet would be adversely and irreparably affected, perhaps even completely annihilated.

The population growth over the past two centuries had been exacerbated by the primary targets' attitude towards, and opinion of, themselves as a species of the planet – that is, divine and eternal – and of the other species of life on that planet. It was, they considered, theirs to abuse in any way they saw fit.

The socio-economic, religious and political systems of the primary target species were highly complex and difficult for the ap-Vanda to comprehend and explain in a truncated form. These socio-economic, religious and political systems were, and had always been, based on the acquisition and retention of power by individual Kaahu animals and by any means necessary – usually by violence, deceit, and division. The Kaahu seemed to cherish division within their species. The main divisive elements within their societies were, from what could be ascertained, religion, nationality, ethnicity, gender, sexuality, colour, mobility and the class, caste or general social status of an individual Kaahu animal – all of these were alien to logical concepts of living. Other species of life, animal or vegetable, were of no real consequence to the Kaahu.

Whilst the ap-Vanda, Vatta and Obiah all recognised that some mammalian-type species, including simians, from whatever planet could evolve utilising an hierarchical social structure, where the strongest animal would control the rest of the societal group by coercion, ideally, in their view, these hell world primates should have evolved beyond this trait. However, they also recognised the Kaahu's difficulty in doing so. The progression of that, possibly necessary, coercion from the earlier periods of their species development to the extreme violence of the present day was, though, not conducive to the evolutionary processes of themselves, other life-forms or indeed, the whole planet. Also, and as long ago as four- or five-thousand years, perhaps longer, it was a recognised military and political concept to divide and rule other Kaahu by creating some form of disharmony between themselves as a group, therefore allowing those perpetrating the friction to conquer and hold power over the rest. There can be no doubt that this stratagem had been utilised prior to that date and ever since – it was still being used with all of those elements. All of these divisions and their consequences had had a profound and negative effect on the evolution of the Kaahu, all other species of life and, by extension, the planet itself – at least in the general opinion of the soon-to-be invading alien species. Actively working against the interests of one's fellow beings, rather than for the general good of the planet and all its life-forms, as illustrated by the circumstances prevalent at that time on the target planet, only endangered life in all its forms on that planet.

There were a multitude of irrational belief systems, the seemingly ubiquitous religions, on the hell world, all claiming to be the one, *true* religion and all espousing love for all, yet separateness from all other, by default, false beliefs. Bizarrely, however, most of these sects purported to worship the same deity as each other. These strange beliefs, their *faith*, and the separation they encouraged, often promoted the compulsion of adherents to kill other religionists not of their doctrine. All of their *sacred* texts and the leaders of these religions, more or less invariably, also encouraged their followers to be separate and to be violent whilst, at the same time, preaching peace and love for all.

The planet had been separated into unnatural, political entities that the Kaahu called *nation states*. Accordingly, just to be a Kaahu, born within the self-defined boundaries of one of these entities, endowed that individual with superior intelligence, courage and fighting skills to those other Kaahu born in other such entities. So much so, it was considered a matter of great pride to kill or be killed whilst *defending* their own entity from another similar, though for the duration of the conflict, *evil*, entity, despite the fact that the *defenders* were often the original aggressors, and were so only for the power and wealth acquisition that such aggression would bring about. The division these entities promoted did not only manifest themselves in military matters; national fervour in any sphere such as sport or trade, the general mistrust of other nationalities, and the hatred of all those non-national enemies, were enthusiastically encouraged by their military, economic and political rulers and, more often than not, their religious leaders too. It is, perhaps, noteworthy that those same evil, non-national enemies, so despised during a conflict, were soon not quite as evil once wealth and power generating trade could, once again, begin between the formerly warring nations and those same religious, economic, military and political leaders could attain more and more wealth and power.

Ethnicity, yet one more totally alien idea to the ap-Vanda, Vatta and Obiah species, was a Kaahu concept related to their individual ancestry – where on the planet their antecedents were born. A national entity, as described above, could contain many Kaahu of different ethnic origins, and conflict within a national entity could erupt because of these differences in ethnicity. The usual dividing ethnic factors on the planet were colour of skin, religion, culture, language or, even, how an individual or group dressed.

Although all of the aliens found it incredulous, there was also an obvious schism between male and female Kaahu, with the male the dominant gender of the two. This split took many, some subliminal or covert, forms and, whilst in the private, domestic sphere it could often be a violent, confrontational and oppressive experience for the female animal, in the public domain, in more liberal areas of the planet, the illusion of parity between the genders was promoted and maintained. But it was just that – an illusion. In some of their national entities, those more liberal areas, legislation had been enacted to protect females from discrimination by males but, in practice, the female was institutionally oppressed throughout all of these entities and, in many, many others, there was no attempt made to disguise the schism by the usually all-male legislators. It should be added here that all of these anti-female activities could always be linked, in one way or another, to the primary target species' irrational religious beliefs.

In the more illiberal locations, in huge swathes of the planet's surface, females fared far worse. Parents in some of these locations would commit infanticide of their female issue, whilst others consented to have their daughters' genitalia brutally mutilated. Many females, planet-wide, were denied even a basic level of education merely due to their gender and millions were sold into virtual, if not actual, slavery every year. The filicide could, generally, be blamed on the inequitable economic systems prevalent at the time – the parents lacking either the wealth or power to afford female offspring as they would have to endow currency or property, or both, to the family of any male who took the female as a *legally-recognised* mate. Male offspring, on the other hand, were, under the same system, a potential source of future wealth. The practice of genital mutilation had both a religious and cultural background but, broadly, it was considered by the aliens to be an attempt by males to, both, subdue females in general whilst achieving personal sexual pleasure for members of their own sex from the females individually – in most instances the labia was almost completely sutured – at the expense

173

of the total lack of the ecstasies of intercourse for the female animal – the clitoris having been removed. It also caused considerable pain for the female of the species who, the aliens had learned, had suffered this barbaric and abhorrent mutilation debasement for centuries.

It could only have been assumed that the Kaahu males feared, in some way, their female counterparts. It had been a little over a century before that, more or less, any females anywhere on the hell world had received any kind of academic education and, even at the current time, there were millions, perhaps billions, of female animals denied any schooling whatsoever. Rather than educate females animals, the male Kaahu sought to exploit them sexually and economically, though even the erudite females on the hell world were not immune from such mistreatment. It was said by the Kaahu that slavery had been abolished on the target world yet, year after year, it seemed that many young female animals of their species were exchanged for currency against their wishes. The females would be sold legally to males for marriage, by their parents, for sexual and domestic purposes, abducted and sold to males for prostitution purposes or, even, sold to males for prostitution purposes by their own parents. An unknown number of female children were raped and sexually abused every day, across the entire planet – by a parent, a sibling, a relative or an adult friend. Images of such abuses were rife on the Kaahu nexus, even at that time. That is not to say that male Kaahu issue were never sexually abused as children – indeed they were and, probably, to the same degree – but, broadly speaking, males did not have to suffer such an over-arching range of assaults to both their person and their dignity.

Approximately fifty percent of the primary target population were female, yet, on that male dominated world, that is where parity ended. This self-proclaimed most intelligent of beings had oppressed half of their population for millennia. As with so many aspects of their supposed evolution into the higher beings they all believed themselves to be, they should have abandoned this illogical trait a long time ago. Along with their ridiculously illogical superstitious beliefs, their vicious murders of their own and other species of animal and their inexplicable abuse of their own children, the unjust domination of females of their own species should have been forgotten well before the present time. The correlation between their irrational belief systems and the male domination over females was irrefutably evident. Generally, their gods were all male, their clerics were all male and, thus, the tenor of their beliefs was also all male.

***

The natural sexual proclivities of individual primary target animals could, and often did, provoke great controversy and division in most areas of the hell world. In many areas, Kaahu that had sexual intercourse with other members of their own gender could be legally imprisoned, beaten or executed, or possibly all three, for this so-called *crime*. Many of those Kaahu animals that did not participate in same-gender sexual intercourse thought that such behaviour was *evil* and against their gods' wishes – the same gods who were, apparently, omnipotent, omnipresent and infallible. If so, how could they create aberrations such as these animals? Surely, if these gods could see all, be everywhere at any one time and never make mistakes, animals that engaged in this type of sexual intercourse could not hope to have ever existed?

Simple, simple minds.

***

The colour of the primary target species' skin was, apparently, of huge importance to their species – another very strange notion when the fact that they were all just different shades of the same colour was recognised, something that, obviously, they had not yet done. This phenomenon was prevalent on the target planet because, perhaps, it was simpler for the Kaahu to discern the otherness of another animal's skin colour visually than to recognise the more non-physical traits of others, their religion, their ethnicity, their sexuality or their nationality, that would suggest an animal different or separate from themselves and, so, worthy of aggression or disdain.

Simplicity of thought was one of the most defining characteristics of the majority of these Kaahu animals.

***

The three species of aliens had been greatly mystified by all of the self-made divisions between the primary target animals, but none more so than those they found in their attitude to the, so-called, disabled members of their own species, whatever their nationality, ethnicity or gender. Although the ap-Vanda, as a species, had eliminated most, if not all, genetically linked physical and mental disabilities, as had the Vatta and Obiah before them, their bodies were not immune to accidental damage which could render a person incapable of, or less able to perform, certain physical or mental activities. They believed they understood how this negatively affected those that suffered such accidents and, as a society, they tried to make life as normal and inclusive as possible for their fellows as they could.

Although the incidence of serious, accidental injury was very low, much research had been undertaken, and continued to be undertaken, on mechanical movement aids for those with physical injuries, at that time enabling even those with the most severe spinal injuries to engage in activities such as walking, sitting down and standing-up with relative ease – albeit wearing some quite ungainly external apparatus.

Brain injuries were more prevalent than serious physical injuries though, thankfully to the aliens, most were not too severe and did not cause mental impairment and could, where required, be alleviated by surgery. Automata carried out all the activities that could be hazardous to animals, such as working in locations where there was a danger of injury caused by falling materials or working in areas of height or other such perilous occupations. The most injuries to the aliens usually occurred during sporting activities such as ball games or scaling high peaks for recreational purposes. For those unfortunate enough to suffer damage that seriously affected their mental processes, however, little could be done, medically, to restore their abilities. These animals would not be ostracised, isolated or ridiculed by their peers. Their families, friends and the wider community would rally round to support their fellow animal, and not only in the short term.

This did not happen on the target planet.

The majority of Kaahu treated those of their own species with physical and mental disabilities as less than themselves – as a different species. As with the gender divide, in some national entities the discrimination, from the public aspect, was indirect rather than out-and-out overt, yet privately was ugly and often violent. Again, the ap-Vanda could only surmise that this was because of the obvious visual differences between an able and disabled primary target to these simple minded animals. This simple-mindedness could, in the opinion of the ap-Vanda, Vatta and Obiah, be extremely hazardous. It could also be said that, generally, the Kaahu treated older members of their societies in a manner similar to the disabled.

***

The vast majority of the primary targets, probably approaching the high nineties in percentage terms, appeared to think of themselves as non-animal entities who would survive their own deaths and live on forever, for eternity. This delusion may have coloured the Kaahu view on the state of their world – why worry about the destruction of the physical world when the *spirit* lives on whatever happens? There was absolutely no scientific evidence to substantiate this unintelligible theory.

As highly unlikely as it appeared to all of the invading aliens, it may well be that, after death, the essence, the life-force of an animal, may be dispersed into the universe – that was certainly true of the nutrients of a corpse – but that was not what the Kaahu believed. The Kaahu religions taught them that their corporeal bodies would be, somehow, reconstituted and returned to them in some, possibly, off-planet paradise – they had nothing to worry about. This appeared to run contrary to any evolutionary theories that the aliens had ever heard.

The fact that so many of the Kaahu disbelieved, or in many instances were completely unaware of, the fact of evolution was because of the irrational superstitious beliefs they held. Those that knew of evolutionary theory were so blinded by their faith as to disbelieve it, whilst those of them that knew nothing of it, probably never would – their religions would not educate them in such subjects. Perversely, a tiny percentage of the Kaahu appeared to accept the evolutionary theory as fact, yet still considered themselves to be eternal beings who will survive after death whilst not bestowing this everlasting attribute to other species of animals who would only exist for their own lifespans and die to complete nothingness. An even smaller minority believed evolution to be a fact and realised that irrational superstitious beliefs in an afterlife were mere delusions, yet still regarded any other species of animals as inferior to their own and did not consider the murder and torture of these different species as criminal, let alone cruel, acts. An even tinier still minority did not believe in any irrational superstitious beliefs, and realised that their species evolved from a common ancestor to all other current animal species on the planet and would not harm or eat those animals. Unfortunately, this latter group appeared to be so small in percentage terms as to not properly register on any statistical chart, and had little to no influence on the majority and other minority groupings noted above.

***

The primary target species' attitude to their home-world simply defied belief.

Up to fifteen-million hectares, perhaps more, of forest were destroyed by their activities every year, mainly to facilitate intensive farming of unsuitable crops or rearing other species of animals for eventual slaughter and consumption.

Kaahu scientists had estimated that up to seventy-five percent of all animal species were indigenous to the tropical rainforests of the planet and, potentially, millions of other species of animal, plant and micro-organisms may have been awaiting discovery by those same scientists. Had the destruction of these forests continued, these millions of species would, surely, never have been discovered.

Rainforests were responsible for the conversion of vast amounts of carbon dioxide into oxygen and storing that particular pollutant within their trunks and roots. It had been estimated that around thirty percent of the planet's oxygen has been through this process at any one time.

Twelve-million hectares of land was lost by desertification caused partly by Kaahu deforestation and partly by their intensive farming of the land. Intensive agriculture could mean either depleting the nutrients in the soil by improper land management, or over-grazing by other species of animals, those unnaturally selected and reared for consumption by the target species.

It was estimated by the Kaahu themselves that their polluting activities, such as the constant burning of fossil fuels and the deceptively named *land use change,* which meant deforestation, had caused there to be thirty-seven billion tonnes of carbon dioxide polluting their planet, and this total was growing by a further ten-billion tonnes every year. Half of that amount was in their atmosphere and was the major cause of global warming and climate change. Twenty-five percent of the total amount found its way into the planet's oceans, causing acidification and the subsequent impact on the food chain to all marine creatures. The final quarter was safely soaked up into the ever decreasing forests on the planet which, at the rate of destruction described above, would not be so safe for long.

***

The three species of aliens freely admitted to being totally perplexed by the intricacies of the Kaahu economic systems, their convoluted financial or fiscal practices. But the aliens did not need to understand them. All three species agreed, however, that these functions were yet more examples of the Kaahu megalomaniacal obsessions with their own personal power and their greed for more and more currency. These pecuniary processes were specifically designed to exploit and confound other members of their species purely for the advantage of the powerful against the weak. But those same weak Kaahu were complicit in the procedures because they allowed their self-appointed *betters* to continue to profit from their timidity in the vain hope that, one day, they too would be in a position to so exploit and confound their fellow animals.

But the ap-Vanda, Vatta and Obiah did not need to expend their energies acquiring an intimate knowledge of these systems. They needed not to delve into the complexities of profit and loss, interest rates and other such nonsenses – what would be the point? All ages – from even the seven and eight year olds to the centenarians of their species – could compute the mathematics and decipher the equations, but these inane processes would soon be wiped away and forgotten on the hell world. Soon their bankers, financiers, entrepreneurs and all other such self-seeking animals would be dead. Soon, reason would prevail and no animal on the planet would be so abased by their fellow species. No currencies would be required, no compulsion to profit from the, perhaps, unfortunate circumstances of another animal. Everything the surviving Temuri and their future offspring could possibly ever require for nourishment, shelter, warmth, education and relaxation would be freely at hand without them ever having to experience hunger, exposure, illiteracy, innumeracy, or back-breaking toil in their lives.

chapter twenty-eight

The babies of the Kaahu were, as with the children of all species of animal everywhere, no matter on which planet they may have been born, beautiful little animals – at the very least, to their own parents. Images of these creatures had been ever-increasing, in huge abundance, on the Kaahu mass communication networks, their social nexus, that were intercepted and viewed by the aliens over the preceding years. These animals, at birth and until they were perhaps, one year old, were innocents. Later, ugliness would insinuate itself into the psyche of the child. After that time they, naturally, began to take on the more unsavoury characteristics of their parents and societies; their irrational beliefs, their competitive tendencies, so often leading to violence, and they developed the taste for the dead animal carcasses so beloved by their species. However, their journey into corruption would start at a much earlier age.

In the majority of cases, and for the first six to twelve months of their lives, primary target children were usually exclusively nourished by their mothers' milk – a mammalian bodily fluid generated by the perfectly natural process of lactation within the female parent. Following that period of natural nutrition, however, most Kaahu were fed a diet of lactations obtained from unnatural sources, predominantly the mothers' milk from bovine species that were kept in a state of almost constant pregnancy by artificial insemination, that forced these animals to be permanently lactating so as to supply their milk for consumption by the Kaahu. One disgusting by-product of this was the fact that the resulting babies of these unnaturally impregnated bovine creatures were, invariably, separated from their mothers at a very early age and slaughtered very soon thereafter, again for consumption by the Kaahu. No consideration was given by the primary targets to either the mother, for the loss of her child, or the, no doubt, terrified and confused baby wrested from the safety and comfort of his or her parent, and viciously killed. No empathy felt nor compassion shown. It was assumed by the aliens that this appalling behaviour was because of the ridiculous notions the Kaahu held regarding their status in the universe; that is supreme, immortal demi-gods, compared to being *just* animals, that is, every species other than their own. They, as non-animals, experienced such things as pain, fear, parental love and loss, yet other species, the animals, did not feel pain and did not experience any emotional traumas associated with the atrocities that the Kaahu perpetrated against them – again, despite a mass of evidence to the contrary having been both scientifically proven and right before their non-animal eyes.

Millions of primary target animals lived side-by-side with millions of other species of animals known as *pets* which, apparently, they *owned* as property. Despite the demeaning legalistic terms, it seems as if many of these cohabitation arrangements were successful and all parties appeared content.

However the circumstances surrounding the supply of these animals, the commercialisation of life itself, was yet another affront to the sensibilities of the ap-Vanda, Vatta and Obiah. As with so many other instances of their interactions with other animals, the Kaahu treated feline, canine and other species as mere instruments of wealth acquisition, as breeding became a production line for the sole benefit of the primary targets. And not all of these cohabitation relationships were happy – at least not for the unfortunate slave-animal, the *pet*. Many,

many millions of these animals were cruelly neglected, left to starve or die of thirst or exposure, tortured and otherwise abused every year by the Kaahu. Many millions more were euthanized by medics every year because their Kaahu *owners* no longer wanted them.

In similar circumstances, though with totally different results from the occasionally harmonious state of affairs mentioned above, millions of primary target animals also *owned* and worked with other species in environments such as agri-factories, laboratories, zoo-prisons, places of slaughter or on activities related to, so-called, sports. Especially in these locations, the intensity with which the Kaahu interacted with these other species and the activities they undertook against them, must have made it patently clear to them that physical and emotional feelings, as well as personality, were present within all of those other animals. Those attributes were never publicly acknowledged by the primary target species undertaking these activities. These other species of animal were tortured, abused and slaughtered.

Those two categories of animals, the pets or companion animals, and those enslaved in agri-factories, laboratories, zoo-prisons, places of slaughter or on activities related to, so-called, sports, would, during the project, be classified as secondary targets by the ap-Vanda, Vatta and Obiah. Very unfortunately, these animals must also be culled.

Besides the Kaahu' predilection for violently murdering other species of animal, they also appeared to be rather fond of killing each other, again with huge amounts of gusto and violence. They did this on an alarmingly constant basis – hardly a second passed on the planet without at least one primary target animal being shot, blown-up, bludgeoned or stabbed to death by a fellow Kaahu animal. The above is not comprehensive list of the Kaahu methods of killing each other. Of course, that cannot compare with the horror of one-hundred and twenty-five thousand land animals of other species that were murdered by the Kaahu for food every single second of every single day.

One primary animal would kill another primary animal at the slightest hint of an excuse, no matter how trivial. Popular excuses offered up by the Kaahu for killing another primary target animal seemed to be because the victim did not believe in the perpetrator's particular brand of superstitious nonsense or held, perhaps, a slightly variant belief of that same nonsense; or, perhaps, the victim did not believe in any of their nonsense – any or all of these could be sanctioned by their leaders and judiciary bodies; the colour of the victim's skin, that is, it was different from the killer's skin colour – too dark or too pale – on the face of it, officially frowned upon but, unofficially, used extensively by political leaders to attain and keep power; the sexuality of the victim did not conform to that of the murderer – also sanctioned by their leaders and judiciary in large areas of the planet; for material gain, be it for the perpetrator personally or for the interests of one of the primary targets' artificial national entities – the latter positively promoted and encouraged; or just plain, insane rage – there was a lot of that about for some reason. All of these abominations had been happening for many hundreds, perhaps thousands, of years and would have continued to occur unless there was some form of intervention.

It appears that all of the primary targets were totally obsessed with weaponry of some description or other and with violence in any form. Weapons and violence were, unquestionably, the main ingredients in Kaahu entertainment and in their fictions.

It also appeared that most Kaahu spent a great deal of their lives intoxicated by one substance or another. Inhaled, imbibed, injected, ingested – there were no ways that the Kaahu would reject to achieve the desired level of befuddlement. This intoxication often played a substantial role in the murders, and other offences, that these animals committed, though by no means was it a requirement to be so inebriated to carry out those crimes. Given the nature of life on the hell world for the Kaahu, the alien invaders could, almost, understand this perceived need for such extreme chemical-based disarray but, as with so many other activities of the Kaahu, they considered it insanity to purposely and continually damage their bodies and minds with these substances. The ap-Vanda, as the Vatta and Obiah, did not partake of any of these chemical recreations. Alcohol would only be used as a solvent in such processes as the recycling of silk or, at a pinch, for medicinal purposes as an antiseptic medium. Neither would they use the other, mind-altering chemicals so abused by the primary target species such as opiates, except, on the rare occasions they were required, as an analgesic.

However, that is not to say that the ap-Vanda did not imbibe stimulants. They drank infusions of many different varieties; herbal, vegetable and fruit, and a beverage produced from the roasted seeds of a tropical plant called kaw-he, which, at that stage, they presumed must be akin to the Kaahu *coffee* drink. This presumption arose, mainly, because of the similarity of the processes used to produce the beverage but it was a conjecture they later discovered to be incorrect, at least when it came to the taste. Some ap-Vanda also joked that the perceived similarity was the result of wishful thinking by some members of their species because the pronunciation of each term was almost identical. Some of those infusions, especially the kaw-he, did have stimulative properties but, comparatively, they were all quite mild.

The ap-Vanda mainly drank water, infusions or, perhaps, fruit or vegetable juices on social occasions. They felt no need, no compulsion, to lose their senses, even to the slightest degree. Neither did the Vatta, nor the Obiah.

Inhaling the smoke of smouldering dried vegetation was, again, an insane concept to the ap-Vanda and their two alien allies; such folly surely could never have been thought to be a good idea, could it? Was it not bad enough that the Kaahu had so effectively befouled the air they breathed; did they also need to exacerbate the situation by forcing other toxic materials into their own lungs?

It was obvious to the three alien species that the Kaahu used all of these chemical substances as an escape – perhaps as a kind of death-wish – from the hardships of their lives, a fact that the Kaahu themselves would admit to, but they had nobody to blame but themselves. They and they alone made their lives, and the lives of countless other species, miserable.

When the Kaahu were not overdosing themselves with inhaled, injected or some other imbibed chemicals, they were killing themselves with the food they were eating. It was, surely, poetic justice that the animal-based diet of the majority of Kaahu on the hell world, a diet only made possible with the associated suffering of billions of other creatures, was, in turn, killing many millions of those Kaahu every year, or if not directly causing their deaths, inducing a myriad of diseases to further add countless agonies to their already miserable lives.

And it was not necessarily only the animal matter they were digesting that were causing the problems; so many chemicals, so many antibiotics, so many steroids, so many growth hormones were artificially introduced to those unfortunate beings of other species before their slaughter, that they adversely affected the health of the Kaahu.

Yet all these foods, produced from the misery of other species, were actively promoted, for the most part, as healthy, as being fit and proper for primary target consumption. Mother's milk from mammals of differing species from the Kaahu and consumed in copious amounts by those animals, yet denied to the children for whom it was originally produced, was promoted as being essential for the healthy development of the primary targets' children, but was also laced with such chemical additives and could induce many digestive and pulmonary diseases and multiple allergies.

But the Kaahu did not seem to care about their children.

Besides being dishonest to them for life, mentally, physically and sexually abusing them or regarding those children as mere sexual commodities, the Kaahu also actively encouraged their children to eat and drink substances that were not only full of those chemical additives, but also adulterated by fats, sugars and salts – none of which could be considered to be healthy by any so-called intelligent civilisation. At that time on the hell world, there was an obesity epidemic because of this abuse – grossly overweight adult and child Kaahu, all across the planet, were contracting all kinds of debilitating illnesses; yet the Kaahu continued to promote these foods and beverages to their children so as not to adversely affect the amount of wealth generated for a very small number of their population that such promotion engendered. Would a species that cared for its offspring gleefully and knowingly poison them as the Kaahu seemed to do?

Whilst irrational to the aliens' eyes, the concept of separate, artificially created national entities were historical and may, in the past, have served to unite the Kaahu populations in times of strife – but those troubles were all self-inflicted. It is safe to say that, for the past one-hundred years at least, these entities had served only to uphold the powers of oppression, greed and mass murder.

The concept behind the most popular of the primary target system of governance, *democracy*, appeared sound in theory but it was undermined by the prevailing economic system, which actively supported corruption, greed and violence, and the type of primary target attracted to those vices – corrupt, greedy individuals prone to extreme violence to achieve their aims, avidly seeking personal power and material wealth.

Such were the Kaahu politicians – all of them.

The primary target's belief in their future technology, fuelled by competition, being the saviour of their planet and themselves – but just themselves – from the excesses of their fellow animals was yet another irrational and unfounded idea fed to them by their leaders. But how could that possibly be so? It was doubtful, but it may well have been that such planet-saving technology could have been developed; but even if it had, vested interests on the planet, those that controlled the production of energy, the manufacture of goods and the extraction of fossil fuels, would not have readily ceded their grasp on these wealth and power generating concerns.

Avarice would not allow this.

All primary targets, perhaps without exception, constantly lied to their own children from birth. Most of these children never realised that they had been deceived but, even if their parents' deceptions had been discovered, they, invariably, would also lie to their own children from birth when that time came. From childhood to death, all primary target animals were deceived, and they themselves lied, on a daily basis. These lies took many forms.

The lie of the supernatural is one such instance. Most Kaahu truly believed in ethereal beings such as angels and saints that protected them, ghosts and spirits that haunted them, infallible gods and goddesses that ruled over them, devils and demons that tempted and taunted them, all living in, what the Kaahu called, heaven or hell. They also believed that *everything* happened for a reason – absolutely everything, no matter how insignificant, to each and every individual Kaahu, was pre-ordained to plan by their deities. The three alien species, in contrast, believed in a physical universe where the existence of such chimeric forces was, at best, highly improbable, and that the lives of individuals were ultimately arbitrary – an animal could, perhaps, control certain elements of their existence but, sooner or later, something random, minor or major, could or would occur to disrupt that life. Evolution happens for a reason – little else does.

Another falsity fed to the Kaahu was the lie of the improbable. All Kaahu, it appeared, were desirous of freedom, equality, security and opportunity. They claimed these concepts as *rights*, that their status as Kaahu entitled them to these freedoms and that the acquisition of these concepts were achievable for all of their species; yet, in reality, on their world no such doctrines had ever existed, nor would they ever exist. Their irrational belief systems and inequitable, to say the least, political and economic power systems had oppressed, discriminated, assaulted and denied them any kind of freedoms for millennia – there was, at that time, no reason to suppose that the situation would change in even the tiniest fashion. The Kaahu insistence that they were possessed of purported free will flew in the face of rationality when those same religious, political and economic power systems were taken into account.

Passion was another lie. The Kaahu could not differentiate between severe mental disorders and passion. The ap-Vanda, Vatta and Obiah animals had a passion for knowledge, for sports, for procreation, for artistic creation and for each other. They did not, would not, could not taint that emotion with violence or dishonesty to justify those sentiments. In contrast, the Kaahu, as a matter of course, regularly defended their own odious murders, violations, deceptions and misbehaviours as being somehow acceptable because they were committed whilst in a state of such fervour. It was even considered a virtue for a Kaahu to possess, for example, a *passion for business* – that is to say an animal was respected by most others of his species because of their zeal in the exploitation of their fellow beings, other animals and the planet. Participants in Kaahu sports that cheated to gain an unfair advantage against their opponents were, generally, applauded for their passion for the game. To the alien animals, these Kaahu excuses for passion were a form psychopathy; the unnatural, unfeeling and selfish actions of mentally ill animals.

The Kaahu obsession with the emotion of love was fascinating, disturbing and somewhat amusing to the aliens. Those delusional ideas of happy-ever-after, eternal or true love, universal love, love conquers all and soul-mates defied all logic – where did they get these ideas from? To live happily ever after must, surely, imply that the animal is content to start with – was that possible on the target planet? The aliens thought not. Neither did they believe that never-ending love was possible save, perhaps, for the love of a parent for a child which disappeared at the death of that parent. And, having said even that, many Kaahu parents sexually, physically and mentally abused their children – or were those things merely an expression of their eternal love? The aliens had no clue as to what meaning the Kaahu put on either *true* love or *universal* love. The former seemed to imply the possibility of false love but there could not be such an emotion, surely, rather an overt deception by those professing such untruths, and the latter was, considering everything the aliens knew of the Kaahu, simply risible. Taking into account the many centuries of pain and suffering experienced by all species on the hell world, it was patently clear that, in fact, love did not conquer all. Whereas greed and extreme violence had ever-triumphed throughout Kaahu history and the mere notion of soul-mates was, to the aliens, so unfathomable on so many levels as to be, perhaps, underserving of comment – suffice it say that the concept that one animal was *pre-destined* to be with another particular animal was yet another example of the incomprehensibility of these barely-evolved, superstitious Kaahu animals.

In a similar vein, though not entirely emotion-based, the Kaahu seemed to have a belief in the innate fairness and decency of other animals of their species, despite all evidence to the contrary. How could that be so? Their superstitious doctrines and their fictions – ostensibly the same thing – perpetrated this myth as a salve against the horrors committed by the Kaahu, and in their name, for centuries and right up to that time. Yes, some members of your species just gassed to death five-million innocent others of your species because they were different, but those who committed the atrocity were evil individuals (who, by some strange coincidence, happened to find themselves together in the same place and at exactly the same time to do such awful acts) not in any way similar to the rest of your species who are just *not* like that – you are intrinsically good. In reality, all of the Kaahu inflicted immense pain and suffering on animals of *all* species and abused the planet beyond the telling – there was nothing fair or decent about this species, innate or otherwise.

Many billions of the Kaahu appeared to have an obsessive, destructive fixation with others of their species – in particular, those who did not share their particular belief-system and, hence, their life-view. In many instances, they were quite prepared to kill these others with alternative opinions or philosophies.

At some point in their past, possibly as long ago as all those thousands of years earlier when the primary target species first evolved as a separate entity from its progenitor, the Kaahu developed what could be described as a *strong versus weak* attitude to life and their fellow species of animal. It is probably safe to speculate that this way of life was created by the *strong*, where the weakest members would be subjugated or bullied. Generally speaking, the *strong* possessed all that the *weak* animals did not and the *weak* envied and yearned for all of the things the *strong* had – in particular, material wealth.

However, no matter how much of this wealth the *weak* accumulated, they would never achieve the level of affluence of the *strong* – that would not be allowed unless they obtained power. Only the *strong* possessed power and they achieved that power through their ancestors', or their own, extreme violence. They had perceived power because they not only considered themselves as superior, but also because the *weak* considered the *strong* as superior, and that view was ever propagated because the *strong* controlled all of the means of communication.

The *strong* also had actual power – the power to shape the lives of the *weak* and of all other species on the planet.

The Kaahu called this *Civilisation*.

chapter twenty-nine

On the ap-Vanda home-world at that time it was not all dry scientific and academic research; it was not all spacecraft or automaton design and manufacture; it was not at all work, work, work for the ap-Vanda animals despite there being many tasks to perform. A number of the aliens not participating in the project, or at least not in a formal capacity, got more involved with the hell world mission as the years passed by and more data was received. As the various languages from the hell world were translated, academies added most, if not all, of them to their educational schedules and students studied them with zeal.

The latest news from the target planet, albeit with a slight delay due to the time taken for it to traverse the great distances between the two worlds and to be translated into the universal language, was transmitted, with sub-titles, around the ap-Vanda home-world every day, and numerous serious debates, and many not-so serious, were held by all of the world's communities on a weekly, if not daily, basis. Amongst the whole ap-Vanda populace, there was a general interest in happenings on that strange, tortured world so far away.

And it was not just the political, military or sociological events of the distant primary target societies that gripped the inhabitants of the planet. Huge interest was also shown in the Kaahu art forms; music, visual arts and, as they were digitised over the years by the Kaahu and translated on this world, their creative writing. By the time literature was captured in some digital format by the primary targets as a matter of course, everyone on the ap-Vanda home-world spoke at least one of those many primary target languages, though it was thought no one person spoke them all, so they could all enjoy, or otherwise, the literature of the Kaahu.

All of the Kaahu art forms fascinated the ap-Vanda. They were enchanted in particular with all of their tele-visual broadcasts about the other species of animal and plant life on the hell world, and marvelled at the beauty of the rare, virtually untouched land and seascapes – such magnificent animals and such idyllic scenes. But as much as they loved these natural documentaries, in the same instance, they were saddened and disgusted by the inherent cruelty shown to other species and the rarity of such areas of untouched beauty depicted in the transmissions. The continuing reports of Kaahu interference that threatened both the viability of those environments and the future of the native species appalled them, and the apathy shown by the vast majority of Kaahu sickened them. Judging by the number of these programmes, no primary target on the planet could say that they were not aware of the damage they were doing. A tinge of regret, however, was felt for the tiny number of those Kaahu animals who were informing the others about the plight of their planet by making these broadcasts – they obviously had much more empathy than the majority of Kaahu. Alas, their cautionary words, amongst those magnificent images, fell onto the deaf ears of an apathetic audience. It was obvious to the ap-Vanda that not everyone on the target planet was as vicious and uncaring as the majority of Kaahu, but they were so few in number.

There had been a theory, posited by some ap-Vanda academics, that there could have been upwards of half a billion primary targets that subsisted only on a plant-based diet. However, they qualified this proposition by also expounding the view that this would not have been a conscious life-choice by a large proportion of these animals as, thanks to the insane value systems prevalent across the hell world, most of those Kaahu could not afford to buy dead animal flesh to consume, but had they been able to, they would have been as likely as any other of their species to consume that flesh. So not an ethical stance by any means.

Some of the other Kaahu tele-visual shows, made, it seemed, for so-called entertainment purposes, caused much hilarity amongst all the population of the planet – in particular, what the primary target animals called *science fiction*. The ap-Vanda populace were greatly amused by many aspects of this writing style; first, the ability of the Kaahu to travel at velocities often far exceeding the speed of light. They knew this was a form of poetic license for entertainment, however some thought it much too unbelievable and ruined their enjoyment of the transmissions for them. The norm in their own forms of visual arts and creative writing was not to stretch the limits of belief too far, but to take the reader or viewer on a plausible, yet enjoyable and interesting journey. But most of the viewing population on the ap-Vanda home-world tended towards enjoying this extreme suspension of belief.

In this *science fiction*, which almost overnight became the favoured literary genre of the Kaahu amongst many of the ap-Vanda populace, it was the sheer number of space-faring alien species encountered, albeit in the author's mind, by the target species that interested the ap-Vanda. These other species were, more often than not, single-mindedly aggressive and always, for some unfathomable reason, intent on *total galactic domination*; and, of course, the protagonist, peace-loving Kaahu would be the gallant, cosmic saviours, which the ap-Vanda found funny on quite a number of levels. Again, they knew such adversaries were created for entertainment value and, if they were honest with themselves, they would have admitted that, as the Kaahu had no experience of extra-terrestrial life, it might have been a fair assumption for them to conclude that there were, indeed, millions of species *out there*, capable of interstellar space travel.

The alien studies of data supplied by probes sent through the Empty Space passage to numerous other solar-systems suggested that most planets containing life that had evolved to a level with sufficient technical know-how to split the atom annihilated themselves either by design or misadventure – nuclear war or nuclear accident. At that time, the probes, alas, were not capable of differentiating between the two outcomes. If, by some remote chance, a planet and its life-forms are not annihilated by either of these two catastrophic types of events, logic suggests that the end will come by way of overpopulation and irreversible and fatal pollution. One of these eventualities was inevitable at some point in the near future for the hell world.

Most ap-Vanda academics advanced a theory that a combination of extreme overpopulation and pollution, leading to conflicts over the necessities of life – water, food, shelter – would, without question, cause violent conflicts – utilising, no doubt, their vile nuclear weapons – between competing tribes, or, on the hell world, nation states, and subsequent destruction of life on affected worlds. It had been estimated by some cosmologists and Empty Space passage academics that a figure of zero-point-zero-zero-one percent of life-sustaining planets will not suffer one of these three types of disaster and these surviving worlds will be spread, in a random fashion, across the vastness of the entire galaxy and, by extension, the whole universe. The odds against meeting these species in space were, as some of those same academics liked to pun, astronomically high. The odds of one of these species being as aggressive as they were portrayed in the Kaahu's science fiction were so minimal as to be non-existent. To pass the self-destructive, nuclear or pollution-ridden stages of evolution and achieve interstellar flight requires a society to be united within itself, which an aggressive, competitive species could never do – they would be far too busy being aggressive and competitive amongst themselves. Either a society falls within that small percentile range or outside assistance would need to be given to it. The theory further postulated that there was no middle ground. Bearing all that in mind, galactic dominance would be futile.

The very idea of Kaahu as the passive, galactic peacekeeping and highly-evolved beings – destined for a higher state of consciousness, whatever that meant – as they liked to portray themselves, was just plain laughable and self-deluding; poetic license taken to its ultimate extreme.

This was both very amusing and very disturbing at the same time.

Anyway, throughout their short history, the Kaahu themselves had only ever travelled to the tiny, satellite moon orbiting the planet on which they resided. Even then, with the aggressive and competitive nature of their societies, they had not returned to the satellite in person for forty or more years; it was too expensive and they had many much more important and costly wars in which to participate. These animals, these primary targets, the Kaahu, may have had grand aspirations of greatness, of evolutionary perfection, but they would never, ever send any of their species to the outer edges of their solar-system, to interstellar space. They would not even visit their stated preferred destination of the fourth planet before the chaos and the self-destruction they had themselves initiated would occur.

With what appeared to be more evidence of their universal self-delusion, the concealment of their true nature was pervasive in all of their literature. They portrayed themselves as, in essence, decent creatures with a small minority bucking that goodness trend. These few individuals were, essentially, evil, as the space monsters in their science fictions were evil, but the decent majority always triumphed over the evil ones – often with the assistance of a hero, often endowed with super powers – whatever they were! There was no tradition of horror, murder or, even, crime in the ap-Vanda written art forms so most of the fictional tele-visual shows from the target planet came as something of a shock to them – but a shock they sort of expected. Of course, these fictions were nothing compared to the violence of their non-fictional news and current affairs programmes – these were far more shocking.

Little or no mention was ever made of the continuing rape and pillage of the planetary bio-systems by the target animals and no mention was ever made of the annual mass murder of billions of animals by the Kaahu – both undeniable evils in which *all* primary target animals were complicit.

All of the primary target species' entertainment on their tele-visual media seemed to be schizophrenic in nature; most of their soft dramas, those without weapons, or their comedies showed only a world of happiness and comfort, yet those transmissions about their day-to-day, real life affairs belied those notions. These showed an unjust world of pain and torment for the Kaahu – hunger, poverty, abuse, exploitation, injustice and murder of their own species were rife, yet those others not suffering these atrocities chose, on the whole, to ignore them, preferring instead to covet the simulated happiness and comfort of the fictional world.

The Kaahu comedic writing was also difficult for the ap-Vanda to comprehend. Much of it was contextual and the aliens had very few points of reference with which to interpret the texts and performances. Some contained concepts that were, perhaps unsurprisingly, alien to them, such as obscure religious or socio-political references, and the aliens could not relate to them. You had to be there, they supposed. They were more comfortable with the visual comedy of, for example, what the Kaahu called *slapstick*, but they did not find it as amusing as the Kaahu animals themselves evidently did. Having said that, during their televisual, so-called, light entertainment programmes, the Kaahu were so unsure of their comedic value that they had to over-dub pre-recorded laughter in the specific areas the writers thought were funny.

Very strange.

There did seem to be numerous crossovers between the two planets in sports but, again, this came as no surprise to them – athletic prowess at running, swimming, propelling spherical objects with various appendages such as feet, hands or pieces of wood, metal or other materials, on grass, ice or other surfaces was surely, and literally, universal. The individualistic nature of the Kaahu versions of sports disappointed the ap-Vanda but, again, this was in no way unexpected. On their world, sports were all about teams and teamwork. Competitors did not participate for personal glory or material reward. Nor did they or would they cheat in any way. They did not take performance enhancing drugs, they did not call foul when no such infringement occurred, nor would they feign injury to disadvantage their opponents – where is the sporting, fair-play element in any of these actions? Admittedly, as far as the ap-Vanda could tell, blatant cheating was not prevalent in each and every one of the target species' sporting endeavours but, at least, bad sportsmanship appeared rife in most.

Was the *man* element of that gender-biased term, *sportsmanship*, a telling factor in their behaviour, they wondered? That was a difficult question for them to answer. Finding female team sports on the broadcast media of the hell world was nigh-on impossible. Even in individual sports, the male competitors seemed to be much more prominent than their female counterparts. There were not as many lurid news stories about female sports cheats even though, from what they had learned, females participated in as many sporting activities as males. The only answers the ap-Vanda could come up with were that either primary females did not cheat at sport or, if they did, no-one on the male-dominated hell world cared.

Males *were*, no doubt, the dominant gender of the target species, as borne out in every sphere of their societies, and, also no doubt, they were genetically imprinted with the urge to succeed. Surely, though, equating that instinct for success at sports by fraudulent means, along with their anachronistic dominance over females, should have disappeared as they and their societies evolved? Evolution, or lack thereof, reared its ugly head yet again.

From the very beginning, as transmissions were first received back on the ap-Vanda home-world, it was noticed that, by far, the most popular sport on that far-away hell world was also the most popular sport on their world. Football. Not the type of football where the ball was not spherical – yet still called a ball on the hell world? – and where this *ball* was predominantly carried by hand and the foot played little or no role in the game; the ap-Vanda inhabitants of this planet called their version of this game, quite naturally they thought, handball – and it was played with a round ball. No, football, as in the spherical ball, was kicked by the foot with the eventual target being scoring more goals, or points, than their opponents – as most games were. The specific rules had slight differences on each of the planets but the game was, essentially, the same, and the inhabitants of this world loved to watch the Kaahu play.

It would go without saying that some of the target

species concepts of sport were not recognised as such on the ap-Vanda home-world. The phrase *blood sport* was a contradiction in terms to the aliens – how could killing other species of animals using high-powered firearms, other high velocity projectiles or the natural instincts of canine or other species, be called a competition between equals? The use of other species for so-called sporting purposes – in reality, more lame excuses for another of those inexplicable Kaahu obsessions, gambling – was also something the ap-Vanda frowned upon. The knowledge that these equus, canine, camelus or other species had been, for generations, bred specifically for this purpose did not help the target species' case – it was yet another negative mark against them. As if there were not enough already!

chapter thirty

As the communication networks on the target planet began to improve, and more information digitised and processing equipment made more widely available to the Kaahu, the ap-Vanda began noticing more and more strange images appearing in the data being sent back to them by way of their orbiting probe. These images displayed target animals engaging in sexual intercourse.

The images showed male and female, female and female, male and male and multiples thereof. Some of the images even depicted inter-species intercourse, the target animals, both male and female, copulating with or performing sexual acts upon other species of animals – obviously non-consensual on the part of those unfortunate, non-Kaahu animals. Yet other images on show proved to the ap-Vanda that the widely-held theory of widespread sexual abuse by the Kaahu of their own children was true. As the years passed, the instances of all such images only increased.

The ap-Vanda had no problem with the images of adult Kaahu engaging in and recording their sexual activities; even they, themselves, had a library of educational erotic literature which included images, though not quite so explicit or prevalent as the data they discovered from the hell world. They had no problem with the more quasi-violent sexual images, again when applied to adult target animals – they did not understand it, but it was of no surprise to them. The whole thing was yet another attempt by the Kaahu to commodify and exploit other animals, something so commonplace on that world that it was hardly remarkable. Yes, the participants in such performances were debased by their actions, as were those animals that took pleasure in witnessing such images, but such degradation of their fellows was both profitable and, therefore, to be expected.

They were, however, deeply saddened by the extension of these practices with the primaries' sexual abuse of other species of animal and of their own children. But, again, it came as no real surprise to the ap-Vanda.

Neither did, in the following years, even uglier, more harrowing images of the primary targets' abuse of each other and, of more importance to the aliens, to other species of life on the hell world. As with every Kaahu interaction, it was all about their own personal gratification, be it sexual or their lust for power or wealth or all of the above.

The technological advances on that world at that time had enabled a greater dissemination of information amongst the primary population, a flow that would only increase, albeit for a short time, into the future, and much more data, both textual and graphical, began to emerge. This progression allowed some, very rare, sympathetic Kaahu to expose, in graphic detail, more information about the abuses of other species of animal and of the planet itself. Unfortunately, yet predictably, these exposures would force the self-promoting, corrupt law-makers, those Kaahu politicians, to protect their pay-masters by enacting legislation to criminalise such public airings.

***

On a lighter note, the whole ap-Vanda population was shocked when images were received from the hell world showing Kaahu males sat with crossed knees. And not just the odd one or two, it appeared that most of them did this. The ap-Vanda were not quite sure how to take this.

chapter thirty-one

At around the same time as the translation of those strange, alien languages began, work also started on the design and build of new interstellar spacecraft and the upgrading of those craft already in service, though at that time, seldom used. However, to achieve this, much more synthetic silk would need to be processed and fabricated. A tree species not native to the ap-Vanda home-world that naturally produced a latex compound containing copious amounts of the silk proteins, *fibroin* and *sericin*, enabled them to manufacture the synthesised silk-substitute which, when combined with graphene, minerals and other materials, had, in the past four and a half centuries, become the basic building-block of not just their spacecraft, but also much of their societal infrastructure. It was a wondrous material; extremely strong yet almost as light as air; flexible in the extreme, adaptable to multiple purposes and, with the correct treatment, ultimately re-usable.

Resources were pulled from such areas as planetary vehicle manufacture, domestic products and college or dwelling construction, both on- and off-world, in order to concentrate their efforts on producing the craft the aliens would need for the venture. For this to happen, they would also need more raw mineral materials, so more ore-processing vehicles and their supporting wagon craft would need to be built and pressed into service. Although all of the elements – minerals and metals – they required were constituent parts of their planet, they were averse to destroying the very environment they and other species lived in to obtain them when the materials were available a relatively short journey away.

There were already two-hundred and twenty-six such ore-processing vehicles, some five-hundred million or so kilometres away, working in an asteroid belt of over ten-billion planetoid objects of varying size orbiting their star. The auxiliary wagons of these ore-processing vehicles spent their time traversing the space between the belt and the planet, delivering the processed carbonaceous, silicate and metallic materials to intermediary storage ports in synchronous orbit adjacent to polymerisation and on-processing factories. The subsequent processed materials would be combined with the vegetable silk to create the desired end-product. For domestic use, the finished products would be transferred to the surface loaded on large planetary transport vehicles. For producing spacecraft, however, the output from the process would remain in orbit to be constructed, by automata, in-space.

The ore-processing vehicles, out there at the asteroid belt, were all autonomous and very versatile machines. For asteroids with a diameter of at least one kilometre, they would land on the object, mine the raw materials and process them on the planetoid's surface. Smaller objects, up to a maximum of one-hundred metres in diameter, would be grabbed by the craft, drawn into the body of the vehicle and the processing undertaken in space. Larger asteroids, in excess of one-hundred metres in diameter but smaller than one kilometre, would be split into smaller pieces by remote automated probes drilling to a pre-programmed depth, and the detonation of explosive charges placed by those same probes. These newly reduced asteroids would also be processed and the extracted elemental materials separated in open space. The processed and separated materials would, at that point, be transferred to wagons for transport back to the planet. The wagons were also autonomous but, as they only trundled from one point in space to another, they were not so versatile.

Synthesis of heavy hydrogen and hydrogen-three, to power the fusion engines of the spacecraft, was also increased. And, of course, new fusion engines and their complementary particulate-drive engines were also constructed.

A copious number of silk-plant seeds had been collected over the preceding few centuries, and the world's entire stock of silk trees and those seeds were all aboard forty-two spacecraft and seven massive, processor-controlled cultivation and auto-manufacturing platforms, of over twelve square kilometres each, in stationary orbit above the planet. The trees on the platforms enjoyed access to constant starlight through their space-tight, transparent silk canopies. In fact, only three of the seven platforms were ever, under normal circumstances, in production mode. The plants on the remaining platforms and on the spacecraft were kept inert, un-growing, by shielding them from sunlight, lowering the temperature on board and limiting the amounts of water and nutrition fed to them.

Vast amounts of the fibroin- and sericin-rich latex was produced every year on the platforms and there was a planned surplus of the harvested substance, but not for emergencies such as was occurring at that time. This total was added to by post-processed recycled silk. The raw latex was a deep dark-brown, almost gel-like, liquid that was transformed on contact with air, gradually reducing in mass as the gelling properties were dispersed into the atmosphere, leaving the black, light and flexible yet astonishingly strong material so vital to their society. It had been found that, when the unprocessed silk was in a vacuum or suspended in water, hardening was prevented until it was required. As with many vegetable organisms, the production of this material was thought to have first evolved as a defensive mechanism to deter predation – small amounts of the latex were exuded when the exterior of the plant was damaged. Regular bleeding of the trees was found to have no deleterious effects on the plants, nor did they appear to lose the ability to generate the desired properties which led botanists to theorise that both the proteins, fibroin and sericin, were produced by the tree itself, an innate process, rather than being extracted from any nutrient fed to the plants.

The trees aboard the four unused platforms would need re-awakening to ensure that enough silk would be produced, and the components for at least three mobile platforms would need to be manufactured for transportation and eventual construction on arrival at the target planet. The dormant plants on board twenty of the seeded spacecraft would have to be activated to be ready in time for the mission.

Graphene production, too, was carried out in orbiting fabrication stations using the separate techniques of sonication of ionic liquids, carbon dioxide reduction and plasma etching of carbon nanotubes with the plasma generated in a controlled environment within the vacuum of space. Carbon fibre production, also synthesised in orbit, was also upped.

Two of the main components of their spacecraft construction were a carbon fibre reinforced titanium-like alloy and graphene lined aluminium, the former offering immense strength for the skeleton of the crafts and the latter strength and pliability to be used in conjunction with silk and graphene for the inner and outer skin. Insulating material was processed from asteroid minerals and used as an interlay between skins – these multiple layers of silk, graphene and minerals protected the spacecraft occupants from any stellar-radiation issues and, in conjunction with a nanoparticulate outer-coating, were crucial to the anti-detection properties of the vessels. This latter attribute was thought necessary despite the apparent lack of threat from other extra-terrestrial species. Logic suggested there would be no such external menace, but there was always a slight a risk so prudence, as always, prevailed.

Procurement and production of all required materials would now be stepped up.

chapter thirty-two

Theirs was an almost fully-automated society. All of the ap-Vanda manufacturing processes were undertaken by automata. Anything that could be manufactured this way was manufactured this way, and the level of technology they were at meant that everything was auto-produced; dwellings and clothes, spacecraft and boots, fusion reactors and footballs, particulate engines and hair brushes. Their species designed both the products and the automata to make those products. Automata manufactured other automata and they, in turn, built the products.

All agricultural work was performed by machine, from tilling the land through to sowing the seeds, harvesting, storage and transportation of crops.

Automated machinery could work in places that were not accessible to animals, or at least not with ease, in the vacuum of space, underwater or in confined spaces. The size of these machines varied from a few centimetres to the twelve square kilometre plant platforms. At one extreme, they were small enough to produce items so tiny and intricate they were only visible with powerful imaging equipment, or at the other extreme, so massive in size and power as to be capable of lifting huge weights over great distances. They could weave fabric, cut rock, weld metal or mould silk. They could fly, swim, climb, cling, dig, pull or push.

All of their spacecraft were automata – they did not require any animal input whatsoever for flight, save for departure and arrival points being programmed into their systems. However, although they were an advanced society in comparison to other species of animal on their home planet, they were also animals at heart and, as animals, it always felt natural for there to be people in the control rooms of these craft at all times during flight. Their planetary transport vehicles, whilst also autonomous machines, would, as a precaution, always be notionally managed by a pilot as the length of flights were comparatively short.

All the ap-Vanda had to do, machine-free, was to eat, sleep, cook, keep themselves clean and concentrate on their work and play activities – just about everything else was automated.

The people of the planet had created these automata in a way that was clean and efficient – they were all, in some way, powered by the numerous fusion reactors both on and off the planet, either connected to a power source or utilising remote power-cells charged from such a reactor, or from the rays of the nearby star. They did the tasks they were designed for – mainly they flew, crawled, rolled, swam, hovered or were fixtures in a manufacturing plant.

The ap-Vanda had never attempted to create an automaton that resembled them physically – a two metre tall, two-legged machine with upper limbs equipped with prehensile, multi-fingered extremities. What would be the point? Such an automaton may well have more strength than its animal counterpart, but bipedal locomotion, in most, if not all, of the tasks such machines were asked to perform, was an awkward, unstable method of movement. The Vatta and Obiah animals had also not bothered trying to build such a machine for the same reasons. All three species regarded the Kaahu's seemingly obsessive desire to recreate themselves in mechanical form as being symptomatic of the primary target species' self-love, so much so that they were compelled to replicate themselves in any way possible, and perhaps had combined that compulsion with a subliminal hankering to dominate another of their species – or at least a facsimile of one.

The ap-Vanda themselves were mammalian-like, bipedal animals that evolved along similar lines to the primary target species, from a simian ancestry. The facial features and body appendages were almost identical, but overall they were larger, on average, than most Kaahu by as much as ten percent. The most noticeable difference between the two species would, in the past, have been the skin colours – the ap-Vanda could be any shade from a pallid grey to a dark grey with hair colours from white to jet-black dependent on which area of the planet they were born. At that point in time, the majority of ap-Vanda were, pretty much, a uniform mid-grey skinned animal because of generations of inter-breeding of divergent populations – though hair colour would still span the entire white/black spectra.

The ap-Vanda population numbered, at that time, slightly under four and a half million planet-wide. They tended to live in settlements of up to thirty-thousand inhabitants across the globe, though there was a gradual move towards permanent habitation on-board orbiting platforms, spacecraft or, for the time being, on one of the satellite moons. Still others chose to live away or in isolation from their fellow ap-Vanda in the wildernesses of the planet rather than in a settlement or off-planet.

chapter thirty-three

Ten years before the prodigious procession of spacecraft left the vicinity of their planet starting their long journey to the hell world, the preliminary conclusions of a report, compiled by various academics in sociology, psychology and exobiology, five years in the making, was published on the planet's electronic information nexus.

In reality, the particular academic areas of sociology and exobiology were, before the discovery of the hell world, at best pure theoretical subjects for study which, in the previous four-hundred or so years, had been almost untouched by academia – they had had more useful stuff to study like quantum mechanics, particle theory, matter/anti-matter interrelations and, of course, the numerous Empty Space theories. So the precise fields of sociology and exobiology had not been at all well represented in academic circles until that incredible, if scary, day the hell world was discovered.

In the past, sociology had not been relevant to the nature of their society which, on the whole, was uniformly organised across the planet. For example, there was not, nor had there been for many centuries now, distinct socio-cultural differences between populations – every member of their species lived their lives based on the same set of principles as their peers. There may have been studies into why some couples opted to cohabitate, or why some individuals chose to live solitary lives, both being contrary to the norm within their society, but these were conducted by psychologists rather than sociologists and they were not thought to be deviant in their behaviour – just quite interesting. There were a few elderly, respected practitioners that had dabbled in both the sociological and exo-biological spheres but, not surprisingly, any research had been minimal and undertaken decades prior to the hell world discovery date; and it had to be said, if there is nothing to study, no new data, no different conclusions to be drawn, what was the point?

For the first couple of years after the discovery there was also little for them to study – linguists had the centre-stage at that time, translating the multitude of languages that were being beamed back in various formats from the hell world – so, when sufficient translated data *was* made available, the opportunity was taken by many students, some already immersed within the psychological and biological spheres of study, to accept the new challenges presented to them. Many youngsters, excited by these new opportunities for study, were also eager to assist and learn from their elders. In fact, the majority of this new report and its conclusions were compiled by those younger research assistants who, at the time of its publication, were professorial in their skills and knowledge.

The only three ap-Vanda animals on the planet at that time with any experience of sociology all of a sudden became very popular teachers in that field – they also, of course, had other specialisms to their names – and, after those few years of translation by the planets linguists, they had many willing and competent assistants to help them research the subsequent data. From the outset, that data was rich, fruitful and bewildering for all concerned, although it may have been not so much of a puzzle for the exo-biologists whose conclusions amounted to the fact that the hell world teemed with a huge variety of flora and fauna, of which the Kaahu were just another species of animal. Pretty simple stuff, really.

The sociologists, on the other hand, had a field

day on the target species – so much to research and to learn; so much to understand and try to explain. But no *deep* research was required to uncover the truth about these animals, as reflected in their observations, and no great, unexpected revelations appeared in their conclusions. And amongst all of their cruelties, greed and irrationalities, that evidence pointed to the fact that the primary target species were weak-willed, gullible animals that, without consideration, without reason, obeyed the instructions issued by their supposed betters who, sometimes subliminally, sometimes not, merely ordered their underlings to make them more wealthy and, thereby, more powerful by trying to emulate them. This they achieved with apparent ease.

Through the use of pretty pictures, depicting a possible happy world lifestyle where the sun always shone, healthy children laughed and played and the ever-smiling parents were not in a constant state of consternation about the future of those children or themselves, be they displayed on the social networks or in printed form in publications and hoardings, the Kaahu would accept all of these perceptions as real and attainable. If not pretty pictures, so-called celebrities or loud, bright, brash colours were utilised to sell them the aspiration of a better life. No such world existed, nor could ever exist, for the Kaahu. They were so easily, so naively, seduced by the images of fellow members of their species pretending to be happy – but none of these animals, anywhere on the planet or of whatever assumed status, was happy.

Everything the Kaahu did, their power and economic systems, their superstitions, their atrocities and their self-imposed, societal divisions, prevented such an idyllic existence – for any of them – be they the few presumed elite or the many supposed inferior members of their species. Obviously, those descriptors were general observations and the academics felt sure that there would be exceptions. That is to say, not every primary target displayed all of these traits – just the vast, overwhelming majority.

The published report came as no surprise at all to the ap-Vanda, neither was it met with astonishment when it was sent to the Vatta and Obiah. All three species knew, more or less word for word, what those learned academics would conclude in their document, even before the exercise was first undertaken in the previous five or so years. So no delay in preparation was ordered at that time, no wait-and-see policy was adopted; the manufacture and build of automata, including the one-thousand plus spacecraft each species would require for the mission, including planetary transport, ore-processing and sundry vehicles, had continued unabated. No delays in planning and resourcing the mission were called for, no invasion-related research was abandoned, not even on a temporary basis, in anticipation of the academic study.

From the moment the ap-Vanda had first discovered the circumstances on that distant, tortured planet, the existence of those cruel, selfish animals and the misery they were, and had always been, suffering and perpetrating, the three alien species knew that action must be taken against the primary target species on the hell world.

chapter thirty-four

Their work was done; everything was ready. Some fifteen years of invasion preparation on the ap-Vanda home-world had, at last, come to an end and it was time to depart.

Each of the one-thousand plus spacecraft had, for many months, been fully laden with all that would be required for the seven year journey. Each craft that carried the animal passengers was endowed with copious amounts of fresh water. Even so, every drop would have passed through those same animals at least three-hundred or more times before they reached their destination. That same water would also have been used on numerous occasions to nourish the on-board plants that the aliens required for their own nourishment. All the necessary cargo had been stored aboard all of the spacecraft, every vehicle, every automaton and every spare part any of them could require. The hundreds of silk trees, brought out of their stasis, were now all growing in their purpose-built craft.

The mission participants, those five-hundred thousand or so aliens, had been transported from their dwellings on or in orbit of the planet to the spacecraft a good two weeks before the scheduled departure date, to allow time for them to settle into their rooms, into their lives in space. Friends and relations were accommodated on the same vessels, though, where possible, never in adjoining rooms, to encourage new friendships and interactions between all the passengers.

Much of the technology utilised on-board the

spacecraft was familiar to all of the passengers with, perhaps, only the usage of protective cocoons during acceleration from fusion power to particulate drive and on to optimum velocity, being foreign to them. There were some passengers that had experienced the cocoons on prior occasions, though they were in the minority. Most of the passengers were between seven and nine years of age and had not yet ventured out into other areas of their solar-system, so familiarisation with cocoon use was very important, though the effects that such acceleration had on an animal body could not be simulated or demonstrated, or even explained. It appeared, however, that younger animals, experiencing the surge of acceleration for the first time, had less trouble than a fully-matured, adult animal would suffer in similar circumstances. It had been posited that the child's musculature and skeletal structures better cope with the stresses because of their lack of development. Of course, others disagreed with this theory, citing the view that younger animals were usually and naturally less stressed than their older counterparts. Until there was empirical evidence either way, there would be a debate on this and all contentious issues. Whatever the explanation, all of the passengers on the spacecraft were about to experience that rush of speed first-hand.

All of the cocoons were three and a half metres in length by one and a half metres in width by one and a half metres in height and were embedded into the floors of each of the passenger rooms on board the spacecraft. Even if an animal was as short as one metre or as tall two and a half metres – although no one on the mission was *that* tall – the cocoon wrapped itself around its occupant with the same protective utility.

Of course, packing for a seven year journey was fraught with difficulty – especially for a seven year old child of either gender. The panel realised this and, thus, each passenger-carrying vessel was equipped with, they hoped, enough materials and the correct machinery, scanning, design and manufacture automata, to make more than enough new attire for each person in the style, colour and size they desired and required.

Some four years further down the line, the ap-Vanda aboard those one-thousand plus spacecraft, had an appointment with a similar number of vessels from each of the Vatta and Obiah home-worlds. In order to make that appointment at the pre-designated hour and day, there was a specific time and date they had to vacate the space around their own home-world and head off to the very edge of their solar-system, almost into interstellar space – but not quite – to the Empty Space passage. And so they did. Those four years spent travelling through their own solar-system were mostly passed in academic study, vigorous exercise and periods of relaxation for all of the passengers, as were the subsequent years traversing the alien system containing the hell world. They attended lectures, worked in laboratories, gave lectures or sat in quiet contemplation and did research. They ran, played football, batball or slapball, lifted weights and pedalled with vigour on their exercise bicycles. They painted, wrote, made music and danced. They congregated in the refreshment rooms, chatted with old and new friends and colleagues, drank herbal or fruit infusions, kaw-he or water. They made new friends, attended parties, sat quietly reading, corresponded with home, gossiped, laughed and cried.

Besides activities such as swimming or wilderness expeditions, their lives were pretty much as they would have been back on the ap-Vanda home-world. The journey was, as expected, unremarkable and incident-free. At first there were quite a lot of homesick passengers and still even more cocoon-sick animals. Both sets of sufferers quickly recovered. Claustrophobia was, however, a huge issue on every spacecraft despite much effort being exerted prior to the journey on alleviating the problem, with planet-wide de-sensitisation programs operating for two years before the fleet departure. Even though these courses had been strongly recommended by not only the mission organising panel but by all of the ap-Vanda that had been on a space flight of a longer duration than the usual orbital jaunt, many of the fleet passengers did not take up the offer and suffered for it. The situation was, however, anticipated. The lower than hoped for attendances had not gone unnoticed and provision was made by the panel to alleviate the problem, but many passengers spent many months regretting their lack of forethought and negligence on their own well-being front.

Despite there being more or less half a million ap-Vanda animals of both genders on the journey, only sixty-three babies were born on the first part of the trip through their own solar-system, though this could, perhaps, be explained by the immaturity of the vast majority of those animals. More babies would be born in the foreign, hell world solar-system as the travelling population matured. There were a mere seventeen deaths throughout the entire seven or so years in normal space and in Empty Space. All of the fatalities were age-related, each of the dead animals having been over one-hundred years of age at the point of demise. All seventeen had been determined to reach the hell world; all seventeen had died deeply disappointed.

Apart from the births, deaths and the claustrophobia outbreak, the journey to the edge of interstellar space, as already noted, was uneventful. The fleet arrived at the pre-designated point in their solar-system at the scheduled date and time, having disengaged their particulate engines two days earlier, and coasted into position near the probe at the entrance to Empty Space and beyond, the hell world. The Vatta and Obiah convoys of spacecraft were on their way to join them, with the former having already exited Empty Space some four-hundred thousand kilometres distant from the ap-Vanda craft, and the latter apparently still traversing the void of Empty Space.

As the ap-Vanda awaited the arrival of their two allies in the mission and launched an automated craft to conjoin with the probe at the Empty Space, so as to bolster the signal transmissions and graviton beam production, much nervous excitement and anticipation gripped the passengers. On a mission of many such novel events, they were soon to be the first of their species to enter that incredible and, at that time, mostly unexplained passage to the wider galaxy. Just a few hundred ap-Vanda had journeyed to that extreme point in the solar-system and fewer still had experienced interstellar space, albeit for a very short period of time. Never before had there been, for the ap-Vanda, a reason to enter Empty Space. All of their previous probes had discovered only lifeless systems that could be explored by automated probes – why spend years in space when automata could do the required investigations? Perhaps if one of the other probes had discovered a planet that once contained life, they would have mounted an expedition to study the remains. But none of the other probes had discovered such a world so, up until that time, the Empty Space passage had been an unknown experience for their species.

All of the ap-Vanda, without exception, were sat, stood or laid in front of visi-screens, agog with expectation, unknowing of what was about to occur. There was to be no time taken by the three allied alien species to meet and greet on this side of the passage – that would have to wait for a few weeks.

When the Obiah spacecraft approached those of the ap-Vanda and the recently arrived Vatta contingent nearby to the Empty Space entrance, processors on all of the vessels, of all of the three groups of spacecraft, communicated with each other and linked. They now knew to the millimetre where each craft was in relation to themselves, which direction they were travelling and at what speed.

As the bolstering craft was docking with the sentinel probe by the gateway to the solar-system of the hell world, three-thousand plus craft, intent on near-genocide and with graviton particles pulsating from their superstructures, were plunging through the membrane of normal space into the total blackness of the Empty Space passage.

part three

chapter thirty-five

Empty Space. They were not kidding. What an anti-climax!

Aboard the Vatta and Obiah spacecraft, life continued as normal, as normal as had been since perhaps two hours, maybe less, after they had first entered the Empty Space passage, sixty-seven days earlier, on their way to the very edge of the ap-Vanda solar-system. They, too, had stared, open-mouthed and wide-eyed, at every available visi-screen to experience the passage in all its glory. All they could see was blackness. Deep, deep, impenetrable blackness; so deep, so impenetrable, that even the powerful lamps, blazing like mini-suns from the front of each of their vessels, made not so much as a tiny impression on the darkness. Other spacecraft, a little more than one kilometre ahead, behind or at either side, were invisible, shrouded in blackness.

For a long time people stared intently at the screens, trying to discern something other than black. They were disappointed. It was as if the mini-suns were in some way defective, or as if there was no power channelling through to the monitors, or as if the visi-screens were turned off, powered-down or otherwise disabled.

Soon, less than two hours after entering Empty Space, everybody aboard the Vatta and Obiah spacecraft had given up on the lack of scenery – the total nothingness on view – and switched to other vistas from the image databases or live-feeds from home or from above the hell world. Or they just turned-off the visi-screens altogether and read, painted, or studied, or went to play some game or other. Everybody except those animals in the control rooms of the vessels – as a matter of course, these monitors were always powered up and displaying views external to the craft. For all the good it did.

It grew to be more and more disconcerting for those animals in the control rooms as each day passed. Not only were there no images on the visi-screens, there was a zero reading on the instruments that normally displayed the current velocity – according to these readings, they were stationary, motionless in an abyss of blackness.

Unlike the ap-Vanda, this was not the first time that members of either the Vatta or Obiah species had traversed the Empty Space passage. That had, however, been about four centuries or so past. So, for this generation, it was the first time ever – or now, following their short visit to the ap-Vanda solar-system, the second time.

Empty Space had first been discovered, as far as they knew, many centuries earlier, apparently quite by accident. It may well be that, even before that time, other species had come across this phenomenon – who amongst them could possibly have known? The first time, though, that these particular Empty Space travellers were aware of was so long ago that the telling of it had become almost apocryphal. No doubt that, somewhere, there would be a detailed record of what occurred – but everybody thought they knew exactly what happened.

The story goes that, at that time, it was an accepted fact that there was no chance, none whatsoever, of interstellar travel because of the vast distances between star systems and the limitations of both their technology and their physicality. Yes they could build so-called generational spacecraft, and the occupants' great, great,

great grandchildren might reach the nearest solar-system. But what kind of life would that have been for those travellers, those born on and stuck inside a box for the entirety of their existence? How many people would they need to send on the journey to ensure there would be a viable genetic mixture by the time they reached their destination? What if the pressures of such extended journeys had an adverse effect on the fertility of those undertaking the expedition, in particular those of the second or third generations? What about all the food and water they would need? Imagine the size of craft they would have to build just to feed, water and support such an enterprise. So many risks, so few, if any, benefits.

Besides, the astronomical data of the time suggested that there were no planets capable of supporting or nurturing life in that neighbouring, yet impossibly distant, gravity well of a star-system. They could, however, explore their own solar-system, and indeed they did. They could also, if desired, send one or more of their number to interstellar space, but for many generations, they had not – the journey would have been excruciatingly long for any passengers with the early form of fusion propulsion they, at that time, utilised. Besides, they had sent automated probes to deep space and they deemed the data they were receiving at that time was sufficient for their researchers' needs.

As their technology improved, and perhaps just so they could prove to themselves that they could, they decided to send missions to the very edge of their solar-system and beyond with members of their species in control of the craft – this was in a time when automation was not as advanced as it was for current generations. The craft constructed to carry those first animal passengers to the extremity of their solar-system were to be propelled by the first generation particulate drive engines but, even so, it would be a seven year trek from, and seven years back to, their home-world.

The passengers on that first journey, four females and four males, were selected based on their fields of study, their ages and, equally as important, the relationship they enjoyed between themselves. All eight were either astrophysicists, cosmologists or specialists in particulate materials. All eight were seventeen years old. All eight were, and had been for a long time, firm friends. Allegedly, four of the passengers were already lovers when the mission began. It was also alleged that two babies were born during the outbound journey to the edge of the solar-system and one more on their way home – or so the story goes.

This was also at a time well before effectual vegetable cultivation and successful waste recycling for long-term space travel was available. Most of their food had to be carried with them, that is, over one-hundred and fifty-thousand meals for five-thousand or so days – a logistical nightmare. Obviously, to accommodate that amount of food, plus the billions of litres of water they required, the spacecraft had to be of massive proportions – and indeed it was.

At around ten kilometres in length by two kilometres high and half a kilometre wide, it, and a sister-craft built at the same time, were the largest ever construction projects attempted by their species. Almost half of the on-board space was dedicated to carrying or growing food and hauling water, with recycling facilities also included. Apparently, however, the passengers were complaining about the quality of the recycled water after just four years, but little was known on this subject all of these centuries later.

Most of the space that was left in the vessel was utilised for the particulate drive engines which were said to be over five times larger than they were on the ap-Vanda, Vatta and Obiah spacecraft.

After around seven years, the vessel and its eight,

or maybe ten, passengers reached the very edge of their solar-system and, shortly thereafter, crossed the threshold into interstellar space for the first time in the history of their species. There was, even after all of those centuries, no doubt about what happened next.

One of the female passengers, her name was Phang, noticed some anomalous telemetry on her monitor as the craft crossed that imaginary line – her companions were glued to images being transmitted from the external visi-sensors of the historic occasion rather than watching the incoming data that other sensors were collecting. The vessel was halted as soon as everyone was aware of the strange readings that Phang had spotted and the group pored over them to see if they could make them make some sense. They could not. The spacecraft was turned around – a long and tortuous manoeuvre due to the sheer size of the vessel – and flown back into their star's gravity-well in the hope that they could, after once more turning around, retrace their previous trajectory with precision to attempt to replicate the events that produced the anomalous data. In fact, they did not, at that time, need to repeat the complete turnaround, as the same odd telemetry was logged as they passed back into the solar-system – despite the fact they were some twenty kilometres or more away from the initial location of that first recorded anomaly. Checking back on the all of the visuals from the external sensors, it was noticed that, as the very rear of the spacecraft passed a certain point in space, a line of blackness – they had no other words to describe it – followed its progress and, centimetre by centimetre, disappeared again.

The female, Phang – who, it should be noted, is the sole member of the mission to ever be remembered by name for the whole event – not only realised that the line of blackness started at the exact point where waste particulate materials were ejected from the vessel, but that, at the velocity they were travelling, the particulate drive engines were idle so graviton particles alone would be being expelled at that moment in time. To further underline why only her name was the one ever remembered, Phang also posited the theories that, firstly, the graviton particles caused some sort of reaction at a particular point in space which she suggested would be at the very edge of the solar-system and secondly, when they measured the distance between each of the two locations of anomalous data and the star at the centre of their solar-system, the results would be identical – or as near as damn it. This latter thought proved to be a correct forecast after careful measurements and calculations were undertaken.

To confirm the Phang graviton hypothesis, the spacecraft re-engaged its particulate drive, thus eliminating the expulsion of graviton particles, and, once again, proceeded to cross the perceived boundary between their solar-system and interstellar space. There was no strange data, no odd images – Phang was, once again, proved correct. At least, that was the story.

What the phenomenon actually *was* would take another couple of centuries and many visits by spacecraft and probes to uncover. All of the initial discoveries were, of course, sent back to the home-world for other academics to ponder and postulate whilst the spacecraft, before continuing its mission to explore the outermost asteroid field in the system, the excuse they had used to justify the trip to themselves, spent a few months at the outer rim of the solar-system, criss-crossing that rim, recording their results and transmitting them home.

On a whim, probably from Phang, the vessel often varied its dimensional orientation from time to time and found that, no matter where on the edge they crossed to or from interstellar space, when gravitons were being emitted from the waste pipe they received the peculiar data and saw, by way of their visi-screens, the line of blackness. Their measurements on these occasions also showed that the distance of each phenomenon to their sun in each instance corresponded with remarkable precision.

By the time the eight, ten or, who now knows, eleven passengers returned to their home-world – to much acclaim – a second mission, dedicated to investigate the Phang Phenomenon, as it had been dubbed – a title it retained for a few short years – had already begun.

Three whole years before Phang and her colleagues had arrived home, an automated craft had been despatched to the outer rim of their solar-system.

Six whole years after Phang and her colleagues got back, that craft reached the edge of interstellar space. This automated craft was a transportation-only medium for an ultra-sophisticated probe fitted with multiple, high sensitive instrumentation, state-of-the-art visi-sensors and a heavy-duty graviton production and projection mechanism. A week after arrival, the probe was launched from the craft. With all devices aboard fully functional and graviton particles emanating from every orifice, it crept towards that precise point in space where the gravitation pull of the star ceased to exert power and where that massive area of interstellar space, free of any pulling power, began. All the telemetry gathered by those delicate instruments, all of the images captured by those hypersensitive sensors and all of the minutiae of the speed, attitude, distance and orientation, down to the nearest micron, was transmitted back to the automated spacecraft and then back to its home-world. Here, countless academics were staring in keen anticipation at visi-screens, agog with high expectation of what was to come.

The visi-sensors on the exterior of the probe began beaming back images of not a line of blackness, but a hole of blackness as it approached that imaginary demarcation line in space. The visi-sensors on the exterior of the automated craft that had brought the probe to this place also broadcast and recorded the effort and, indeed, those very same sensors witnessed and transmitted the scene as the probe, projecting gravitons as it went, approached that hole of blackness, entered the same and, along with the hole of blackness, disappeared without trace.

The academics back on the home-world watched in stunned silence, aghast, as all the visi-screens blackened and the data coming from the probe ceased abruptly. This was not at all what they had expected.

Of all the prevalent theories that had been advanced at the time of, and following, the discovery of the Phang Phenomenon, the most widely accepted idea speculated that the expulsion of concentrated gravitons made dark matter, imperceptible to their instrumentations beforehand, visible and, for some reason not yet postulated, this visibility was only achievable at the very edges of solar-systems. They had all, almost without exception, accepted this proposition as being the most feasible explanation and were fully expecting to be soon examining the mysterious dark matter material first hand. Further dissemination of the news caused much excitement amongst the academic populace at large – if it was not dark matter, what was it, where did the probe go and what happened when it got there?

Over the following few years, as new missions to the Phang Phenomenon were being planned, resourced and constructed, thousands of hours were expended by academics poring over those last few seconds of available data from the missing probe, attempting to somehow explain the disappearance but, at that time, no credible explanation could be offered. Eventually, five years after that first automated expedition and some eighteen years since it was first discovered, a new experiment was designed, built and sent out to investigate the Phang Phenomenon – but would take a further eight years to reach interstellar space.

During that time, back on the planet there were many advances. An updated version of the particulate drive engine was developed which would cut the time taken to reach the rim of their solar-system by at least two years and, complimentary to this improvement, great strides were taken in upgrading the acceleration-protection devices that were required at ultra-high velocities.

Also during that time, one academic team first advanced the theory of Empty Space, and the still highly speculative and lesser-known concept of Gravity Bubbles.

Well before the Vatta and Obiah entered the Empty Space passage on their journey to the hell world by way of the edge of the ap-Vanda solar-system, much of the Empty Space hypothesis, first expounded all of those centuries earlier, had been proven to be correct. The Gravity Bubble concept was at that point, as it is still, paradoxical, almost esoteric, in that it posited the notion of massive gravity-producing matter, such as stars and their associated systems, creating bubbles exterior to, yet surrounded by, Empty Space. This would partially explain the appearance of lines or holes of blackness, when bombarded by gravitons, at the confluence of solar-systems and interstellar space which, in effect, is as desolate of matter as Empty Space. However, the theory had always failed to properly explain the differences between open, interstellar space and the previously unobservable Empty Space. Gravity Bubble exponents could only offer the view that Empty Space was trans-dimensional whereas normal space, as they knew it, was fixed in this dimensional realm. As the years, decades and centuries would pass, this multi-dimensional aspect of the Empty Space theory would become less cogent as all of the solar-systems they would eventually, discover and explore were irrefutably in the same galaxy, the same dimension, as their own.

By the time the second automated craft arrived at the Phang Phenomenon, therefore, the Empty Space theory as a gateway to other star systems and, perhaps, other galaxies had gained prominence and the planned experiments had to be changed – rather than taking the examination of the graviton-created hole from a distance, a sensor-packed probe would enter the blackness but, this time, a second probe would attempt to keep the aperture ajar by also bombarding the area with graviton particles. The experiment proved to be a huge success mixed with, at first, slight disappointment.

With the particulate emissions from the two automata, a picture emerged of an environment comprised, it appeared, of two distinct, separate bits of stuff – a deep black interior but, if it was possible to be so, an even blacker edge to the hole in normal space. Alas, neither probe was able to measure any of the characteristics of either bit of stuff, and neither were able to gather any samples despite them being so equipped. In fact, the probe that entered Empty Space almost disappeared altogether with the only hint of its non-destruction being the telemetry being received, still, from its on-board instrumentation. However, that data was less than informative with nothing showing from the visi-sensors and both the velocitometer and odometer transmitting back zero in both instances. All of these data convinced the academics back at the home-world that the probe was stuck just the other side of the Phang Phenomenon, marooned in the hole of blackness. On several occasions over the following weeks, attempts were made to put the stricken probe into reverse, but to no avail.

Then, all of a sudden, the received telemetry changed. Nine and a half weeks after first entering the anomaly, the images transmitted by way of the graviton-producing probe at the still-open hole in space at the rim of their solar-system and, an instant later, by way of the craft that transported both probes to that place, to the home-world displayed stars for a few seconds. Then all images and telemetry disappeared.

Initially, the academics monitoring the mission assumed that their attempts to coax the stranded probe into reverse had succeeded but, on reviewing the data from the two automata at the phenomenon and triple-checking it all, there was no record of the probe re-entering their system. A review of the images and mapping the positions of those astral bodies, captured in comparison to their position when viewed from their own solar-system, showed that the probe had emerged at a system some seven light years distant and, of far more importance, the Empty Space theory had been proven to be correct. It would be many decades and a few automated, exploratory missions at different locations on the rim of the solar-system before they confirmed to themselves what they had discovered – a passage to the wider galaxy; a route to areas previously denied to them. But that route would be useless unless they could return from those faraway solar-systems to their own in complete safety.

So even more decades passed and still more automated, exploratory missions sent through the passage before they had the mastered the processes of both outbound and inbound Empty Space travel. Over one-hundred and fifty years after the discovery of the Phang Phenomenon and over one-hundred and twenty years after the first hint of them finding Empty Space, a craft controlled by animals of their species plunged through a graviton-induced hole in the space at the very edge of their solar-system and, sixty-six days later, emerged in an alien system many light years away. They did not, however, linger for any great length of time. Just one hour after arriving, and ensuring that they re-entered Empty Space at the exact position they exited and at exactly the same angle, they headed home through the total blackness.

Since the first probe that had, albeit by accident, journeyed through the Empty Space passage and emerged in another part of the galaxy, much thought was given to *how* the automaton had been propelled there, in particular when taking into account that the speed and distance instrumentation had both displayed a zero value. The most favoured theory at the time was that it was the mysterious and elusive *dark energy,* so long searched for by their academics that had driven their craft through the passage. What was evident after the return of the spacecraft piloted by members of their species, was that this energy was multi-directional and that the angle at which an object entered the Empty Space passage governed that direction of travel.

It would be many centuries before another life-sustaining world was located and, when it was, it was found to be a planet suffering similar single-species abuse as the hell world the ap-Vanda, Vatta and Obiah were, at that point in time, travelling towards. A further century passed before a decision was made to act – as the ap-Vanda, Vatta and Obiah were now about to act on the hell world. Obviously, it had not been a simple decision. They had, on two or three expeditions to other systems, come across worlds that had been devastated by obvious nuclear conflagration or some other environmental catastrophe and they reasoned that this planet, the first life-bearing planet their probe had found, would also suffer such a disastrous event at some time in the near future. Should they or should they not intervene? And, if so, how?

They could not easily solve the problems on the alien world; they could not take away the nuclear power or nuclear weapons, they could not miraculously clean the atmosphere or oceans, they could not change the economic, superstitious or dietary cultures. The solution they, at last, decided on was, to say the least, radical and, perhaps, could have been construed as unethical but, considering the dire circumstances they had found, it was the single most logical course of action they could take. Cull them all – well, more or less.

The rest, as they say, was history – which is kind of stupid because everything that happened in the past is history, is it not?

part four

chapter thirty-six

What could be assumed, with some degree of certainty, to be the entire Temuri population of the planet – of anywhere in the universe, for that matter – sat in twos and threes and waited in front of their personal monitors at home or in some recreation room or other. Or they were in larger groups of up to three-hundred of their species before large screens in various lecture rooms or work stations. They were all somewhere on the planet surface, in one or other of the settlements, or on one of the orbiting platforms. All waiting for the proceedings to begin.

Sat or stood alongside the Temuri audience, in all the locations, were the people they had grown to know as not only their guardians, tutors and mentors, but also as their friends and colleagues; the ap-Vanda. There were also a few animals of the Vatta and Obiah species at each venue, but the majority of the aliens were of that former species.

On a raised dais at the front of one of those lecture theatres sat two female aliens waiting for the correct time to commence their presentations

In a separate room, in orbit of the planet, sat a third alien female; seated alone in front of visi-cast equipment, also waiting to speak.

***

The Temuri were the children of the Kaahu, but, excepting only the undeniable fact of their physical appearance, any other similarities between themselves and their parents ended there. Thanks to their alien guardians, they had not been distracted by any of the inane trivialities that their ancestors had had to contend with for countless generations. From the moment they were first saved from death by the aliens and up to that point in time, the education of the Temuri had not been hindered by imagined differences or by irrational concepts. All of the Temuri children were equal. No longer on this planet would children have to suffer little or no education based on absurd economic, religious, skin colour or gender differences. There could now be no child denied an adequate level of schooling because of lack of wealth whilst others, with wealth, enjoyed all the benefits such learning afforded. There was no need for monetary wealth any more.

As on the ap-Vanda home-world and those of the Vatta and Obiah, and in complete opposition to how the Kaahu had managed their lives, nothing had an economic value. Some things did have value, life had value and education had value, but neither could be expressed in terms of the profit or loss of material wealth for another being. The Kaahu had always thought otherwise – this had been an ingrained belief, fostered over millennia, and, thus, altering this world view could not have happened without the cull.

There was no indoctrination of these children, no nonsensical supernatural or political philosophies forced down their throats. Their studies were not confused by fantastical stories of non-physical beings that, amongst other things, created the universe, exchanged currency for displaced teeth, tormented a Kaahu animal for eternity after death for the slightest perceived wrong-doing, or brought universal joy and peace – but, perversely, just on one particular day or other a year. Their lessons did not, could not, include pseudo-scientific notions of a universe created around the planet they lived on, created a mere few thousand years earlier, created intelligently by a chimera, by a so-called god. The lives of the Temuri were not blighted by such preposterous falsehoods – they were taught that the universe, and everything in it, was a physical entity and that the study of the various branches of physics might one day, eventually, explain the universe. But probably not. There would always be questions – always.

There could be no gender stereotyping, no specific or enforced differing styles of dress for males and females, no replica weapons for the male infants or pretty dolls for their female siblings. There was no segregation based on gender, all of the children were schooled to the same level in the same lectures and seminars in the same locations.

There could be no discrimination based on physical appearances such as the colour of another animal's skin – all of the Temuri children were raised and educated in environments where animals were of all shades, from the palest pink to the deepest brown, which had included Vatta children, the greys of the ap-Vanda children and the greenish tinges of Obiah offspring, those of a similar age to the Temuri.

The Temuri children had never suffered abuse, at least, not since they were rescued from the Kaahu twelve years earlier. No physical assaults, no mental torments or sexual violations had been committed against them.

Medical examinations on the Temuri as they first arrived as babies at the spacecraft had shown that at least ten Temuri had been physically and sexually abused, even at such young ages, at the hands of their Kaahu parents or others of their species and, because of that, these unfortunate individuals had been returned to the planet to be culled with all the other condemned animals. The rest of the children, however, would require constant monitoring in the form of continuing psychological analysis, throughout their lives. The invading aliens did not want the offences of their parents to be imitated by the children, albeit subconsciously, in later life.

Neither the ap-Vanda, nor the Vatta, nor the Obiah were ever lied to or abused as children, nor had they ever lived divided lives based on wealth, gender, religion or colour, so they did not lie nor did they inflict these differences on their Temuri charges. The aliens recognised that the Kaahu had themselves been mentally, physically and sexually abused all of their lives, that many of them had endured extreme poverty and that they had been indoctrinated from birth to believe the absurdities of the supernatural fantasies of their parents. The aliens knew well that many or most of the Kaahu had been bombarded with the lies of never-ending commercial messages all of their lives, telling them they were inadequate as animals, that they were bad parents, that they were old or ugly and, to mitigate those inadequacies or to improve their parenting skills, that they and their children should purchase this service or that product. They realised that the Kaahu had learned all of their irrational prejudices against animals of differing species or gender or colour or superstition from their equally abused and indoctrinated parents and grandparents – that such learned behaviours had been prevalent for centuries. The ap-Vanda, Vatta and Obiah knew all of these facts but could not condone their continued abuses by the Kaahu.

The Temuri had no such distractions, abuse or propaganda forced upon them. Their lives had been so different from those of their antecedents. Education was paramount. From the first time they were introduced to their new ap-Vanda guardians, virtually everything they did had an educational value for the Temuri. Whilst they were awake, they had the constant companionship of at least one of those guardians and, for the first three years, even as the children slept, data and questions were conveyed audibly to them. Visi-aids were not wasted on trivia – there were no pointless, flowery pastimes, no inane so-called child entertainment. There were no games that glorified and sanitised extreme violence or dishonesty. Once the universal language had been mastered, the Temuri moved on to mathematics and, a short time later, the sciences.

They were not taught in classrooms with thirty or forty or more other students, but rather in groups up to a maximum of five pupils. They did not have to struggle to find processors to access appropriate texts or databases, every resource they could ever require was there for them at all times.

The Temuri did not have to endure *weekends*, no such concept existed for the ap-Vanda, Vatta and Obiah. Breaks and vacations were taken at any time – firstly at the instigation of their ap-Vanda guardians but, later, at their own choice. Instead the children learnt and played seven days a week.

As soon as they could walk upright, the Temuri were introduced to sports; football, batball, slapball, handball, running, swimming and more. They played these sports every single day – unless they decided otherwise for a day or so – either in the facilities aboard the orbiting habitat platforms or on the world below them which, for the first few years, they would visit once or twice a week, depending on the planetary meteorological conditions.

Out in the wildernesses and oceans of the planet, away from the Temuri settlements, away from the art and science cities, all other native species of animal and vegetable life were recovering, surviving and, soon, would be thriving once again. Those land-living and aquatic animals that, so recently, were so close to extinction because of the selfishness and greed of the Kaahu, now had recovering populations. Those previously decimated rainforests were, once again, seeding those areas usurped by foreign vegetation and grazing herds of doomed mammals. There were great hopes that the trees, now no longer under the threat of deforestation, would reclaim most of those sites for themselves.

chapter thirty-seven

As the Temuri and their alien guardians waited patiently by their visi-screens, all around them, all around the planet, both on the surface and in orbit, most of the other members of the three species of alien animal, the ap-Vanda, the Vatta and the Obiah, were hard at work, as they had been so employed for the past twelve years.

In orbit of the planet, great strides had been taken in ridding the area of all the debris that had accumulated in the fifty or so years before their arrival. It was, nominally, a joint operation by the three alien species but was, in the main, managed and undertaken by the Vatta. Such great steps were taken that the area of space surrounding the planet was, except for the orbiting paraphernalia of the aliens, virtually free of Kaahu junk with only the odd few bits and bobs circulating the world. These would soon be captured and consigned to fiery destruction in the corona of the local star.

Work on the planet below, directed and undertaken in the main by the Obiah, was also reaching the point where little more, from a practical point of view, could be done. From the outset, twelve years earlier, all of the efforts of the aliens had been concentrated on, as best they could, cleansing the planet of materials that were hazardous to all animal and vegetable life forms, creating safe environments for the settlements of the Temuri and clearing the areas around those eight locations chosen as art or science sites. Military, chemical and biological weapon facilities, nuclear power generation plants, oil and gas drilling or storage areas, seaports and airborne planetary transport terminals, everywhere hazardous materials could be found had been divested of such substances. Even though the aliens could not possibly know the whereabouts of all such materials, they were, after those twelve years, confident they had removed most of it. Throughout those preceding years, both of the two massive automata, designed and constructed with that one task in mind, to heave large loads from the planet surface to the void of space, had each taken that up-down journey thousands of times. Lugging millions of tonnes of death and pollution delivery vehicles in the form of naval and airborne craft such as ships of war, sub-oceanic craft, intra-atmospheric nuclear or, so-called, conventional missiles, oceanic fossil-fuel carriers and the like, these giant elevators dropped-off their cargoes in space to be combined into one long procession of vessels. Tonne after tonne of explosive materials from military installations, their means of delivery, hand-held, vehicular or otherwise, were also transported into orbit. Automata had been assigned to manufacture containers large enough and secure enough to hold these lethal cargoes on both their short journey from the planet and that of their long, slow trek to the local star.

All of these Kaahu abominations of death and destruction would be cobbled together by automata, using materials previously lying unused and unwanted on the surface of the planet, mainly strong metal girders once required for construction, to form a convoy of garbage to be, eventually, dispatched to the heat of the nearby sun.

Great strides had also been taken in ridding the open surfaces on the planet of dead primary and secondary target animals – most disposed of by automata, but many in person, face-to-face, as it were, by the aliens and their cremator weapons. Whilst vast swathes of the planet were still polluted by the rotted corpses of both the primary and secondary categories of target, in terms of areas likely to be used in the near future by the Temuri, including the art and science sites, their settlements and the areas surrounding those locations, the risk of disease from decomposing animal remains had been eliminated – so much so, the animals, both indigenous and alien, could even remove their environmental suits when visiting the cleansed areas.

Within perimeters of between five to twenty-five kilometres of the designated areas of such habitation and study, structures had been demolished and levelled, transportation arteries such as bridges, rails and roadways had been dismantled or ploughed through – there would be no need for any of these Kaahu methods of travel ever again. Where possible, settlements for the Temuri would have been built in areas not previously inhabited by their antecedents, though, it appeared, not a centimetre of land on the planet surface had escaped the Kaahu touch of death. There were remote spots where few of the Kaahu had ventured, but these were deemed to be quite unsuitable for prolonged habitation; too cold, wet and barren or too hot, humid and overgrown, and settling in the either area would not have been acceptable because of the damage the newcomers would have caused to local ecosystems. Thus, some of the Temuri settlements had had to be founded on land previously befouled by their ancestors and, with the assistance of a multitude of automata, the technologies and experiences of the aliens, settlements were constructed and land cleansed for arable farming. It was, however, nine years before crops were considered toxin-fee and suitable to eat by both the Temuri and the aliens.

The ap-Vanda, primarily, had managed the care and education of the Temuri. They helped supervise the construction of, both, the orbiting residential and academic platforms and the settlements on the planet. They also assisted in the management of the automata that had been set to cleanse the soil that would, at some point, grow the food for the Temuri and themselves.

Other robotic machines would build the infrastructure required to enable the growth, harvest, process and delivery of these foodstuffs.

The Temuri children had, for the first year or so after their extraction, been raised on the spacecraft they were first taken to after their removal from the planet surface. There they were, on a one-to-one basis, nourished, nurtured and educated by two ap-Vanda animals – usually one female and one male, though not exclusively – whilst still being in close proximity to others of their species also transported to the same vessel. Within that first year, the orbital platforms were constructed and made ready for the Temuri. Much of the materials had been pre-constructed at, and transported from, the three alien home-worlds and only required assemblage by the build-bot automata, but more platforms would be needed for the future.

To enable this, the silk trees, from both the fifty vessels containing the dormant plants and those kept active aboard the rest of the fleet, were pressed into service and, whilst none of the wagons had yet returned from the asteroid belt where the ore-processing vehicles were busily mining, there were enough of the other required minerals, for the time being, in storage aboard the other automated ships to complete the initial construction tasks. There would also be useful minerals already on the surface, thoughtlessly gouged from the ground of their home-world by the Kaahu.

On the surface of the planet, those selected areas were cleared of Kaahu debris and work commenced erecting or installing dwellings, schools, laboratories, power-generating fusion reactors, water filtration plants and other structures and facilities to better expedite the lives of the future Temuri inhabitants. In a large, desert area on a trans-equatorial continental mass, a project to build a massive solar-power generating facility also began. At the same time, the soil-cleansing automata began their laborious task.

It had been decided, long before the three groups of spacecraft had left their home planets, that not all of the Kaahu technologies were to be discarded. Much could, perhaps in a few years, be utilised and even improved by the Temuri, none more so than the astronomical observation equipment developed by the Kaahu and, during the second year of the alien occupation, these facilities were firstly cleansed, then restored and upgraded. As an adjunct to those restorations, twenty-four probes were dispatched from orbit to encircle the planet in a protective move designed to observe, map and, if required, alert current and future inhabitants of the planet of any rogue asteroids heading their way from any area of space. Armed with that fore-knowledge, those inhabitants could decide on the best course of action to resolve the situation. At that time, there were always four of the alien space vessels ready to intervene with their on-board repeller implements.

During that second year, all of the ten-thousand plus Temuri moved from the spacecraft to the now completed orbital platforms where they would live, learn and play for a further two or more years. The surface facilities of the settlements in all the designated areas were all completed during the last of those two years but they could not be considered as permanent.

The atmospheric conditions, a result of the negligence of over two-hundred years of industrial and domestic pollution by the Kaahu, had de-stabilised the meteorology of the planet to such an extent that there was not a single area left untouched by the abnormal weather patterns. Whilst one land-mass area may have been experiencing extreme drought, bush-fires and unseasonably high temperatures, another area of that same continent may be suffering blizzards and ice-storms, or torrential rain and flooding. So although the structures that comprised the new settlements were robust enough to withstand the rigours of the weather, or most of them, the Temuri, their ap-Vanda guardian-teachers and their Vatta and Obiah allies would spend only part of the year on the planet – why suffer the discomforts of excessive cold or heat of a planet surface when there were climatically-controlled alternatives circulating the world?

chapter thirty-eight

Just after the thirteenth hour of the day, a female face, familiar to most of the assembled Temuri animals and their alien companions, appeared on all of their visi-screens. The female face smiled and her head nodded ever so slightly.

'Hello everybody – I apologise, I am late appearing.' She paused, seemed to shuffle awkwardly in her seat and, again, smiled, but this time with just a hint of embarrassment.

'As everyone here can attest, I was ready – but I could not properly work the technology... again!'

At every venue across and above the planet, there were knowing smiles of recognition from at least one of the Temuri animals in each of the audiences and from most of their non-native companions – she had a bit of a reputation when it came to technology. This was all the more strange when the fact that the alien technology was, principally, voice activated was taken into account – such things, apparently, seem to happen regularly to certain people!

'I think all of you know who I am – if not, where have you been for the past twelve years?'

Again, she smiled but this time straight into the visi-censor and with a hint of comic mischievousness. Much laughter ensued across the planet, but for no more than a few seconds at most.

'Just in case, then, I am Hentanayre. I am, first and foremost, a teacher of engineering and biology, but many of you may know me as the coach of the Tecumseh settlement football team. I am also, now, a member of the organising panel and, like all of my colleagues, have been here with you for these last twelve years – since all of you were infants. Those colleagues have asked me to address you all today and, as you can see, I have accepted this task.'

She smiled again and continued.

'Of course, they first asked my friend Sissonæ, but because she is so heavily pregnant at the moment – well, the stress and excitement of addressing every single one of you, all at the same time, would not have been advisable for her or her new baby.'

Hentanayre looked to her left and saw her expectant friend smiling, somewhat smugly she thought, at her from the audience – she returned the smile, nervously, and continued to speak.

'I am not pregnant, yet that stress and excitement seems overwhelming to me as I speak to you all now. But I must press on.'

Hentanayre looked down at her visi-screen, took a deep breath and began.

'We have now entered year thirteen of the New Era.'

Pause.

'As we have always said, myself and some of your other guardians will be here, perhaps, for the rest of our lives. We made this commitment many years before we arrived here and we have no intention of dishonouring that promise. Our own children may, one day, wish to return permanently to our home-world, that will be their decision; but as they too were born on this planet, or on the journey to get here, and know no other way of life, that course of action is far from a certainty. I suspect that many will choose to spend their lives here along with *their* children and grandchildren in the future. It *is* a beautiful place to live.'

Hentanayre, again, paused momentarily before continuing. 'You are all now in your twelfth or thirteenth years. You are all healthy and strong. In a few years you will no longer need our guidance, teaching or protection to advance as individuals or as a species – not on a day-to-day basis, at least.'

'We believe we have taught you how to live and stay alive on this beautiful planet and we hope you will, between you, create a healthy and strong Temuri population in the future. But, most important of all I think, we have taught you that it is the health of the planet and all of the many millions of its divergent species, including your own, that is of paramount importance and that all of those factors are symbiotic and inextricably linked. No one species can be, nor should be, dominant; all have a right to life and to thrive, or otherwise, in the natural, evolutionary order of things.'

'To that end, we have shown you how to grow food with sustainability and, where necessary, to process those vegetables, pulses, herbs, spices, fruit and fungi for food in a sustainable manner rather than preying on and exploiting other species of animal. Your species has now gone past that evolutionary stage where the slaughter and consumption of other animals was thought natural and essential to life. It never was either natural or essential – not for your species.'

'We believe we have also taught you all the many skills you will need to live fulfilled, peaceful lives and pass that knowledge on to your children, who, in turn, can teach your grandchildren, and that process can continue into the distant future.'

'I know many of you have studied your own and other species' physiologies, including my own ap-Vanda aetiology, and are well on the way to being more than competent medics – indeed, I myself have taught part of this subject to one or two of you – whilst still others are acquiring expertise in physics, engineering, chemistry and multiple other areas of the sciences. All of you will soon, and justifiably so, claim to be specialists in at least two or three distinct disciplines and your skills will only improve with study and experience. You are either already, or soon will be, fully-fledged pilots, biologists or roboticists; surgeons, cosmologists or geologists; botanists, engineers or particle-physicists and, although there are only slightly over ten-thousand of you, all of the practical disciplines needed for your species to thrive have almost been mastered.'

'Those of you with the aptitude also excel in your chosen areas of the arts – myself and the others have often been moved by much of your written and visual works and, as you know, we regularly try and dance to your music, much to your amusement.'

Smiles abounded around the world.

'We have shown you how to maintain the spacecraft in orbit of the planet and how to build new ones from the silk material and the asteroid minerals.'

'We hope that, with the education we are passing on to you, and that you will pass on to your children, you will soon be able to improve the specifications of these spacecraft – their design, instrumentation and propulsion systems, perhaps – so that, when the time is right for some of you to visit *my* home-world, it will take you considerably less than the seven years it took us to get here to yours.'

Hentanayre stopped her speech for a moment, appeared to be deep in thought and slightly troubled but, eventually, said, 'I put the *visit my home-world* bit in there as an example of what you *could* achieve – none of my species would actually expect you to spend so many years in space just to please us or for a vacation! Please do not take that literally.'

She smiled and, once again, looked down at the notes on her screen and continued talking.

'But your well-being and education, or perhaps one day paying a visit to my home-world, are not the only reasons we have taught you these things. There is another, very important task that later generations of your species may be asked to undertake at some point in your future – that will become apparent to you later.'

'The language you all speak, the language we have taught you since early childhood, is spoken on many worlds in the galaxy and, in a way, this connects you to all of those worlds even if you and their inhabitants never meet. You are as one with us and all those other worlds.'

'But, a summary of the past ten years and a hint of what *may* occur at some point in your future is not the main reason I am speaking to you today.'

She paused, took a sip of water from a handy receptacle, then carried on with her message.

'The vast majority of the knowledge we have imparted to you originated, of course, on my home planet or it was data collected from your predecessors by our peoples before and during our journey here, with the relevant material selected and translated for your academic purposes. But there was more data, so very much more, that was not translated at the time of collection. We selected only the information, mainly of an academic nature, that we thought relevant for you and much of that material has since assisted in your education. Your predecessors, who I will get to shortly, had amassed a great deal of physiological data on many, perhaps most, species of life on this planet, the geophysics of the planet and other, more contemporary, information on such topics as the adverse effects of their activities on the general ecology of the planet. But, as I have mentioned, there was oh, so much more.'

'For the last twelve years, both on our home-worlds and, to a much greater extent, here on yours, we three species have been attempting to translate as much of that mass of data as we could and, to be honest, we have hardly scratched the surface. The textual documents we *have* translated, though, will now be made available to you for study, as well as most of the audio-visual material, which we have not translated – music, of course, should be universal and not really need any interpretation, though there may come a time when you will want to know what your ancestors were actually singing about. Much of the visi-documentation appear to us, in their original languages, to be quite inane but, one would hope, a better understanding of those languages would improve one's perceptions of them. So, there are many tasks to undertake for all of you budding linguists out there.'

Hentanayre employed a serious face.

'I should tell you there will be a multitude of concepts that you will find in the translated textual documents that will be very difficult for you to comprehend, if not impossible – if I am honest, I still cannot come to terms with some of them as, to me, they defy all attempts at logic.'

'You have all shown yourselves to be responsive to rational thought and would, I believe, reject any absurd notions you may read, but in this data you will discover a huge number of beliefs and concepts that are so completely irrational that you may not believe them to be true. I promise you that everything you read is completely authentic and everything I am about to tell you is entirely factual.'

She, once again, paused, took another sip of water, then continued.

'We have no words in our language for most of these irrational concepts – why would we? – so the data you will read will be interspersed with phonetic representations of old words and phrases from your progenitors' languages; words and phrases we could not translate. I could list them verbally here and now but, instead, I will tell you some of the facts of these concepts we have, over the years before we arrived here and since that time, discovered from the amassed data.'

'Most of these were ideas underpinned by ancient superstitions that should not have had any place in a society that had evolved to the intellectual level your predecessors professed they had achieved. These superstition-based theories were considered the norm to your parents and their predecessors. But I must, first of all, tell you a greater truth.'

Suddenly Hentanayre felt nervous.

'Please try to keep an open mind whilst listening to what I am about to tell you and look at the situations from both sides, both the actions of your predecessors and those of myself, all the people from my world and those peoples of the Vatta and Obiah home-worlds'

'My colleagues and I, obviously, are not like you. My species, as you know, is ap-Vanda. Our appearance and physiology is significantly different to yours and, naturally, you all noticed that from a very early age. We have told you where we came from, how far away that is, how long it took us to get here and that we were here to protect, nurture and educate you all. Over the years, many of you have asked about your predecessors – your true parents. We have, in the past, prevaricated.'

She was prevaricating at that moment.

'We disliked keeping the facts from you – as we have always said, the truth is very important to us – and so, now is the time for that truth. What I am about to tell you will be difficult for me to say and will not be easy for you to hear.'

Her mouth started to dry-up; she could feel and hear her heart pounding in her chest.

'Some of you may accuse me of using over-emotive language in my story, but this was, and always will be for us, a highly emotive subject. I, and every other member of my species over twelve years of age, either back on my home-world or currently on this planet, grew up knowing what your predecessors had done and continued to do to this planet, to other species of animals and plants and to themselves. All the Vatta and Obiah animals also discovered those things at the same time as we did. We learned to pity and to despise your ancestors in equal measure, so I think that to be unbiased will be difficult.'

Hentanayre paused momentarily to sip some more water.

'I will begin with the most shocking revelation. We arrived in this solar-system some twelve years ago when your parents were alive and, you could have said, in relatively good physical health. As soon as we arrived here, we killed them all.'

chapter thirty-nine

In the ensuing few seconds after this fact was finally made known, though to Hentanayre, it felt much longer, she scanned the faces of the Temuri children, those she could see in the audience at her location, trying to discern their reactions to this momentous revelation. She saw a few exchanged glances between the Temuri youngsters, a couple of frowning faces and – perhaps surprisingly, perhaps not – quite a few of them seemingly nodding their heads as if their suspicions had been confirmed. These were intelligent children. As they travelled around the planet they had all seen the evidence of the Kaahu's failed societies in the numerous and unmissable ruins of their ancestor's former cities; they had all seen the many educational visi-presentations, albeit translated into the universal language, featuring animals so similar to themselves and so dissimilar to the aliens that they all must have known that these people would not have just disappeared for no reason.

Hentanayre glanced at Sissonæ, but her friend, too, was looking around the room trying to gauge the children's mood, so failed to catch her eye.

Hentanayre took a deep breath and continued her monologue.

'And it was not just *your* parents – there were over seven-billion of this species alive on this planet at the time and we destroyed them all, with the exception of ten-thousand or so infants – you. We also had to kill some twenty-five to thirty-billion individual animals of other species. We did not do any of this lightly. We hope that, when you hear our explanation for undertaking this course of action, you will understand our rationale and not judge us too harshly.'

'Our purpose was to, first, prevent this world from becoming just another lifeless lump of rock orbiting your star. My species and the Vatta and Obiah peoples have found many solar-systems that only contain a few gas giants and multiple lifeless lumps of rock of an assortment of sizes. As far as we can tell at this point in time, there are precious few planets in our galaxy capable of sustaining life in any form. Even fewer contain multiple ecosystems with the wonderful diversity of inter-dependent life-forms such as this planet, my own world and those of our allies, the Vatta and Obiah people. We could not risk the chance of there being one less of such a rare planet.'

'The dominant species of the period before our arrival, your parents and predecessors, were, to put it bluntly, a malignant cancer eating away at the very life of the planet – that was not an analogy, that was a fact. They had spread uncontrollably to almost every non-liquid part of this world, destroying anything and everything that got in their way and, we believe, destroyed more or less every living thing they touched. And not only on land. The oceans, rivers, lakes and aquifers, the very liquid water necessary to create and sustain life on the planet, were emptied of many life-forms. Many lakes and aquifers were drained and each and every ocean, lake, aquifer and river was severely contaminated by the toxic waste your progenitors created. Trillions of litres of fresh water were irretrievably polluted by them to extract even more of their beloved fossil fuel to power their wealth-creating schemes – undermining the very fabric of the planet just to burn the released gases and, by doing so, despoil the very air they breathed. The atmosphere, that reservoir of those life-sustaining gases, was being ever-polluted by their chemical and particulate waste matter, by emissions from their inefficient agricultural, industrial and domestic processes, clogging the air with carbon-dioxide, methane and a multiple of other noxious pollutants. Much of those pollutants also aided the depletion of the ozone layer, that stratospheric shield against harmful radiation from your local star, harmful to all life on the planet. Also, at that time, they were destroying hectares of vitally important rainforest every single day – the very same forests that they themselves called *the lungs of the planet*. Incredulous as this must sound, your predecessors were knowingly and gleefully destroying their own home. Every year, upwards of one-hundred and fifty-billion other animals, not of their species, were being slaughtered for food, including marine animals, avians and mammals.'

Hentanayre paused and shook her head.

'Think of that number – one-hundred and fifty-*billion*. Every single year. Every single year for the previous twenty-four years that we knew about. That is three point six *trillion* animals killed for food in less than a quarter of a century – just think of that!'

'This crime also defied belief. With their agricultural expertise and the levels of technology they had attained, they were more than capable of growing enough vegetable produce to feed all of their own species without murdering others for sustenance. The irony is that they *did*, indeed, produce enough plant crops to sustain themselves, but instead they fed most of those crops to those other species of animal which were then killed, usually in childhood, and, in turn, eaten by your ancestors. Yet millions of them still died every year because of lack of sustenance whilst, in other areas of the planet, millions of others were massively overweight or very ill due to their diet of, primarily, dead animals.'

'Every single year for decades, billions of young mammals would be separated at birth from their mothers, or very shortly afterwards, and kept in cramped, indoor environments, pumped full of growth hormones and antibiotic chemicals. *Finished* animals, that is, after they had been over-drugged and overfed, were slaughtered when, depending on the species, they achieved a predesignated weight – when they were only between three or four months to one and a half to two years of age. The animal species that perhaps suffered most were avian, though, of course, suffering is subjective. Tens of billions of these animals were born, confined, drugged, fed, mutilated and slaughtered after just a month or so of life each and every year. Multiple millions of females of this species would be kept alive merely so that your parents and predecessors could consume the unfertilised ova of the animal's menstrual cycle; then, when these avians were considered *spent*, when their cycles were considered unprofitable, they would be slaughtered, at, more or less, just over one year old. In the wild, in theory, these animals could live for thirteen or so years – but so few actually were living wild at that time that nobody could verify that fact.

The males, by nature unable to menstruate, were destroyed, ground to pieces whilst still alive, as soon as their gender was confirmed.'

'Marine life, on the whole, lived in the oceans and died after being caught in netting and dragged to the surface where they suffocated. In terms of numbers, it had been estimated that around one-hundred billion of these animals were killed for consumption by your predecessors every single year. It could be said that, at least, most of this number were born free – unlike the avian and mammals I just mentioned. Others, however, were born and raised inside so-called *fish farms,* which were little more than an area of mesh in the oceans that would contain millions of creatures, tightly packed in, eating their own faeces and the drug-laced remains of their fellow species, until they were large enough to be killed and consumed. Millions of ocean marine creatures, in further examples of your predecessors' irrationality, would be caught in the netting but thrown back into the water, dead, if they were of the wrong species, marine reptiles or mammals, for example, or if the particular species had no *commercial* value. Other species were caught purely for a particular appendage and, after being caught and the limb amputated without anaesthetic, the animals would be thrown back into the ocean, still alive, unable to properly navigate the water, to die a slow death – no doubt in extreme pain and bewildering for the unfortunate creatures. Most marine mammals were recognised by your ancestors to be highly sensitive and intelligent species but, still, these animals were hunted, killed and eaten – unbelievably it was asserted by some of your predecessors that these murders were committed for scientific purposes.'

Hentanayre shook her head, not for the first or last time.

'As I said earlier, most of the old terms I am using do not have synonyms in our universal language so the words from the old languages of your planet – such as *profitably, sold, commercial or economic viability* – can all be discussed at a later stage.'

Again, she paused for a second or two, then carried on.

'We could not, and still cannot, understand how any society could treat fellow animals in such vile and cruel ways. Neither could we believe that your predecessors did not know that these species felt the same sensations of pleasure, pain, loss and love as themselves. Your predecessors often had other species of animal living with them in their homes and, from what we can tell, in most instances regarded these animals as members of their own families. At the same time, however, they endorsed the depravity of mass-murdering other species by also consuming the flesh of those animals. Most of the companion animals they allowed in their homes were either completely carnivorous, such as felines, or mainly carnivorous, such as canines, and therefore also fed on the same processes of multiple mass murder. It must be said, however, that in some areas of the planet no such distinction saved canine or feline animals from being slaughtered and eaten by the Kaahu. Strangely, this killing and eating of companion animals caused great consternation to many of those other Kaahu who purported to be, so-called, *animal-lovers* – obviously a highly subjective term.'

'On a personal level, amongst all of these appalling atrocities committed by your predecessors, I find their apparent addiction to the mother's milk of other mammals the most disturbing and, quite literally, sickening – I was only about four years of age at the time, but I still remember that I vomited when I first heard of this practice, and that was before I knew what lengths they went to, and the suffering they caused, to obtain it. As I am now a mother, the mere thought of my child being stolen from me at birth, or shortly thereafter, and having no idea why he was taken from me or where he was, fills me with dread – to have these child-thieves also feast on my body fluids adds utter disgust to my terror.'

'Of course, those child-thieves slaughtered and ate those young animals.'

A shudder, sigh and a pause.

'At least one-hundred million animals of other species were used in pointless, totally anthropocentric laboratory experiments and killed every year by the Kaahu – the experiments were designed solely to benefit your antecedents, yet the physiology of the species they tested and dissected differed significantly from their own. The vivisectionists, who were sponsored by the pharmaceutical manufacturers, knew this; the pharmaceutical manufacturers, who greatly profited from the sale of chemical products tested by this method, knew this; and the politicians and their advisers, who regulated the violation of these other species, knew this. They all knew there were more reliable ways to find safe products – data-processor models for example – but for purely greedy, personal, economic reasons, these alternatives were hardly ever considered, never mind implemented.'

'The acquisition of personal wealth made your ancestors' world go round. The motives behind their every action appear to have been selfish – for their own personal gratification or self-promotion – and wholly anthropocentric, regardless of the cost to other animals, to plant or other life-forms or to the planet.'

'We considered the notion that this was not their fault – things had always been this way and there was nothing they could have done to change their attitudes. But these were self-professed intelligent beings. They all *knew* of the suffering they caused to other beings, but chose to ignore it. They all *knew* of the damage they were doing to their planet, but chose to ignore it. In both instances many of your predecessors, despite all the evidence to the contrary, denied any culpability. However, even if we could have found any mitigating circumstances, there would still be seven-billion of them on the planet, most of them still reproducing.'

'Propagation of and by a species is a wholly natural impulse, we understand that, but to wilfully continue the process in full knowledge of the consequences of overpopulation on both other species and the planet itself, was, in our opinion, unforgivable. It could also be said in mitigation that the planet's Kaahu populace were living in different time-periods, three or four completely different centuries, all at the same time. Vast numbers of these animals, as intelligent as any other of their species on the planet, had, at most, only a basic education – enough perhaps to read and write – and some did not even receive that level of tuition. They were illiterate and innumerate. Conversely, and in close proximity to the majority of the local uneducated population, there would be vocational or scientifically trained individuals. The difference between them was, more often than not, an accident of birth, rich or poor, and an economic system based on personal greed. Millions of others were living and working through a new industrial revolution in a type of bonded slavery; working for a pittance and living in squalor whilst their masters reaped the benefits of their labour and lived in luxury. An ideology concerned only with personal enrichment – they called it betterment – at whatever cost to future generations of all living beings and the life-nurturing environments of the planet.'

'There were also other politico-economic systems in other areas purporting to be based on justice for all; but besides the *all* only meaning their own species, these ideologies were, manifestly, focused on the accumulation and retention of power and wealth in the hands of certain groups or individuals by any means possible – just the same as the predominant world economic order – raping the planet of precious, non-renewable resources, encouraging over-consumption by a pliable, gullible population, desperate to emulate their *betters'* perceived success, to slake their avarice and engaging in extreme violence to maintain their wealth or increase it by conquest. Looking back throughout their history, greed, the lust for power and brutality were all common denominators.'

'Half of the dominant population appeared to be bloated with obesity, the other half were starving to death with hunger. Most of those obese animals had no self-control; the starving animals had no choice.'"

Up to ninety-five percent of the dominant population, and probably more, held wildly irrational beliefs in supernatural, all-powerful deities, both good, the god or gods, and evil, the devils and demons. All faiths were based on texts written thousands of years earlier but were still considered to be relevant, the absolute truth – despite scientific scrutiny proving otherwise. In most cases, these *religious* beliefs bordered on psychotic and were not only almost exclusively anthropocentric but also ran contrary to any need to conserve the planet's ecosystems. Why save this world when, by following one of their *gods*, there would be a much better place guaranteed to them in some perceived paradisal afterlife? There would be no death for this life form.'

'These animals, and these animals alone, apparently possessed an extra bodily organ of some kind, a *soul*, that was invisible to the naked eye or, for that matter, any form of medical investigation, and most importantly, this soul was immortal. No other animal species had souls – including me, I suppose – only your ancestors, because this species did not consider themselves to be animals – they were *special* – their arrogance was stunning. At the end of an immortal non-animal's life, in most of these religions, this soul, this immortal appendage, would be miraculously transported to a paradise somewhere in the universe– unspecified, of course – where it would spend eternity adoring its creator or sometimes just sitting around, doing nothing except praising their deity, depending on which of the stories they believed.

'No single illogical superstition was more or less delusional than the other, though – all of their species would live on after their lives had ended. And what kind of *after-life* would that have been for the Kaahu in one of their magical paradises? Apparently a never-ending existence of constantly praising their almighty creator, forever on their knees in reverence, or forever prostrate – on a cloud perhaps? – in awe before he, she or it. But for the whole of eternity?'

'Still other superstitions espoused reincarnation;

being re-born as a member of another species until complete enlightenment was achieved, for example – but how that enlightenment was attained by this method was not, for us, satisfactorily explained. Also, considering the billions of animals of other species slaughtered in early childhood each year by these cruel, spiritual animals for their food, this form of transmutation may not have had the desired effect. Imagine what kind of enlightenment you can find being reborn as one of the avian species that are de-beaked, fattened, drugged and slaughtered before you were two-months old.'

'Blaming anything bad that happened to them on the evil perpetrated by supernatural devils and demons was the norm for these creatures – it was never their fault. In fact, the sad truth was, the only *evil* things on the planet were your ancestors.'

'Somewhat ironically, those Kaahu who were deemed to be *evil* by the majority – perhaps those few who employed reason to view their world or those that were described as *homosexual* – would spend eternity in a blazing inferno being punished for their *sins* by supernatural creatures known as *demons* or *devils*. Were you to look on the Kaahu social nexus, you could find a list of these crimes against their religions and, perhaps, note that the entire species would infringe these edicts – maybe they are all there now! But I digress.'

'The illogicality of these religions was compounded by the cruelty and violence they employed against members of their own species that were believers of other faiths or, incredulously, some of their own adherents. None were averse to massacring groups of other animals with the same basic beliefs as themselves but whose philosophy differed, ever so slightly, from what *their* particular cult considered to be the *truth*. These other animals were thought of as heretics and, because of their alternative interpretation of the main group's ancient text, must die. In many areas of the planet, animals of different religious beliefs were, seemingly, legitimate targets for violent assault or murder and, in these and many other parts of the world, it was likewise unwise to be homosexual or atheistic due to the risk of imprisonment or execution for these *crimes.*'

'Huge areas of the planet were governed using these old books as guides to how entire populations were to live their lives. Constitutions demanded allegiance to these deities and binding laws were enacted to protect against insulting or questioning them, with imprisonment, beatings or even death the punishments for non-compliance. Religious wars and conflicts were rife at the time of our arrival, as they had been throughout the two-thousand years before that time – perhaps even longer. Fifty percent of adherents were, effectively, excluded from full participation in all of the religious groups, based on gender alone – essentially, as in most aspects of these strange societies, the dominant voices were aggressive, power-hungry and, more often than not, male.'

Hentanayre paused in thought for moment and added: 'For some of you Temuri girls who were born in certain areas of this planet, you do not want to know what these males would have ordered to be done to your genitalia.'

She shook her head slowly before she continued.

'These religious beliefs were not only pernicious, they were beyond illogical with no scientific basis whatsoever. When astronomy determined that their planet was not, in fact, the centre of the solar-system with the sun and other planets orbiting it, nor, indeed, that it was not the centre of the universe, it was heresy. When evolution was first posited, it, too, was also considered heretical.'

'Consider the premise: In an observable universe of approximately one-hundred and seventy-billion galaxies, each containing between one-hundred billion and five-hundred billion or more stars, these deities – or at least one of them – chose this particular, nondescript galaxy and, not only that, selected a minor star in an obscure area of the galaxy to create the only planet in the entire universe to host life; and, on that world, though billions of years later for some reason, created a non-animal life form in their own image who could treat the planet and its other inhabitants as it desired. Alternatively, their god, or gods, first created this world six-thousand years ago and added the rest of the universe a couple of days later. Such were their beliefs.'

'More than anything, these irrational beliefs in superstitious nonsense held back their own evolution and adversely affected or completely curtailed the evolution of other species on this planet. None of these superstitions encouraged independent thought, rather they actively suppressed it. Although they all purported to preach of love and tolerance, those qualities were not extended towards other species of life and, when it did not suit them, they were not even extended to their own species. Whilst they all encouraged the unfettered procreation of their species, they were not averse to killing similar animals in the name of their particular deity in relatively small numbers, usually on an hour by hour basis. As they were born in the image of their creator, this made them, in their own minds, perfect, god-like beings deserving of certain rights not bestowed on inferior species of life nor the planet they all lived on. These *rights* legitimised their ability to exploit their own species for personal gain and other species and the planet for whatever reason they desired. These *rights* enabled and encouraged them to procreate to the point of destroying their own world. These *rights* encouraged and endorsed belief in nonsensical philosophies. All without limitation. There could be no mitigation.'

'We believed we had three choices – we still believe

this: Firstly, we could have chosen to continue our observations. Sit back and watch as the population of the dominant species on the planet continued to grow unchecked. Do nothing as all the natural resources were gradually exhausted or became so rare as to cause mass conflict between tribes of these so-called intelligent and civilised animals with weapons of mass destruction at their disposal. Just sit on our home-worlds, witness and catalogue the outcome of thermonuclear war on the differing species of life and its aftermath. Twiddle our collective thumbs as nuclear winter took hold and total darkness engulfed the planet for decades, annihilating most species of vegetation and animal life, if not all. We rejected this choice.'

'Secondly, again, we could have chosen to continue to observe. Sit back and watch as the Kaahu population of the planet continue to grow unchecked. Do nothing as even more fossil fuels were burned and more and more pollutants released into the already thickening and sickening atmosphere, and watch on, unconcerned, as global warming took effect. Watch as all the natural resources, fresh water and food, were gradually exhausted and, if the war-like factions did not take any action, witness mass starvation and disease affecting all species of life take hold. Twiddle our collective thumbs as more mass extinctions took place in front of our eyes, desertification become widespread and ocean acidification being intensified, causing disastrous adverse effects on all marine life as that acidification led to more and more carbon dioxide being released into the atmosphere. Were all this to be allowed to continue, we believed there would, sooner or later – we think sooner – be a massive breakdown in atmospheric conditions, leading to a near-total evaporation of all the vital gases it contained and the consequences that would inevitably entail for all life on the planet. Again, we rejected this option.'

'The third choice was to restore the process of natural evolution which had been restricted so severely on the planet and, in many instances, unnaturally interfered with or prematurely ended by your predecessors. At the same time we wanted to allow the planet and the other species of life the time to recover from the over-exploitation of your ancestors that they had endured. We knew, if left alone, the natural order has an incredible capacity to bounce back. So, the only way to achieve this was to cull the problem species, your predecessors; your parents. This is the option we chose.'

Hentanayre glanced at her notes displayed on an ancillary visi-screen to the right of the main screen in front of her, the latter which also served as the visi-sensor that was transmitting this speech to the Temuri. She saw that her main part in this dark day of revelations had been completed.

'We should take a break,' she continued, 'and return in, perhaps, half-an-hour, when we will be joined by Sis from the Obiah people.'

chapter forty

A short recess was taken; a mere half-an-hour for the Temuri population to ingest and try to absorb, perhaps, the most devastating, the most painful, information they had ever had to hear or were ever likely to hear again; and just half-an-hour for the alien female, Hentanayre, to compose her thoughts for the next session of revelations.

Her first thought, though, was to urinate – she had been too nervous to eat at all that day and all the water she had drunk before and during the visi-cast appeared to have gone straight through her. She gestured to her female companion, indicating her destination, and left the platform whilst her friend continued to busy herself at a separate visi-screen.

After she had relieved herself in the toilet room at the rear of lecture theatre stage and had washed her hands, Hentanayre returned to the dais, sat down and tried to review the transmission she had just made.

Primarily, she was concerned about how the children, their much-loved charges, were taking the news of how and why their parents had died – well, had been murdered, there could be no other way to see it! She imagined there may be shock, grief and anger, but, in all honesty, other than her perceived notion that they had already surmised the truth beforehand, she had no idea what the children were feeling – how could she? She had never personally lost even a family member. The only person that had died that she had known was an older professor who passed away on the journey to this place and, really, she had not known her that well – she was more a friend of a friend. Her sense of loss at that time must pale into insignificance when compared to the loss, the trauma, which the Temuri children must now be feeling – even though, because they were so young at the time, they could not have any conscious memories of their families. But she could not conceive of what emotions they were experiencing.

She began to question her presentation. Was she too direct? Should she have shrouded the information in more vague, less direct terms? No, she concluded, there would have been no point in obscuring the facts behind ambiguity; that would reek of deception and would have raised more questions than it answered.

The remaining minutes seemed to pass quite quickly. Sat at the desk, Hentanayre took yet another sip of water and touched the top right hand corner of the main visi-screen in front of her and said the name of her Obiah colleague.

'Sis?'

Almost twenty seconds passed before the image of the Obiah female appeared.

'Apologies, Hentanayre, I was not at my desk.'

'Do not apologise,' the ap-Vanda female replied. 'Are you ready?'

'I am.' Kobensis responded.

chapter forty-one

'I am Kobensis – although everyone just calls me Sis – and I have been part of the coordinating team attempting the restoration of your planet for the past twelve years.'

The Obiah female's face loomed large on the visi-screens across and above the planet. She smiled, although it looked kind of forced. It was forced.

The Obiah were described by the ap-Vanda, the Vatta and Temuri as *mainly* mammalian. The Obiah characterised themselves as pure mammals; they live-birthed, their offspring were breastfed and they were warm-blooded, but their skin was tinged with a greenish hue and they had no visible ears, though their hearing was exceptionally acute – much more so than their alien or Temuri counterparts. Rather than nostrils, they possessed a horizontal t-shaped slit in the centre of their faces and their black eyes were angled more around the side of their faces than were forward-looking. They were also quite hairless. It was, perhaps, little wonder that their alien allies thought them lizard-like – albeit in a light-hearted, non-offensive way. Smiling did not come easily to the Obiah – they did not have the facial muscles needed to perform such an expression.

Although these Obiah bodily features may have been similar, perhaps, to some of the wilder imaginings of the Kaahu with regards to alien life, this species were not tiny, spindly creatures with huge or pointy crania – and they wore clothes. But, otherwise, they did bear a startling resemblance to some of those fictional aliens thought up by the Kaahu.

The Obiah were, self-admittedly, a less than sociable people, even amongst their own kind. Unlike the Vatta and unlike the ap-Vanda, the Obiah did not particularly like to congregate in large groups to discuss this topic or that issue – unless, of course, it was in an academic or other learning setting. They had, it appeared, no desires to display their talents to others, be they musical or any other sort of creative talent that required public view. They made music, they wrote poetry and prose and they created artworks, but something in their genetic make-up seemed to prevent them from being able to show their artistic talents or themselves off to their peers. However, ask them to present an academic paper, discuss a scientific theory or tutor a study group, and they would be in their element.

Kobensis continued.

'I am here to talk to you about education and evolution. Hentanayre has, quite rightly, expressed our great sorrow, our deep regret, at having to kill so many animals on this world, but as she said, we only had three options – two of which would have decimated the planet. If we had not taken the action we did, you Temuri may not have lived beyond forty years and, however long you existed, you would no doubt have suffered the consequences of your former species' behaviour, either by the irradiations from their unconscionable weapons or by the poisonous effects of their noxious pollutants – most of which, of course, were directly associated with their odious consumption practices, particularly of other species of animals. So, perhaps we did not have three options – they were just philosophical implements. We did not sit around a table to argue about whether or not to watch your antecedents destroy the planet one way or the other. We had no choice but to act, and although the psychological consequences of our actions will remain forever with all the Obiah, Vatta and ap-Vanda who participated, the greater crime would have been committed had we done nothing.'

'Although we cannot say for certain that your former species would have been completely wiped out in any ensuing catastrophe, we can categorically state that many other species of life *would* have been made extinct. The Kaahu animals, your parents, had already caused that state of non-existence, that total annihilation of an entire group of life-forms, to be suffered by many species; and even at the time of our arrival, many, many more were teetering on the edge of extinction, including even some of your own simian near relatives, because of the greed and apathy of those same parents and their fellow animals. Consider what they did or were about to do. How would those life-forms have evolved had they not been wiped so carelessly, so nonchalantly, from the surface of your world, from existence forever? Nobody will ever truly know much about those who suffered that devastation, but now at least, those close to the edge of such disappearances have a chance to progress and future generations of Temuri will have the opportunity to observe their advancement.'

'From my words, you will see that we did not come here to save you, in particular, from extinction. Your species was just another group of animals in danger – except in your case, that peril came from yourselves as a species. Neither did we, nor could or would we ever, consider making your species extinct as a punishment or other such excuse – that would have been unconscionable and unpardonable.'

Kobensis paused, but only for a second.

'Your task now is to never allow those vile events that occurred in the name of your ancestors to happen on this world again. We are confident you can achieve this. You are more well-equipped to undertake the task than any of your predecessors ever were or could ever hope to have been. Without exception, you all have enquiring minds, you will not allow an unproven theory to go unquestioned or be regarded as fact simply on the word of another. Your education has been firmly grounded in scientific methodologies rather than irrationality, and we expect you all to teach your children and grandchildren to think along similar lines so that the upwards spiral of knowledge-seeking continues into the future. This is what we understand as evolution in animal species.'

'"Yes, it has been a physical process throughout the lifespan of yours and every other species that has ever lived, and that process is more likely than not continuing, but, in our view, evolution in animals is also about intellectual progress. Without that intellectual progress, a species cannot recognise its mistakes, cannot learn from those mistakes, and continues to make those same mistakes for the entirety of its short existence. Physically, they may be near perfection with every part of their bodies ideally suited to their environment, but if a species does not also adapt themselves mentally, no matter how intelligent they may think they are, they will fail.'

'There are a number of planets in this galaxy that can bear witness to this fact. Planets that were once green, wet and teeming with life are now irradiated beyond redemption or are atmospheric death-traps because a so-called advanced species of animal could not or, more likely, would not, use their intelligence to avoid the extinctions of not just themselves and other species, but their entire planet."

"We believe that education will overcome these issues, and a continuing commitment to knowledge attainment will result in further evolutionary advancements as well as, of course, greater scientific and academic advances.'

'But that education cannot be a mishmash of fact and fantasy, cannot be limited by accident of birth nor be dictated by the prevailing point of view – political, economic or superstition based. All are counter-evolutionary. To have any merit, education must be based on theories that are demonstrable, that can be tested, either positively or negatively – to teach anything other is but a lie. Always bear that in mind as you grow and learn. Do not take everything at face value – question everything put to you as fact; interrogate everyone who insists those presumed facts are true; always ask for proof and settle for nothing less.'

'Everything Hentanayre and I have claimed to you to be fact today is provable. The Kaahu documents that we are asking you to translate will back-up the assertion of their atrocities as proposed by Hentanayre. You will read of their base treatment of other species of animals, their neglect of their own planet, to the point of catastrophe, their insane beliefs, their inexplicable internal divisions and their universal sadness. It will be all there, recounted by the Kaahu themselves, in page after page after page of self-reflection – but very little remorse.'

'For my part, I can show you documentary evidence of destroyed worlds and how they were destroyed – though, unfortunately, not by whom.'

'As for my proof of the evolutionary benefits of a correct education, I need only present myself, Hentanayre and every other alien on or around the planet – plus many more on worlds far away. Naanich will explain shortly.'

'Before I finish, I must tell you all that the Obiah will soon all be leaving. Our work here is almost complete and we all miss our home-world very much. Both the ap-Vanda and the Vatta had suggested we hold a series of farewell parties to include you, the Temuri; but as I am sure you know, we Obiah are not particularly fond of such festivities so, on behalf of my species, I wish you all well for the future. Also, and I am sure I am not revealing any great secret when I tell you, the Vatta, who, it seems, are genetically predisposed to party, will soon be leaving for their planet, too, so there will be many celebrations up until that time.'

'I would like to say that, those of my people that have worked with you, have all greatly enjoyed the experience, and I am sure you will always be in our thoughts.'

With that, the visi-screen returned to display an unprepared Hentanayre who, for a brief moment, stared out blankly at the watching audience.

'Oh,' she recovered, 'that was unexpected – thank you, Kobensis.'

Hentanayre gave a wry smile to camera and continued.

'So finally today, I will introduce my friend, Naanich. We travelled together from the Empty Space passage exit point at the edge of this solar-system to your planet all those years ago and we have remained friends ever since. As Sis mentioned, the Vatta will also soon be leaving – I will miss her.'

The visi-screen image shifted and the face of the Vatta female, Naanich, appeared, looking rather timidly out on all the attendees, most of whom, of course, she could not see – even those in the same room.

She laughed.

'Well thank you, my friend,' she said with some irony and added, with somewhat more sarcasm, 'And my gratitude to Kobensis for giving us such ample warning that she would finish so abruptly!'

chapter forty-two

The Vatta were even more similar, physically, to the primary target species, and therefore to the Temuri, than the ap-Vanda. Their build, facial features and, at one time, their skin tones, were almost identical, though the Vatta were now all a mid-brown colour rather than the range of colours, from pale pink to dark brown, that the Kaahu had once been. The position of the Vatta home-world in its solar-system corresponded, in terms of distance from its star, almost exactly to the alien world they had first arrived at twelve years earlier. To the naked eye, the only discernible difference between the Vatta and the Temuri were the larger hands and feet, caused by the one extra digit on each of those appendages possessed of the Vatta.

Like the ap-Vanda, and very much unlike the Obiah, the Vatta were predominantly quite gregarious as a species; they liked to laugh and they liked to enjoy themselves – preferably in groups.

All of the individual animals of the three invading species were possessed of a self-confidence born of being aware of all facts known to their species, and of never being lied to or deceived. This knowledge made them almost unflappable, so even when taken by surprise, any lack of composure would be momentary. There would be no temper-tantrums, no seething rages, no thoughts of revenge, so even though Naanich was slightly taken aback by her unexpectedly early appearance on the visicast, she thought no more of it.

Because of the aliens' easy self-possession, the

Kaahu would, no doubt, have described them as *arrogant* or *smug*, but then again, had one of the Kaahu species been in a similar situation, the possibility that they would go on to murder the person that caused them such embarrassment could not be entirely ruled out. Such had been the Kaahu character.

'Hello everybody,' Naanich continued with a broad smile. 'As my good friend, Hentanayre, has just said, I am Naanich and I am Vatta – but I think that most of you know me or know of me.'

Throughout the individual monologues of Hentanayre and Kobensis, Naanich had been sat next to her ap-Vanda friend on that same raised platform in that same space filled with Temuri children and members of the three alien species. She had, as best she could, tried to scan the faces of the Temuri audience as Hentanayre had recounted the roles of the aliens in the deaths of the Kaahu, the parents and relatives of those same Temuri, but she learned little. The room itself had been quite dark and she could only see the first few rows of faces in front of where she was sitting. She saw no tears in the eyes of the children she could see and she heard no gasps of surprise as the news was imparted. Most of the children had just looked at each other as the awful facts emerged, some looked at their alien guardians or companions and some kept their eyes on Hentanayre. Naanich was glad that, as far as she could tell, none of the Temuri had looked at her, though perhaps somewhere in that room, or most definitely in another location, there were children she had taught and to whom she felt close to. Although she did wonder whether or not those children – all the children – were feeling betrayed by the ap-Vanda, Vatta and Obiah at that point, she knew the Temuri were rational, intelligent animals and, more than likely, had predicted beforehand everything they had been told, and were about to hear. What other circumstance could possibly have arisen that resulted in ten-thousand children being cared for and raised by three different species of animals from other planets? Naanich thought that today would, perhaps, be an affirmation for many of the Temuri – but she could not be sure of that.

The Vatta female had paused for a couple of seconds after her introductory remarks. She took a deep breath, and continued her monologue.

'I realise that what we have told you today was perhaps very shocking to you, and I am also sure that many, if not all of you, will have noticed the inconsistency in our informing you of the facts concerning your parents and our stated promise never to lie to you, never to wilfully deceive you. Yet by failing until now to tell you of the killing of your predecessors, we have lied to you, have deceived you all, by that act of omission – but, as Hentanayre said, we had to wait until you had reached an age when you could better understand our reasoning.'

'But I must also now tell you that this was not the only time, nor will it be that last, that information has been, or will be, kept from you on purpose. There is a truth about the home-worlds of the ap-Vanda, the Vatta and the Obiah that, again, I am sure most of you may have already surmised.'

'The term we now use for your species, "Temuri", as you know, means "new-born" in an old, dead ap-Vanda language – just as the word "Kaahu" we applied to your antecedents came from the same tongue. But what you did not know is the term "ap-Vanda", also meaning "new-born", is from an ancient Vatta language, and the term "Vatta" originated on the Obiah home-world and, too, means "new-born". "Obiah" is an old Crais word meaning – but I am sure you have already guessed. All of us were culled of our ancestors by aliens from distant worlds. The sole differences between our three planets and your own are the years it occurred and the species involved in the various projects.'

'Over one-thousand years ago, a planet was culled by three species of aliens called the Crais, the Skriit and the Pourn. They extracted ten-thousand or so children before killing the rest of that species, and those ten-thousand or so extracted children formed the basis of what we now know as the twelve-million animal Obiah population. The Obiah, in conjunction with the Crais and the Skriit culled my home-world around seven-hundred and fifty years ago and, in turn, the Vatta, Obiah and Crais culled the ancestors of the ap-Vanda about five-hundred years later, which was around four-hundred and fifty years before we all came here to your home-world and culled it. All of our home-worlds would have been once designated as hell worlds, just as your home-world was.'

'It would come as a surprise to many of my species, and to many of the ap-Vanda, that both our worlds were so similar to the one previously dominated by your antecedents that they were almost indistinguishable. The Vatta and ap-Vanda people look to the future rather than the past, so few studied the available older data on their species – I am no exception. Throughout my early life on the Vatta home-world and the journey here, I had no idea of the relatively recent history of my species – we were as greedy, vicious, superstitious and stupid as any Kaahu from your world, as were the ap-Vanda predecessors. The Obiah ancestors, I have learned, were living in totalitarian servitude rather than the individual greed power-systems of our three planets, but their society was also based on obscene cruelty, wild superstition and deep stupidity with power-greedy leaders. But any one of these oppressed animals would have, with much gusto, exchanged positions with those leaders without any qualms whatsoever, so they were no better than my antecedents, nor those of Hentanayre, nor yours.'

'We, as children, were not taught these things as we grew. Neither, as far as I am aware, were my parents or grandparents – I am somewhat sure that the same is true on the ap-Vanda home-world. In contrast, the Obiah, or so I am told, include learning about the culling of their home-world as a matter of course in their education. Phew – excuse me a moment.'

Naanich picked-up a three-quarter full, large glass of water and took a long drink. She put down the glass and continued.

'Apologies – I was quite dry mouthed for some reason!'

'As far as we know, this planet, your world, is around the fourteenth in the galaxy to be culled in this way over the past four-thousand years or so. The exact details are a bit cloudy – such a long time has passed and, quite frankly, we do not know for certain if there were other such culls before those fourteen; and neither do we know anything about who started the process all those years ago except for the name of the person who discovered Empty Space – and even that is, perhaps, just apocryphal. We do know of seventy-two other solar-systems that once contained life-bearing worlds but now are devoid of such planets because of the activities of their former, now forever extinct, dominant populations. Indeed, my people discovered such an empty solar-system with a devastated planet orbiting its star not long before we found the former hell world that is now home to the ap-Vanda.'

'Over the course of the past four millennia, not a single life-sustaining planet has been found that did not include a species of dominant, so-called intelligent, life, such as your and my antecedents, that were not threatening the future of other species and the life of the planet itself. In telling you these things, I am not saying that we, any of us *aliens*, can in any way, appreciate what you are feeling at this moment. There are old documents, from both ap-Vanda and Vatta sources, recorded after each group had been informed of the earlier culls which speak of great shock, sadness and disappointment, but most were composed years after the actual date of the revelations.'

'But we do have many textual, audio and visual documents created before, during and after each of those three projects – those culls – just as we have textual, audio and visual data from the past thirty-five or so years detailing all the planning, execution and post-cull operations undertaken here. All of this information, plus data from earlier culls, will also be made available to you now.'

Naanich paused for a couple of seconds, but before she could resume her talk, she sensed movement at her side and the image on her visi-screen, all of the visi-screens taking the transmission in fact, split down the centre and Hentanayre's face appeared on the opposite side to Naanich's image. Naanich turned and looked quizzically at her friend.

'Apologies, Naanich' the ap-Vanda female said, 'I think you are close to finishing? A number of interesting questions have been posed by our audiences and I wondered if you would help me to respond, please? When you have finished, of course.'

A cheerful laugh was heard in reply.

'Of course I will, Hentanayre,' she said, 'I was just about to finish. Though I must confirm the rumour started by Kobensis that the Vatta will, indeed, be also returning to our home-world soon and, yes, we will be holding parties to celebrate that fact.'

Throughout this good-natured dig at her Obiah colleague, Naanich gave a mischievous grin to camera.

'What is the first question, Hentanayre?' she asked.

chapter forty-three

Over the following hour, Naanich and Hentanayre answered a few questions from the Temuri but most were referred back to the newly-released Kaahu datasets.

The first question they answered in full asked what advances in space travel there had been over the past four millennia. Naanich replied.

'Very little. Although we can build propulsion systems that would more than exceed the current top speed of just under one-million kilometres an hour in our spacecraft, we cannot yet build spacecraft that can withstand the pressures that rate of velocity produces, nor could we animals withstand those pressures.'

She smiled at the visi-sensor so all could see but it was primarily aimed at her ap-Vanda colleague.

'Hentanayre can attest to the discomfort suffered whilst in the dreaded cocoons we have to take shelter in whilst acceleration to the cruising speed of the particulate drive engines – most of us have to knock ourselves out to endure it. The thought of extending the time in those contraptions frightens me! You will all understand what I am saying soon enough, when you experience it!'

Naanich grinned widely and Hentanayre joined in the conversation.

'In any event,' explained the ap-Vanda female, 'until we can improve the materials used on the spacecraft and overcome the horrors of the cocoons – both of which researchers of all our species appear to be forever attempting – there is little to gain from expending time and effort on developing faster passenger-carrying vessels. It is very rare for any of us to leave our own solar-systems anyway, unless a hell world is found. We do, occasionally, visit the Empty Space research vessels at the edges of our solar-systems but we have no reason to send animals into the void of interstellar space because automated probes provide all the data from that area that we require – or so we believe at this point in time. When we do need to visit another solar-system in person, every four-hundred or so years, we use the Empty Space passage and, somehow, we appear to achieve light speed or above. So, to echo the response to the question given by Naanich, I would also say that very little progress has been made – but perhaps sometime in the future, one of you may discover ways to develop the silk material, or devise a brand new material, to enable progress in these areas.'

'And, if I may interrupt,' interrupted Naanich, 'your species now have all the tools required to visit the realms of other stars – even reaching the edge of this solar-system was something that the Kaahu would never have achieved, even if they had managed to exist for another four millennia!'

The next question answered had asked if there were any planets discovered, to their knowledge, without a Kaahu-like dominant species, perhaps one in an earlier stage of the planet's evolutionary progress. Hentanayre admitted that she did not know but, in preparation for this day, Naanich had researched a number of topics and one such area had dealt with the results of exploratory probes launched into Empty Space by each of the ap-Vanda, Vatta and Obiah. More digests than comprehensive texts, these documents summarised the discoveries that each of their probes had made in alien solar-systems.

'This is a very good question,' began Naanich, 'and, as I only have data going back around one-thousand years, I can only answer for that period. As far as the Obiah, ap-Vanda and Vatta are concerned, no such life-sustaining world devoid of a Kaahu-like, dominant, self-destructive species has ever yet been found. The questions to ask now are, of course, why not and what would you do if such a planet *was* discovered?'

Silence.

'Thank you, Naanich,' Hentanayre said when her friend had been quiet for enough time for her to realise that she had, perhaps, finished her response; though even then Hentanayre was not sure. When there was no reaction to the contrary from the Vatta female, the ap-Vanda female continued the session.

'The next question asks; was it necessary to kill *all* of the Kaahu?'

Hentanayre paused for a couple of seconds before replying to her own query.

'I am afraid so. All of the Kaahu, all of your parents and families, were tainted, corrupted, by *their* parents and families, *their* teachers, *their* self-proclaimed betters. Their indoctrination was so deep, so insidious, that, had we not taken the actions we did, it would have been impossible to rid them of the delusions they were under.'

'Of course,' interjected Naanich, 'we do not know for sure if *all* the Kaahu were culled or if some survived the process, or if they did indeed survive, are they are still alive today? There are vast areas of this planet that nobody has visited for at least twelve years now – nobody from our three species, that is. We do have probes in the air, but they are scanning for the life-signs of multiple indigenous species, including the Kaahu, rather than just *for* the Kaahu. It is not beyond the realms of possibility that one or more populations of Kaahu are still living on your planet. This is not exceptional. On my own home-world, a tiny population of my ancestors survived for some sixty years after the cull. There were also individuals, those unable to find other survivors, but they fared less well and died within five years, according to the records. One group of four animals managed to procreate and produce three young, but alas, the offspring were all male, with the obvious outcome. They were only discovered some thirty-five to forty years after the cull and were studied, surreptitiously of course, until they became extinct. From the observations, it was noted that they retained all of the irrational superstitious beliefs, the cruelty and the greed of their contemporaries despite their circumstances. They prayed to their gods, they hunted, killed and ate other species of animal and they attempted to dominate each other, with violence, throughout – even though there were, at most, only seven animals.'

Again, Hentanayre was unsure.

'Have you finished, Naanich?' she asked.

'Yes, replied the Vatta; then, abruptly, 'no, just one more thing on this, please. All of the relevant information on the Kaahu is stored in the databases that have now been made available to you – plus *so much* irrelevant information about them – that you should read about them and make up your own minds whether or not they should all have been culled. That is all I have to say on this.'

There were other questions about the Kaahu and, on each occasion, Hentanayre and Naanich also referred the Temuri to these newly-released databases. There was one question they left until the end of the session – what next for the Temuri?

Naanich was first to take up the challenge of answering this question.

'There are between one to two-hundred billion galaxies in the observable universe – that we know about, that we can observe. Each one of those galaxies will, no doubt, contain upwards of two to three-hundred billion stars, perhaps more. Trillions of stars means trillions of questions. Each and every one of those stars is a potential opportunity for discovery, for research, for acquiring knowledge.'

'You, the Temuri, now have before you a whole universe of unknown facts to uncover and you can do that unencumbered by the petty differences, the illogicality, the viciousness and the ignorance of your ancestors. You can explore your world and all of its natural wonders, your star and its solar-system. You can, eventually, explore other solar-systems previously unvisited by other species.'

'You can, perhaps, answer as yet unanswered questions – what is Empty Space? Is the theory of trans-dimensional gravity bubbles viable? If so, is there an opposite trans-dimensional effect within the bubble? Your antecedents did much research on the origins of the universe – the *Big Bang Theory* they called it – but were they on the right track? If so, what preceded that great burst of creation? If not, what are the origins of the universe?'

'Of course, other problems to work out could include asking why no planets have yet been found in the past four millennia in the early stages of vegetable and animal evolution. Is it because of the age of our galaxy or this particular part of our galaxy or some other reason? And what should be done if such a world was found – what would be the ethical consequences of settling on that type of planet, for example?'

'Nearer home – are there Kaahu still alive on this planet and, if so, what is to become of them? Would you study them, contact them or cull them? So many questions!'

Silence.

'I am finished, Hentanayre,' Naanich concluded.

'Thank you, Naanich,' said the ap-Vanda female. 'I will fill-in some details.'

Hentanayre paused for a second or two before

continuing.

'Both the Vatta and the Obiah, as you all now know, will all be leaving within the next few months and, sometime in the following ten years, most of the ap-Vanda will also return to my home-world leaving around only thirty-thousand or so of us here on your planet. We, the guardians, your surrogate parents, and about ten-thousand others will stay for, perhaps, the rest of our lives. In that time we will continue to educate and guide you as best we can. As I think we have stressed today, we believe that education is the most important aspect of your evolution as individuals and as a species – but we will not just feed you knowledge as and when a theory is substantiated, you must acquire this knowledge by your own work. We will lead you to a certain level but the rest will be up to you. That has been the way things are done for over the four-thousand years that we know of and continues to be done, even now.'

'There exists between the Obiah and Vatta, as well as between the Vatta and ap-Vanda, a knowledge-gap. These gaps are natural occurrences, bearing in mind the amount of time each species has spent in study. For example, the Obiah had a five-hundred or so year knowledge advantage over the Vatta when they culled the latter's home-world. The Vatta were educated by the Obiah to a level that approximated a knowledge-gap of about two-hundred years – so a huge leap in learning *was* involved – before they left them, as we ap-Vanda will leave you, to return home or die. From that point on, the role of the Vatta was to self-improve themselves with study, research and experiment. But even after the Obiah had left them, they were not alone. At set intervals, the Obiah would contact the Vatta with various hypotheses or theories, equations or questions, asking the Vatta what they made of them. The Vatta, in turn, would ponder the possibilities for as long as they required and return their responses. In the event of their not being able to make head nor tail of the posed problem or, perhaps, they were on the wrong track, the Obiah would ask them to keep trying. When the Vatta sent a correct response, the Obiah would congratulate them and send another problem. On odd occasions the Vatta would receive some data that, again, they could not make sense of and the Obiah would agree that it made no sense to them either. This data may well have come from the Crais, the former guardians of the Obiah – even though their ancestors went through the culling process over one-thousand years ago, their guardians, the Crais, were, and are, still in contact with the Obiah, which shows you that this process of education is an eternal, on-going process.'

'Exchange Vatta for Obiah and ap-Vanda for Vatta, and exactly the same processes apply to my people and our relationship with Naanich's people. And this, in the future if you so choose, can also be a similar link between you, the Temuri, and we, the ap-Vanda. And we ap-Vanda, Vatta and Obiah want to extend these kinds of interplanetary connections into the future. We want to save other paradises from other Kaahu-like species intent on the annihilation of their own worlds leading to the extinction of all life upon those worlds – and we want you to assist us. But that will necessitate, one day in the future, your descendants taking part in a cull on some as yet undiscovered hell world in another part of the galaxy – and, more than that, your progeny making that discovery possible by sending their own probes through Empty Space. But as I said, that will not be for a few hundred years.'

'You, your children and their children – all future Temuri – now have wonderful lives ahead of them. None of you will be encumbered by mistakes of the past; none will be held back by preposterous divisions or absurd superstitions; none will starve or die young because of avaricious and psychopathic economic systems nor be killed in other animals' power struggles.'

'You and all future Temuri will be able to paint, write, compose, work and play with none of the concerns of your antecedents and, unlike those antecedents, you can be happy. But, most of all, you must study and learn in order to evolve. And whilst gaining knowledge, you must build up your population – and all of those as yet unborn Temuri must also study and learn. All of the time you are studying and learning and building up your population, remember, also, to enjoy your lives.'

***

Less than two hours after it had started, the presentation was over.

Less than half-an-hour after that, the Temuri and their alien companions that had been sat listening to the words of the ap-Vanda, Vatta and Obiah females had left the confines of the meeting room, leaving only Hentanayre and Naanich still sat on the raised platform.

Naanich turned to Hentanayre and said, quietly, 'We really should have rehearsed this.'

chapter forty-four

Just short of two months after the most important
meeting in the lives of the Temuri, the Obiah and their
spacecraft, with little ceremony, left orbit of the former
hell world and headed out for the edge of the solar-
system and the Empty Space passage, and onwards to
their home. It was less than a month after the Obiah
left that the Vatta, after much celebration, followed
them. Before they left, before the multiple farewell
parties, the Vatta set the massive flotilla of Kaahu
garbage on its course toward the corona of the local
star a mere one-hundred and fifty-million kilometres
away; all the destructive, radioactive materials, most of
the polluting vessels, all the weaponry they could find,
the debris that was spiralling around the planet when
they arrived – all of it in one long convoy dispatched
for fiery disintegration. Of course, all that detritus
would never actually reach the star, it would be burned
up and destroyed well before getting anywhere near it.
Which, of course, was the whole point of the exercise.
It would also take many years for this procession of
refuse to reach its destination as it moved under its own
momentum, having been put into motion by both large
elevator-bots tugging at it until the movement began
along the entire length of the snaking mass. The journey
had also to commence at a precise time and date so as to
avoid the gravitational pull of both the second and first
planets between its starting point in orbit and the star.
But it would get there, one day.

part five

chapter forty-five

There was no longer a physical ap-Vanda animal presence anywhere in the Temuri home solar-system; they had long since gone back to their own planet or died. Even the technologies they had left behind had become obsolete and were replaced by smarter, leaner Temuri upgrades. But their influence, of course, was everywhere.

Most of the original five-hundred thousand plus ap-Vanda had left some twenty or so years after the cull, but at least thirty-thousand stayed on for life as they had sworn so to do. They continued to protect, educate and advise the original Temuri population as it matured throughout their lives and, at the same time, have children, and in many instances grandchildren, of their own. But those same ap-Vanda children and grandchildren, ever alien on that alien planet, all left to find the home-planet of their own species following the deaths of their mothers. But even after the last ap-Vanda had died and their bodies disposed of; even when their progeny had left to discover their own heritage, light years away, the Temuri were not alone. As promised all those years before, there was regular contact – by way of the probe tethered at the edge of the Temuri home solar-system and its companion probe in the ap-Vanda system – between the two species.

As well as the challenging hypotheses, equations and propositions that would arrive every now and then as part of the on-going educational requirements of the Temuri, the ap-Vanda would often send news of their society and those of their allies in the cull, the Vatta and Obiah animals. In return, the Temuri would relay any news of interest back to the ap-Vanda; for example, 'We have begun to construct an agricultural facility on the fourth planet which we hope will help with our desire to utilise less space for our own purposes on the home-world,' or 'Our latest probe through the Empty Space passage has just been launched heading, we hope, for a solar-system some nine light years away'. The ap-Vanda would pass this information down the line to the Vatta and the Obiah.

The population of the latter of those species, the Obiah, were still, mainly, living on their home-planet as opposed to them all relocating to orbital platforms or settling on other worlds in their solar-system, unlike their allies the Vatta, ap-Vanda and, now, the Temuri. It would, however, have been very difficult for the Obiah to migrate to another world in the vicinity; the only other rocky planets in their system were much too far from the star to support life without their expending a great deal of effort and suffering significant discomfort. The two planets nearest their own world were both moon-less gas giants and the Obiah themselves also had no satellite moons orbiting their world.

However, some good fortune was with the Obiah; their planet was considerably larger than those of their friends in the other solar-systems and, combined with the fact of their innate slow birth-rate – the gestation period for a female animal was sixteen months – and their reluctance to produce more than one offspring per female leading to a comparatively small population, their impact on the planet, from an ecological point of view, was quite limited. Yet, although over nine-million of the Obiah still lived on the surface of their home-world, a further four-million or so were permanently resident in space.

The Vatta on the other hand had elected to relocate

away from their home planet, save for a few thousand animals engaged in academic research, and were settled into communities of millions on orbital platforms, both of the satellite moons and on the two previously lifeless worlds closest to their home-world in the solar-system. All-in-all, the Vatta population had reached almost thirty-seven million animals with over three-quarters of them being born either in space or on a planet not their own. It would perhaps have been incorrect to describe the Vatta home-world as being, at that time, nothing more than a vacation spot for the majority of its former inhabitants, but whoever described it as such would not have been *too* far wide of the mark.

Whilst the ap-Vanda could also be described at that point as being first and foremost space-dwelling animals, there was still a sizeable number of their species living on their home-world. They had every intention of one day fully vacating the planet surface but, at that time, they had other things on their collective minds. During the previous century, their long-range imaging instrumentation had discovered a planet in a distant solar-system which appeared to be different from other worlds they had found – the chemical properties they could discern, under certain conditions, strongly suggested the presence of liquid water and, if the traces were detectable from that distance, in great quantities. They had greatly improved the efficacy of all their tools since the time of the last hell world discovery.

As had always been the case within those allied species that spoke the universal language, those aliens that had been culled and went on to cull, the search for other hell worlds ceased after such a planet was located. From that point onwards, their commitment to such exploration had been fulfilled and the gauntlet of such discovery would be eventually passed on to the newly-culled planet, despite the acknowledged fact that there would invariably be a cessation of such effort for at least four centuries. It was unfortunate but had always been deemed necessary due to the stressful nature of the exercise – just as an allied species would only be expected to be involved in three culling operations even though each mission may have a gap of up to half a millennium between them.

However, there was something about this new planet, albeit intangible, that intrigued the ap-Vanda academics, so much so that they sent a probe through the Empty Space passage to investigate and discovered that most elusive of entities – more rare than a hell world – a pristine world devoid of a single oppressive, dominant species.

For more than thirty years now the ap-Vanda had been observing and studying the flora and fauna from the non-contaminating distance of planetary orbit utilising sterile probes and automata to visually and audibly record the multiple species of animal life, sample and analyse soil, rock and water specimens and undertake thousands of other experiments in the atmosphere, oceans and land-masses. One-thousand five-hundred ap-Vanda animals had travelled to the planet and were circulating above the untainted world studying the data being returned from the automata and compiling a huge repository of knowledge of the age and origins of this unique environment. Not one of the ap-Vanda animals entered the atmosphere of this new world – not one of them ever would. Their probes and automata were powered by the local star and were emission-free; they were all constructed in the vacuum conditions of space and not one spent more than thirty days and nights on the surface or in the atmosphere or oceans before being recalled to the orbiting research laboratories and replaced by new machinery to avoid the possibility of breakdown, crash and contamination. This procedure also allowed for the collection and delivery of non-animal, physical samples from the various locations on, above and below the surface of this wonderful world. In the truest scientific sense, they were there only to study, to record and to learn – not to interfere, not to pollute and not to damage life-forms.

Every day, back on the ap-Vanda home-world, there was exciting news of new species or sub-species of some life-form or other; mammals, reptiles, aves, arthropods, plants and protists. A wonderful, new taxonomy of species to study and share with their, equally excited, allies on the Obiah, Vatta and Temuri home-worlds, as well as, no doubt, much further, as the Obiah could be relied upon to pass the data back down the line to their former guardians and teachers, the Crais species. Who knows how much more the information was disseminated?

chapter forty-six

On the planet surface of the Temuri home-world, as well as in orbit, automata of all shapes and sizes carried on unaware of any other activities the animals or most of the other machines were undertaking – they were, after all, just a conglomeration of all manner of metals, the silk material, a power source and a myriad of electronic components. They scuttled, hovered or rolled about the place, cleaning and washing, scrubbing and polishing, cutting and welding, lifting and carrying, up and down, screwing and unscrewing, weaving and wafting, ploughing and planting, irrigating and pruning, reaping and threshing, kneading and baking, storing and delivering, building and demolishing. Or they lurked, unseen, in dark alcoves or brightly lit termini, awaiting new commands or undergoing a power recharge. All of the largest automata, those containing and nurturing the silk plants, were floating serenely some four-thousand kilometres from the mass of habitat and academy platforms in stationary orbit of the Temuri home-world, the former hell world.

Adjacent to the silk plant producing mega-structures were the manufacturing constructs that supplied the Temuri with most of their material needs, combining the silk with metals and minerals mined out at the solar-system's asteroid belts and delivered straight to their door, both by automata of multiple skills. The mining-bots grabbed and crushed, sieved and sorted the extra-terrestrial materials into separate containers that were loaded onto the delivery-bots that trundled between the floating boulders in the middle of nowhere and the factory-platforms and their automata high above the planet.

Most of the eight-hundred or so fully automated spacecraft, those to be used for travel within and beyond their own solar-system, were in a parking orbit of the world. A few of them were out towards the edges of interstellar space, either coming or going, assisting their animal passengers with academic research projects on or around those planetary and planetoid bodies at those outer limits of the gravitational influence of the local star. Six other vessels were kept close by the Temuri home-world, on constant standby in case of stray asteroids discovered heading towards the planet.

Multiple planetary transport vehicles, automata all, regularly scooted here and there – flying above the planet surface or in its nearby space or from various points in orbit to various points on land and back again. Yet other automata, comparatively tiny machines next to the spacecraft, or even the planetary transport vehicles, would spend most of their time hovering above that land to assist in the husbandry and study of the planet and its multifarious life-forms, animal and vegetable, tracking and recording the lives of the animals and the spread of vegetation in many areas of the world, its mountains, plains, forests and deserts. And on that same land, in the wildernesses that now covered most of the planet surface, all of those species of animals had thrived since the disappearance of the Kaahu.

Other species of ape, whose numbers could be counted in the shamefully low hundreds of individuals during the final throes of the Kaahu domination period, had now recovered to a healthy population size and were flourishing. None of the remaining three species of mammals characterised by their magnificent nose-horns were now found dead with dreadful facial wounds and those horns missing, though a fourth had, unfortunately, gone extinct just before the cull all those years before. More good news was that the three species of the largest terrestrial mammal on the planet could now march through their natural habitats whilst proudly displaying their splendid tusks without fear of the actions of that cruel, ignorant species of simian with their greed and high-powered mechanised weapons; the Kaahu.

Various species of felidae, once hunted down by the Kaahu for their fur or, insanely, their penises or bones, had also recovered from near-extinction and could be found in areas far exceeding the prior limitations imposed upon them by Kaahu incursion and activity. On the huge landmass that spanned the equator, below the vast area of desert, migrations of herbivorous mammals of a magnitude not seen in many, many centuries was now an annual event as the animals followed the rains across the continent to feast on the new vegetation. Feasting also were the many carnivorous species of felidae, canidae and hyaenidae who had choice pickings of the old and infirm or the young and naive herbivores whilst scavenging animals, aves, arthropods and those same felidae, canidae and hyaenidae, would clean up the remains.

Across the ocean, in the upper area of the continent that spanned almost the entirety of both hemispheres, large, dark bovine creatures also enjoyed mass migrations across their feeding grounds, tracked remorselessly by canidae species that preyed on the elderly and young animals of the herds.

Everywhere on the planet, in the wilderness and below the surface of the oceans, lakes and rivers, once extinction-threatened species were all enjoying their space and their freedom from mass slaughter.

Some of the former companion animals to the Kaahu, especially canidae and felidae, those that escaped the culler weapons of the ap-Vanda, Vatta and Obiah peoples, had adapted to life in the wilderness without their former slave-masters and were also thriving.

Much to the disappointment of some of the Temuri, and to the relief of many others, no trace was ever found of any Kaahu that may have also survived the cull. It was posited that, if any had indeed managed to avoid those fatal energy beams, they would likely have been individuals, thus unable to reproduce. Or they were groups of animals that perhaps were killed by diseases generated from the multitude of corpses of their fellow species that must have littered the areas where these possible survivors took shelter. Either way, the Temuri were sure there were no Kaahu on the planet – at least, not any more. And now the oceans were awash with marine life, the skies were crowded with aves, the land teemed with mammalia and everywhere there were arthropods.

Where once stood massive Kaahu settlements, now were mostly ruins of a past existence overgrown with vegetation and time. Some structures survived almost intact – the taller ones usually, those not demolished earlier – they had been built to withstand the rigours of the weather and seismic cataclysms. They could not, however, resist the proliferation of plant life that engulfed them, leaving eerily beautiful green towers, ideal for nesting, at the higher levels, or lairs further below.

Generally, all was well for the planet and all its live inhabitants on the Temuri home-world, this former hell world.

chapter forty-seven

Four and a half centuries or so had passed since the cull. The planet had started to gradually repair itself as soon as the wanton production and disposal of pollutants had been ceased. Given the opportunity, nature seemed to have a way of claiming back its own equilibrium if not overwhelmed by circumstances as it had been for that, relatively, short time the Kaahu animals had held sway on the planet. All of these many years later, the forests on the planet had recovered sufficiently to be able to safely inhale and retain much, if not most, of those pollutants wilfully thrown up into the atmosphere, exhaling clean, pure oxygen in its place.

The rivers and oceans, once conduits and cesspools of mixed excrement, toxic chemicals, oils and other poisons, were now, with the exception of the seemingly unending occurrences of non-biodegradable synthetic polymer articles that were constantly being rediscovered, removed and disintegrated, running comparatively as clean as they had a millennium before.

The descendants of the species responsible for all of that past harm now numbered over three-million individuals. Some people still lived in settlements scattered here and there across the globe yet there was a growing trend for them to move living quarters from the planet surface to orbiting residential platforms circling the planet. Most had already done so. Their relocation was not necessarily for altruistic reasons alone. Although they recognised that they, as individuals, occupied far more planetary space than individuals of other species, a circumstance that could only increase over time, there was also the question of their safety and comfort.

Much of the polar icecaps had long since thawed, long since melted away to mingle and merge with the world's oceans to inundate some coastal areas of land – but not as much as might have been had the reckless pollution of their antecedents not been halted.

Yet many remaining, non-submerged areas on the planet were either too hot or too cold; too dry or too wet. There were swarms of flying, biting invertebrates or strong cyclones; cataclysmic seismic events or paralysing blizzards; destructive wildfires or deleterious droughts. Events that, even with their technologies, could not be prevented from occurring or halted once in progress. They could, with some accuracy, predict the timings of almost all of those instances of natural inclemency and tremors but were powerless at their prevention.

On the other hand, life on the residential platforms in near space, whilst by no means ideal, was comfortable and controllable. It was always dry, could be as warm or as cool in their personal space as anyone could desire and none of their number were subject to the vagaries of meteorological conditions or geological faults. Up there, room for the inevitable expansion of their population and society was limitless, clean and harmless to other species – if nothing else, space is, without question, spacious.

Alongside, though separated from, the many residential platforms and their ubiquitous academic and scientific laboratory structures were a multitude of fully-automated manufacturing plants that continued to supply their material needs in all their diverse natures: socks and spacecraft; toothpaste and telescopes; footballs and fusion reactors and, of course, relatively close by to both residences and factories were all of the silk tree craft providing the material that underpinned their society and those of a myriad of other species across the galaxy. Animals living aboard the orbiting platforms often only ventured to the surface when required for their agricultural needs, academic study or recreational purposes. They could have, if they so desired, completely detached themselves from their home-world – the Temuri had always possessed the technology not to be wholly dependent on the vagaries of those complex and ultimately, fragile ecosystems just a few thousand kilometres below them.

The people responsible for their species' survival – the saviours of their entire world – the ap-Vanda, Vatta and Obiah, had journeyed to this planet almost half a millennia past, on spacecraft that were designed to collect and convert all internal atmospheric moisture to water and recycled all of it with the water used by the passengers for growing food, drinking and washing. This same water was also used to create oxygen during the reclamation process. Even before that time, the technology had been developed to safely create their own water from the asteroidal materials mined further out in the solar-system using fusion power to bind the hydrogen and oxygen molecules. These water creation techniques were, however, not utilised by the aliens during their journey to the planet all those years ago as there was no easy access to the required minerals. Had they so desired, they could have completely removed themselves from their home-world – they could manufacture their own water and oxygen. And, with those two vital elements, they could live anywhere. However, they were still animals. They had thousands, perhaps millions, of years of evolution on the surface of that world behind them; a genetic, innate, deep connection to the planet that could not be easily broken. Not yet. Maybe a few thousand years living in space would change that. Maybe not. So, they still grew most of their food, did much of their research and took their vacations on the planet.

Automata, as had been normal for the past four and a half centuries, still managed the husbandry of food production Down Below, as their home-world was now popularly known to those living off-world, and some of these people would still prefer to journey to the surface to collect the freshly harvested crops rather than have the automata deliver them, as they still did for the smaller populations still living on the planet. Although it had never been a particular hardship to travel between the planet surface and the inner space of the orbiting satellites or the factory platforms, recent advances in propulsion technology had made such journeys shorter and more convenient. Further miniaturisation of fusion reaction engines had greatly increased the velocity capabilities of all of their vessels, be they spacecraft, probes or planetary transport vehicles. From their initial starting-point in space, no destination on the planet surface was more than ten minutes away. The journey times within the atmosphere were slightly longer but most trips between settlements were no more than half-an-hour.

At any one time there would be thousands of the off-worlders on the surface of the planet for academic purposes; monitoring and studying other species of land or marine animals or undertaking research into their antecedents utilising the old, fragile printed materials housed at one of the many preserved art and science cities located across the planet. Others, adept at or studying archaeology, would be at digs in those villages, towns or cities not preserved or at sites of interest from much further back in time.

At the same time there would be many vacationers enjoying their home-world. Snowboarding in the high mountain ranges or, perhaps, sailing and diving in warm, blue tropical waters, or maybe viewing the exhibits in the galleries and museums of one of the art or science cities. They may have been strolling hand in hand through meadows in unspoilt wilderness or enjoying the other sights of natural beauty at its finest on this world in a hide somewhere.

Some three-hundred and seventy-thousand of their species had remained resident on the planet, for a variety of reasons. Some were unconcerned by the trials and threats that planet-life often presented; some did not like the idea of flashing through the atmosphere at unmentionable speeds, others disliked the necessary sterility of space-life, yet others felt connected to their dwellings or the locales in which they lived. Whatever their reasoning, there had been no compulsion for them to relocate to space nor could there be, or would there be, in the future.

Just as on all of the thirteen other home-worlds known to speak the universal language, any form of coercion was unheard of. There were no felons or hoodlums within this society, no psychopaths or sociopaths, no paedophiles, murderers or thieves. There was no law enforcement, there were no laws, because the Temuri society was not a sick society. It was in truth what their ancestors, the Kaahu, would have called *civilised* – a state of being that that particular incarnation of the species had never achieved. This new species – for that is what they undoubtedly were, although they may have been physiologically no different from the Kaahu, psychologically they were completely separate animals – were a confident bunch of mammals. There was no fear for the Temuri.

They feared not that another member of their species would, for example, take control of a planetary transport vehicle and crash it into an orbiting habitat or laboratory platform or such structures on the planet surface – not that the on-board data-processing systems would allow such an action. They feared not that the inhabitants of one habitation platform would declare war on a neighbouring platform. They had no concerns about their children playing outdoors or of them being abused or attacked by relatives, teachers or total strangers. The populace had no fears of being punched, stabbed, shot or blown-up by any of their species, neither would they be lied to nor ridiculed.

The only risks of death or injury they faced were voluntary risks taken by the Temuri themselves and usually associated with their leisure activities – climbing, swimming, caving or, perhaps, vacationing in the wilderness where other species of animal could attack them, though such attacks were quite rare. There were still areas on the planet where other dangers yet lurked or could lie in wait for the unsuspecting visitor; areas still irradiated by neglectful use of fissionable materials by the Kaahu centuries earlier; areas still contaminated by possibly explosive materials from that same violent era of the past.

The Temuri had no military forces because there were no enemies to wage war against, they were as one as a species – the same values, the same language and the same goals. They also knew, or, more accurately, believed, they faced no external threat. They had taken on board the theories of their guardians, the ap-Vanda and the other alien species, reviewed and queried their data and concluded they were, more than likely, correct – no overly-aggressive, ultra-competitive and selfish animals would survive their own actions, let alone make space travel a viable enough project for them. The Kaahu, those animals that, to the Temuri, best epitomised those failings, espoused the virtues of competition between themselves, claiming that progress could only be gained from such struggles whilst decrying mutual cooperation as unproductive. Everything that the Temuri had learned about their ancestors seemed to disprove those assertions – unless, of course, progress can be defined by the amount of wealth generated by the already powerful for themselves alone rather than for the benefit of all life on the planet in general and the planet itself. The Kaahu would, undoubtedly, have destroyed themselves and, probably, the world they lived on but they were prevented from doing so by the ap-Vanda, the Vatta and the Obiah.

Thus, losing sleep about such alien creatures with violent conquest on their minds, invading their peace, was not something the Temuri suffered, it was such a highly unlikely scenario that they slept easily in their beds. The Temuri were, simply put, happy. It was a happiness borne of the self-confidence that their society engendered. They were secure in the knowledge that they would never be hungry or cold, or in fear of their lives through lack of care by their peers. They were secure in the knowledge their consciences were clear of the baggage of their recent ancestors – the atrocities committed against their own and other species of life on the planet and against the planet itself. No species of life had been rendered extinct by the deliberate actions of the Temuri. No animal had been killed for food, clothing, fun or any kind of pseudo-scientific experimentation since the Kaahu were eliminated.

There had been no forestry depletion whatsoever, nor had there been any excavation of minerals from on or below the planet surface. Neither had any noxious substances been expelled into the atmosphere since the time of the Kaahu – their power generation requirements, for domestic use and transport on the planet, was emission-free, save for oxygen and water-vapour. All their mineral requirements were mined at the nearby asteroid belt and all mineral processing and manufacturing was undertaken in orbit. All waste products generated by these processes were stored in space and were regularly, every ten years or so, sent for incineration at the very edges of the corona of the local star.

The Temuri were also secure in the knowledge

that there were no false divisions within their society. Yes, everybody was an individual, though no-one was separate. There was a clear recognition amongst all the Temuri that the divisions of the past, of the Kaahu, were specifically created by some of those animals to engender disharmony amongst others to achieve power over the separated. No gender, skin-colour, so-called ethnicity, disability, sexual orientation or any other Kaahu-created diversity had any relevance to the Temuri and neither, of course, did the differences caused by absurd superstitious beliefs – none had done so for centuries.

The Temuri were so secure, so self-confident in themselves as a society that, some forty-seven years earlier, they had begun their own exploration of the galaxy by launching their first probe into Empty Space – they had accepted the challenge thrown down by the ap-Vanda, Vatta and Obiah species all those years ago to assist other troubled worlds in distant parts of the galaxy.

Forty-four probes later, after their latest probe had picked up the slightest of chemical traces indicating the presence, somewhere in the alien solar-system, of liquid water, the entire Temuri population was agog awaiting its arrival at the planet on which that precious liquid was thought to exist. The traces were detected when the probe first exited the Empty Space passage and now, some three and a half years later, it had almost reached its destination. Would it find a dead world devastated by nuclear war or smothered by atmospheric catastrophe? Or would the probe discover a planet dominated by a single species of animal, billions of them. So many that they would be blithely destroying the very ecosystem that they and every other species on that planet depended upon for life?

A hell world?

Author Profile

The author is an ethical vegan and maintains that veganism is not a diet – it is a way of life; it is a commitment to respect all forms of animal life (human and non-human) and the planet on which we all live. The author strongly opposes any and all manner of animal exploitation.

n o o n e is an anarchist (in the classical sense) and an atheist who believes that all things supernatural are totally illogical, delusional and, ultimately, destructive. Also an environmentalist, n o o n e cannot comprehend the idea that human animals are nonchalantly destroying the planet – an action which can be likened to people steadfastly hacking away at the foundations of a borrowed house and constantly defecating in every room whilst kidding themselves that they can pass that house on to their children.

The author shares a home, 'half-way up a small island on a small-minded planet', with two cats. *the hell world* is their first publication.

Publisher Information

Rowanvale Books provides publishing services to independent authors, writers and poets all over the globe. We deliver a personal, honest and efficient service that allows authors to see their work published, while remaining in control of the process and retaining their creativity. By making publishing services available to authors in a cost-effective and ethical way, we at Rowanvale Books hope to ensure that the local, national and international community benefits from a steady stream of good quality literature.

For more information about us, our authors or our publications, please get in touch.

www.rowanvalebooks.com
info@rowanvalebooks.com